Filling in the Pieces

Filling in the Pieces

WOMEN TELL THEIR STORIES OF THE TWENTIETH CENTURY

WRITTEN AND EDITED BY

MICHAELA CRAWFORD REAVES

California Lutheran University

cognella®
SAN DIEGO

Bassim Hamadeh, CEO and Publisher
David Miano, Senior Field Acquistions Ediotr
Jordan Krikorian, Editorial Assistant
Michelle Piehl, Senior Project Editor
Alia Bales, Production Editor
Jess Estrella, Senior Graphic Designer
Trey Soto, Licensing Specialist
Natalie Piccotti, Director of Marketing
Kassie Graves, Vice President of Editorial
Jamie Giganti, Director of Academic Publishing

Cover image copyright © 2020 iStockphoto LP/Christian Horz.
Design: Copyright © 2012 Depositphotos/zeber2010.

Printed in the United States of America.

3970 Sorrento Valley Blvd., Ste. 500, San Diego, CA 92121

CONTENTS

DOING ORAL HISTORY

Before each part, a map and timeline has been provided to help situate the interviews within their historical context.

In 1979 Neil Putman Sigmon stated, "You don't have to be famous for your life to be history."[1] This notion then suggests that historians heed the call to give a voice to the voiceless. The historical focus away from just king lists and battle victories to social history began in the nineteenth century and grew more popular in the twentieth century, in part because the events of the twentieth century, including genocides, famines, and domestic purges, focused so much on individual groups of people rather than the hierarchy. In most cases the people who died did not necessarily qualify as famous, but their participation, willing or not, makes them vital to the historical record. One of the groups least likely to be noted throughout thousands of years of

---

1   Jacqueline Dowd Hall, interview with Nell Putnam Sigmon, December 13, 1979 (H-143), Southern Oral History Program Collection #4007, Southern Historical Collection, University of North Carolina at Chapel Hill.

history is one half the world's population—women. Although the occasional queen or "wife" gained recognition, the daily female householder often passed into history without much fanfare.

As the industrial revolutions of the nineteenth century changed how people lived and worked it became apparent that the "cogs" in the machines were more than the metal of the machine tools but included the person who worked those tools. At the end of the century historians turned their attention to the faceless workers and investigated labor history, which became a part of social history that did "bottoms-up" rather than the "top-down" history of kings, potentates, and generals.[2] Fundamental to this change were the improved tools of archaeology and the science of anthropology, also formally introduced in this time period. One leader in the field of this "new history" was historian Carl Becker (1873–1945), who became the president of the American Historical Society. In that role he made his annual address to the association in 1931 in which he stated, "History is the memory of things said and done."[3] Who better to remember those things than the people who said them, including the women of the twentieth century?

Human creatures have the ability to mentally record and remember events that happen, as may other creatures, but we do it in ways that can be verbally expressed, a gift that makes our memory particularly retainable. Memory then became the first "digital" recording device of humankind. People with exceptional memories were selected from tribes to become the recorder and retainer of those events and to share them with the next generation. In most cases, a village elder would single out a young person or persons and begin telling them the lore of their tribal group. Before the invention of writing, these memories recorded religious canon, natural disasters, and oral law. The oral history of one Aboriginal Australian people called the Gunditjmara describes a volcanic eruption that may be the oral history of an event that took place more than thirty-seven thousand years ago. Research seems to support this date. This means that oral history events record history more than thirty thousand years longer than written history, which most likely was introduced in the Middle East in the fourth century BCE. Over the next centuries the words of rabbis were recorded in the Old Testament, the words of the bard Homer became the *Iliad* and the *Odyssey,* the *griots* of Africa preserved epic heroes like Sundiata, and the lessons of the Buddha became the *buddhavacana* and *Abhidharma.*

Fast forward five thousand years and the Great Depression offered a chance for an organized and state-sponsored oral history project. The Federal Writer's Project, a segment of the WPA or Work's Progress Administration of Franklin D. Roosevelt's New Deal, used the opportunity to record the experiences of men and women during the Depression while also recording the Slave Narrative Collection,

2   Jesse L. Lemisch, "Jack Tar in the Streets: Merchant Seamen in the Politics of Revolutionary America," *The William and Mary Quarterly* 25, no. 3 (1968): 371–407.

3   Carl Becker, "Annual Address of the President of the American Historical Association, delivered at Minneapolis, December 29, 1931." *American Historical Review* 37, no. 2, (1932): 221–36.

the oral history of formerly enslaved persons in the antebellum South. During this period, one historian, Allen Nevins, established the first center for oral history at Columbia University in 1948. His reasoning stemmed from his time as a newspaperman watching obituaries roll by each day. At the time he thought, "Year by year, they died, and I said to myself as I saw the obituary columns, 'What memories that man carries with him into total oblivion, and how completely they are lost.'"[4] Although this quote is again about the leaders of society, the idea rings true for the women of the twentieth century.

In the early 1990s it struck me that the women who witnessed the century of two world wars, landing on the moon, and invention of technology that gave us the internet were growing old. Those born in the earliest years of the century were approaching their centenary and so many eyewitness accounts would be lost if no one took the time to ask some questions. I already knew that in my own family I had "lost" part of my history because I was too young to ask my grandfather, "What was Paris in 1919 really like?" With that in mind I introduced to my Women in American History course an assignment on oral history. The students were asked to find a female relative or friend (although some just called retirement homes for a "blind" interview) over the age of 65 and ask them to tell their story. Each student received a similar set of questions and instructions. Little could I know the breadth of the stories we would receive over the next twenty years by asking questions of the women attached to just one class in a small liberal arts college.

Oral history typically includes personal narratives, correspondence, and visual aids, like photographs, medals, and other material artifacts. Therefore, students often made photocopies of pictures and mementos. The interviews were always recorded in the early years by handheld voice recorders and in the later years on iPhones. Once the students had the story, the next decision was how to present it. The first option was to tell the story as if the woman were sitting in the room through the use of first person. The best known of this style may be Charles Dickens's opening line in *David Copperfield*, "I am born." The second option was the interview format in which the student asked the questions and the interviewee answered. The "when were you born" format, then used second person. The third option was for the student to transfer the question-and-answer format into a third-person oral history by saying something like "Mary Henry was born in 1935." All of these methods tell the story, but the choice of the recorder becomes important since the style reflects the point of view of the author; in other words, the story of the oral history comes through the narrator's voice. In these oral histories, therefore, the reader will find that the voice changes from one to the next. Although the names have been changed, the relationship of the interviewer to the subject is accurate.

The interviews themselves record the large and small events of one person's life. More than that they record changes in social mores, political organizations,

---

4 Quoted by Norman Hoyle, "Oral History," *Library Trends* (July 1972): 60–82, https://core. ac.uk/download/pdf/4815997.pdf.

and technology. In another facet they record what the person being interviewed deemed important. Most women remembered their childhoods and teenage years very clearly up until they matured. Whether life turned out as expected, most of the women turned to duty, jobs, and child raising for the adult portion of their lives. Only after the age of sixty or so did the limelight switch back to the women themselves.

Because private events can be painful, all the students were cautioned to be sensitive and careful while talking to their new friends. While people in 2010 may be very comfortable discussing birth control, women in the 1930s were not. The questions were to be asked as openly as possible and without judgment. At the end of the interview, usually when the older woman tired, the student obtained a release so that the stories could be incorporated in this book. In very few cases, usually ones that included crimes, the older women did not sign the release.

As you read these stories you will see the ways in which life a century later has changed and the ways in which it has not. In a few cases political change in 2020 made it necessary to remove some oral histories due to a possible threat to still living family members. If you stop and think for a moment, using my grandfather as an example, he was born in the age of the horse and buggy, before his town had a telephone, and lived to see a man walk on the moon. For many of the women in these histories they were born in countries that no longer exist and places that are forgotten. In all cases, every attempt has been made to identify the places of which the women speak in both the "older" way and with the newer name.

Finally, how did these class projects become a book? The stories were kept in hard copies in my office until a large enough set was compiled. They were then digitized, although the first third of the stories all had to be retyped by departmental assistants into a digital format and with news identifiers. I owe those students a great debt of gratitude for their collaboration on this project over a decade or more. They are Eleanor Barker, Allison Berman, Kelli Campa, Dora Cardona, Brianna DeValk, Katelin Eich, Cristina Farias, Leanna Garcia, Laura Mele, Liana Minassian, Emily Quin Ortega, Jennifer Robinson, Kathryn Sizemore, Megan Suhosky, Morgan West, and Mary Kate Willis.

In addition, the students whose oral histories are included must be acknowledged: Natalie Paniagua, Carol Little, Jeneanne Navarro, Laura Stark, Heather Kennedy, Vahe Khachatourian, Samantha Frank, Hamza Mujaddidi, Glynnis Jones, Emily Trefethen, Jennifer Palimino, Philip Payne, Jason Young, Jake Morayniss, Sue Scudder, Noi Scheild, Melanie Cornejo, Wenqing Luo, Danielle Balderama, Matthew Minick, Haig Tchamakian, Dora Cardona, Darby Schuett, Brandon Hill, Caitlin Fransen, Alex Hacker, Wren Cherney, Jeff Meyers, Brittni Thomas, Fabian Shapourmanesh, and Mary Kate Willis.

Enjoy "filling in the pieces" of twentieth-century history!

TIMELINE

- **1892–1954**

  Ellis Island processes 12 million immigrants to USA

- **1893**

  Women get the vote in New Zealand

- **1908**

  Belgium annexes African Congo as Belgian Colony (until 1960)

- **1910**

  Mexican Revolution

- **1911**

  Chinese Revolution ends Qing Dynasty, Republic of China born

- **1914–1918**

  World I begins with assassination of Austro-Hungarian heir by terrorist organization (Black Hand)

- **1915**

  Armenian genocide in Turkey and 21 Demands from Japan to China

- **1917**

  Communist Revolution leads to Treaty of Brest Litovsk and founding of the Union of Soviet Socialists Republics (USSR)

- **1918**

  Invasion by Germany and USSR of Estonia

- **1919**

  Women get the vote in Afghanistan after achieving independence from Britaind

- **1927–1949**

  Civil war in China Mao (Communists) vs. Chiang (Kuomingtang)

- **1929–1940**

  Great Depression

1900–1918

Introduction

Historians often refer to the nineteenth century as the "longest century," not because it lasted over one hundred years, but because the world remained much the same in terms of power and behavior from 1789 until 1914. The first date represents the ratification of the US Constitution and the French Revolution, while the latter represents the beginning of World War I, or the Thirty Years War with Germany, as it is sometimes called. The nineteenth century is typified by worldwide revolutions, the growth of industrialization and immigration, steady world population growth, and the final heyday of both colonialism and the British Empire. When the Edwardian world of 1910 came to its bloody end in August of 1914, the world that emerged after the First World War in 1919 looked very different.

One easy way to visualize the changes in life and ways of thought is to picture the representative artwork of an artist like Thomas Gainsborough with his *The Blue Boy* in 1770 and the revolutionary work of Marcel Duchamp, *Nude Descending a Staircase*, at the Armory Show in 1913. Gainsborough's painting is clearly representative, while Duchamp's painting is modernist and nonrepresentative and suggests movement in a static painting. So what happened at the end of the nineteenth century to change the perception of those who lived through it?

The technological progress of the two centuries before 1900 gave the world the steam engine, replaceable parts, a method to limit smallpox on a worldwide level, and inventions from gas and electric lights to steel girders. Communication increased with the telegraph, train travel, and the telephone, while death rates dropped, allowing more children to live to adulthood. The advent of both industrialization and the concomitant growth of cities encouraged migration on a global scale, while shifting population in the United States from over 90 percent agrarian in 1800 to approximately 40 percent in 1900. In the twenty-first century that number is under 2 percent. New ways to process steel allowed the cities to grow vertically, changing the horizontal patterns of human settlement and compressing populations into acres rather than miles. New and cheaper production, like the "penny press," allowed ideas to spread faster and farther, while philosophers tried to make sense of a world in which the average worker lived in crowded tenements and run-down cottages.

In terms of world power, Great Britain began its reign at the end of the sixteenth century with the defeat of the Spanish Armada. By 1900, Spain had lost its empire and Britain's Queen Victoria ruled over an empire on which the "sun never set." In 1901, over one-third of the world's population descended from Anglo-European roots and the ideas of the classical world were the litmus test of philosophical thought, art, and beauty. One hundred years later over one-third of the world's population lives in India or China. Imbedded within this system, however, lurked problems of social and economic inequity, the shadow of colonialism, and the ever present application of new technology to weapons and war-making.

Clearly, the dawn of twentieth century heralded a time of change and growth. Ideas from those of Darwin to Freud colored the interpretation of the actions of the inhabitants of earth. In many places, the dominance of religion began to slowly erode despite the "Great Awakenings" of the nineteenth century, as feelings of hopelessness gave way to nihilism and existentialism. The shift from a feudal-bound labor model to an industrial labor model gave the world Franz Kafka's *Metamorphosis* but also allowed for the rise of Karl Marx's proletariat and labor unions demanding better treatment for workers around the globe. As the old empires began to break up, ideas of nationalism and the contest for resources reached new heights and redrew the maps from Europe to Africa and Asia. In the wake of these changes, revolution and war roiled through the world. The revolutions included new ideas about who should control human power structures from the board rooms of the skyscrapers to the kitchens of the workers.

Most women born at the dawn of the twentieth century still married young, bore many children, and anticipated being "governed" by their fathers, their husbands, or their sons. But some women attended college, a few women could vote, and others would demand equal rights for the females of the world. Nowhere was this more evident than in the demands for the enfranchisement of women as, around the globe, from New Zealand to Afghanistan, women sought the right to vote. For American women the right to vote was achieved with the Nineteenth Amendment to the Constitution in 1920. The women in the first set of oral histories were born into this turbulent time.

Although the period from 1900 to 1914 appeared peaceful enough, underlying problems existed as states fought for world power status, millions of peasant farmers were moved off of their land, and millions died from famine in China, North Africa, Russia, and India. Pressure on populations encouraged many to attempt to migrate to other areas. For the United States this influx of immigrants from 1890–1900 came primarily from southern and eastern Europe. The numbers of immigrants peaked by World War I, and such large numbers would not exist again for a century. Ports of entry in the United States, including Ellis Island, built large facilities to process these immigrants, who, unlike earlier immigrants of the nineteenth century, tended to remain in urban ethnic enclaves called ghettos. These immigrants represented not only a less educated class of migrants but also new religions, particularly Jewish and Roman Catholic immigrants. These groups faced persecution and social ostracism in the United States, but others, like Armenians of the old Ottoman Empire, faced genocide. In Mexico, the entrenched Catholic Church confronted anti-clericalism as church lands were nationalized, and in much of Eastern Europe and Russia, Jewish *shtetls* present in those countries for centuries faced *pogroms* and antisemitism.

Religious differences were not the only issues as millions of peasant farmers lost their lands, settled in urban areas, and formed a poor, restive, and sickly population. The fact that land ownership in much of the world, from China to Russia, and from Europe to South America, concentrated the bulk of wealth in feudal-style landholdings caused large-scale revolutions to break out. In 1911 the Mexican Revolution began as Porfirio Diaz, who had been in power in Mexico for over thirty years, was forced to leave the country. In Cuba, one of Spain's last imperial holdings, rebellion set off the Spanish-American War. The Qing Dynasty in China that began in 1644 collapsed by 1912 as a new era of competition ensued between leaders of the Kuomintang. Similarly, the Romanov Dynasty of Russia that ruled from 1613 to 1917 ended with the assassination of the czar and his family by the Bolshevik Revolution. Countries from Saudi Arabia to Japan and Columbia experienced the overthrow of old systems in the nineteenth century and had yet to come to terms with the change by 1900. As the old empires of Europe began to wane, large areas of Africa, Asia, and the Middle East found the breakdown of old boundaries led to ethnic and religious conflict.

For American girls and boys born in 1900 the world seemed full of new inventions, and the nation looked forward to great success. Model Ts chugged downtown streets, telephones became available in homes, the Wright brothers demonstrated that human flight was possible, and most of the country supported ending child labor in mills and offering a high school education to the masses. College sports were the new pastime, along with professional baseball, girls wore their hair in pompadours, and young men still carried canes as a fashion statement and wore straw "skimmers" on their heads. Newspapers were largely controlled by publishers like Joseph Pulitzer and William Randolph Hearst, who thought nothing of reflecting their own opinions strongly in their press. Native-born Anglo-European Americans soon had access to prefabricated homes, iceboxes, and labor-saving devices like vacuums. Immigrants could hope to move from New York's impoverished Eastside to the new "suburbs" of the Bronx and Brooklyn. Although many immigrants still had large families of eight or more children, those children were being given a chance to "better themselves," get an education, and raise their families' standard of living. The internal African American migration from the South to northern cities like Chicago also offered hope for a better life to persons enslaved only fifty years before. But as bright as the future looked, underlying problems were about to plunge the world into war.

European kingdoms historically waged war with zeal, but many of these wars involved professional armies and were not primarily aimed at disrupting civilian life. For Europe that last great conflict had ended with Napoleon's defeat, and the Concert of Europe had imposed order in 1815 on European powers that opposed new revolutionary ideas, including nationalism. Despite the incorporation of both Germany and Italy as nation-states by 1880, the national boundaries of Europe lasted until 1914. At the time, traditional powers, including Britain, France, Germany/Prussia, Austria, and Russia, remained the "balance of power" brokers on the continent. Choosing to ignore national and ethnic insurgencies, these powers tended to avoid confronting issues like those in the Balkans and Eastern Europe. Eventually a series of secret pacts among the emperors, coupled with radical politics in areas like Serbia and Russia, led to the implosion of the nineteenth-century European structure.

While Europe teetered on the edge of disaster, the Far East faced its own series of upheavals. Beginning with the division of the Qing Dynasty by European potentates, the dynasty weakened. It declined further through the opium wars with Britain, the internal Taiping Revolution, and the Boxer Rebellion. The large Chinese population of peasants faced the threat of famine and a lack of upward mobility. Young Chinese students sought ways to modernize the state and strengthen it so that Chinese territorial integrity would be honored while Western missionaries sought to create strong Christian communities in China. Although European incursions in China expanded, imperialism became the main threat for China but came closer to home, across the Yellow Sea.

In 1868 the Meiji Restoration in Japan restored the power of the emperor over the Tokugawa Shogunate that had ruled since 1603. Fundamental to its success was the exclusion of foreign interference, which changed in 1853 with the visit by Commodore Perry to Japan. Over the next fifty years, Japan rapidly modernized and by the early twentieth century achieved significant world power status. Due to limited natural resources and a growing population, Japan began a series of incursions onto the Asian mainland. The first Sino-Japanese War occurred in 1895 over the Korean Peninsula, leading to the cession of the island of Taiwan and the Liaodang Peninsula to Japan. Later, in 1905, Japan and Russia faced off on the Korean Peninsula and Japan won, thus weakening the czar's position in Russia. Despite efforts by President Theodore Roosevelt and the Treaty of Portsmouth, by 1910 Japan extended its rule onto the Korean Peninsula. By 1915, Japan used World War I as an opportunity to impose the Twenty-One Demands on China, insisting on "special privileges" on the mainland.

Although the world of 1900 can be defined as a global one in terms of trade, large portions of the globe still remained under the control of colonial powers, including imperial powers of both Europe and Asia. Conflicts for both European and Asian hegemony would dominate the twentieth century. For most Americans, however, knowledge of Asia, Africa, and even Latin America was limited. Strong xenophobic ideas dominated the American press as native-born Americans decried the number of immigrants. The numbers were so significant that only one person in ten was a native-born citizen in the New York of 1900. Americans, nearly all of whom were immigrants, nevertheless feared the new immigrants who flooded the cities and worked for low wages. In addition, Americans of the Protestant faith distrusted "Papist" Roman Catholics, as well as what they perceived as eastern European Jewish immigrants who often embraced the ideas of radical socialism and significant labor reform.

For Americans, the later nineteenth century witnessed the American Civil War, two economic "panics" in 1873 and 1893, and labor crises, including significant labor violence in the 1880s and 1890s. The new century offered a sense of new birth and economic wealth. Having weathered the last century, Americans embraced reform in both the political and social realms. The expanded government limited trusts and oligopolies, new state and federal laws granted women and minorities the vote, the Progressive era highlighted social and civic improvements, the new generation could plan to

Michoacàn, Mexico (1905)

As told to her granddaughter.

FIGURE 1.1.1 Farmer and Ox, Mexico 1911

Alejandra Ines Vega Santos was born on August 10, 1905 in Puerto De Cabras, Michoacán, Mexico, a town of about one hundred families. She was given the name Alejandra Ines Vega but most everyone called her Ines. She was born to Jesus and Teresa Vega and was one of their 13 living children. They had 18 children, and Ines was the third from the last. Her mother said that she was born at a time of inconvenience because she was born while her mother was walking three miles to get the water needed for the day. Her mother left home that August morning with an empty water jug on her head and returned with a full jug of water and a baby at her breast.

A year after Ines was born, her sister was born, and a year or so after that, another sister. Those two sisters were the ones Ines played with during her childhood. She did not go to school, and neither did anyone in her family. There was no school nearby and the children were going to become farmers, so there was no point of getting an education. Ines's parents called their children the children of the soil because most of their time was spent learning how to tame the land. Ines's brothers did the heavy work while the girls did the light but difficult tasks that involved brains and heart. By the age of five, Ines had her own section of the garden to raise corn and potatoes for her family. She was in charge of cleaning, watering, and feeding that area. Ines had to work to eat and she was taught that hard work brought plenty of food and warmth. Her education did not involve going to school where she was taught the proper way to write or talk. She said, "It was being in my house where we were taught how to survive."

Ines's life was like that of any child, with chores to do and exploration to occur. Her life was normal until 1911. In that year, Ines's brother was taken away. When she woke up that particular morning, something did not feel right. Even at age six, Ines knew something was wrong. She heard a noise and asked her older sister what it was. The sister did not know, so Ines got out of bed and found that her brothers and parents were out of their beds trying to find out what caused the noise. Once she saw who it was making the noise, Ines knew why he was there. Ines's brother had defied their father and had a relationship with a married woman. Her husband was the man who stood outside in her honor and to the family's horror. The husband called out for Ines's brother, and despite the family encouraging him to run and hide, Ines's father would not allow it. The brother had not listened to what his father told him, so he had to face the consequences by himself. Ines's father forbade the children from helping their brother, telling them he would disown them if they did. One by one Ines's siblings returned to bed, as did she, but she stayed by the crack in the door. Ines's mother blessed the brother and left for her room. Ines did not have to see what was going on outside to know what happened. There were sounds of a struggle, some screams, moans, and then silence. Ines's mother opened the door in the morning and screamed. Her brother was on the ground, beaten and dead. He was brought into the house, cleaned, buried, and never spoken of again.

A new chapter began for Ines in 1913 when she was eight years old. Her family had lived in peace for the two years since her brother's death. They lived in happiness on their rancho, and, as a child, Ines did the normal things of milking the goats and cows, killing the chickens, and cleaning. One day as she walked to get tortillas from the next town, everything seemed to be the same, but as she returned home, it felt as if she should walk home a different way. She decided to walk a different way and discovered her brother on the church steps, shot. A girl Ines knew called for her to get her father, and at first Ines could not move. The girl repeated the request again, and Ines ran home. Her parents were sitting down for lunch and her mother asked for the tortillas. Ines said nothing because she did not have the strength to tell her mother that another child had died, but she knew. The plate that her mother held was on the floor, and her father was out of his chair, yelling for his horse. He asked where the brother was, and Ines could only manage to mumble "church." Her mother was distraught and wanted to know why her son was killed.

Her father angrily replied that the brother was stealing horses again. Ines's father left and came back in about an hour. The burial happened the next day because there was no way to keep the body from beginning to decompose. Ines's family never tried to find out who had killed her brother because they knew that he had done something to deserve it. Her brother had stolen horses many times but very rarely did he get caught. Most of the time, Ines's father beat her brother and sent him to return the horses. That time he was caught and was taught never to steal again.

The death of a third brother began the new year and a new chapter in Ines's life. It was January or February of 1917 and Ines was twelve years old. Having lost two sons already, Ines's mother felt it would be best if her other sons found jobs elsewhere. The older ones did find jobs, and the three sons who remained were the youngest. The oldest of the three was 16 and was the next to leave. The night before he did, the man from across the way invited him for a few drinks and a few games of cards. Ines's mother asked the brother not to go, but he wanted to as it would be the last time he saw his friends. He left with no goodbye or farewell kiss. Later that night, Ines and her younger sisters woke up and saw a light coming from their parents' room. As they opened their door, their mother fell to her knees in tears, because the sheriff had informed her of the shooting that had killed her son. Another brother had left, another brother who would never return. He had been shot in the back because the men he had played with became drunk and were angry that the brother had won a few games of cards. The men were found and punished for the death and Ines's father let the family mourn for the death.

After 1911, the Mexican Revolution raged over the political leadership of Mexico. The Villistas, or Pancho Villa's men, were hiding out in the mountains near Ines's rancho. They would come every night to steal from the rancho. Ines was not allowed outside, and food was hidden underground, and at night, the women hid. The Villistas would come down and steal the food from the crops, horses, money, and women, and sometimes even land. The women would return, but not the same way in which they left.

Ines's sisters experienced the effects of being taken by those men. Her father and his farm hands had left for the day to work in the fields when an unexpected raid surprised the women who had stayed at home. Ines's mother heard the Villistas coming and tried to hide all of the girls and the food. There were seven girls, but she was only able to hide three and the food. Ines was one of the three who had been hidden and she watched in horror as her sisters were taken as the men entered the house. All were taken except her mother who they said was too old and it would be a compliment if they took her. They were pleased with their prizes, so they and the rest of the men left the town. Ines's father returned too late, for her sisters were already taken, and they mourned their loss for two days. The sisters returned after two days, but everyone knew what happened to them while they were taken. Ines's oldest sister was the strongest, and she was the one who lasted the longest. They all stayed in bed for a few weeks as Ines's mother took care of them. One by one, they all passed away. Depression took all of Ines's sisters in the span of two years.

Around the same time, the rancho was burned to the ground. The revolution was happening all over Mexico and one day the Mexican government passed through Ines's family rancho. One night, she woke up to the smell of fire. Her father and the farm hands were already awake and running to the river, which was their only supply of water. Ines and her younger sisters got out of bed to help. The whole rancho was on fire. Ines ran to the river with her bucket as fast as she could, and she ran back and forth between the river and the rancho many times. By the time the last flames were extinguished, it was midday. It was difficult to determine what time it truly was because the smoke was so thick and a gray haze was over the rancho. The house was not very damaged, but the crops were. Over the following years, people rebuilt their homes and ate, but Ines's family starved. During the same period of time, the revolution also took the lives of Ines's last two brothers. Both left to fight against the government and both perished. One was shot and the other disappeared and was never heard from again.

The family finally managed to get back on their feet in 1933. Ines had met her future husband, who was a hand on the farm. His name was José Santos, and even though he was younger than Ines, they became true friends. At the time, it was not proper for a girl to go out by herself with a gentleman, and for Ines and José, there was nowhere to go. They would stay around the rancho and talk and work. Ines was 28 and the time for her to marry had past. She was considered too old to start a family because most had begun theirs at 18. That did not bother them because the year she was 28, she and José married.

On Ines's wedding day, she had no time to rest. She had to make the food and cake for the party after the ceremony and clean her house and the rancho. She was the oldest now because all of her older siblings had either left or had died. After she finished her chores, she finished the night's dinner, completed her wedding dress, and got ready to leave. She heard the church bells ring the first warning of Catholic Mass and she was on her way; the church was in the next town, which was three miles away. Ines had to walk the three miles in her wedding dress, and it took her 45 minutes, which was barely enough time.

From then on, Ines had illusions of her life being of peace, since her childhood was the definition of suffering and pain. She was married to her husband for two years before they had a child. The first was a boy who was born in 1935. She had him in the field as she gathered potatoes for dinner. When the boy was two years old, Ines had another child. This time, it was a girl who brought much joy into Ines's life. She lived for about a year when she was bitten by either a spider or a snake. Ines did not notice how hurt the baby really was until her leg got swollen and turned blue. Ines used home remedies in order to cure her, but they only prolonged the baby's pain. She lived for about a month that way until Ines finally took her to the doctor. It was too late. The poison had made its way through her tiny body. The doctor said that all they could do was wait until her body could fight no longer. A few months after her second birthday, the baby died, and Ines blamed herself. Ines felt that if she would have taken the baby to the doctor sooner she may have lived longer, but Ines trusted in her garden and home remedies over a man called a doctor.

Ines did not have any more children for about five years. She did not want any more loss to affect her family. In that time, in addition to caring for her husband and child, Ines started a corn-milling store. People preferred to walk for miles rather than work for their own food. One April night in 1942, Ines gave birth to a son. Her mother was with her and helped her deliver a large baby boy. After she gave birth, Ines fell ill. She was asleep for two days with a fever. Her husband later told her that the doctor visited, but she had no memory of it. When she woke up, she was told she would not be able to have any more children. With her two sons and her husband, they lived off the money from corn milling. Life was the same until 1950 when Ines gave birth to her last son. She was 45 when she had her son on June 22, 1950. She gave birth to him between one tortilla batch and another. She finished her day's work and finally had rest at eight o'clock that night. By that time, her other sons had left Mexico City for a trade school. Her sons were the first to leave the rancho to get an education, and Ines was proud of that.

Time went on until Ines's youngest son left and went to school in Mexico City. It was 1968 when they decided to move to Las Vegas to live with their older son. Ines and her family moved to coastal California in 1971. José and one of their sons found work dealing with strawberries. Ines stayed at home alone while everyone left to work or go to school. Ines started to get out of the house and go to church. At church, she found many different people who taught her some English and Bingo, and even though she did not know much about the town, she still went out. Once she got lost as she took her grandchild to school and the police had to take her home. The police also were called when she was accused of stealing food from the local store. That was when Ines stopped venturing outside. She instead spent her time knitting and cross-stitching. Ines and José lived on money from Social Security and from José's job, which provided them with enough money to afford an apartment. They lived there until their youngest boy got a house and started his own family.

Ines lived with her youngest son for nearly ten years. Around that time, José fell ill and Ines cared for him. After a long period of joy and good fortune, fate took her husband in the bed where they spent their first and last nights together. José turned, said Ines' name, and passed. Her husband's death was the last chapter in Ines's book of life. Ines felt that she had enough death and pain in her own life that her children and grandchildren would not be left with any of their own. She lived in hope that her 96 years of pain would teach her children that strength will conquer all.

CREDIT

Singapore (1913)

As told to her great-niece.

FIGURE 1.2.1 Women Building Brick Barricade in Singapore (World Photo Walk) Twenty-first century street art in Singapore's Chinatown district memorializes the "red-hat" women who constructed modern Singapore. These mostly Hakka women from the Chinese Guangdong province became known as "samsui women" since they spoke Cantonese and referred to their home as "samsui" or "three waters." During the 1920's and 30's the British attempted to balance the sex ratios in Singapore by limiting male immigration. Since Guangdong and its neighboring provinces were poor, young women between the ages of 18-10 took advantage of the opportunity to migrate to Singapore and send money home to their families. At the end of their long journey they occupied four-to-a-room flats over Chinatown stores and lived a life of celibacy for the next five decades. Each morning they donned dark blouses and pants to work on construction sites. The dark color served to hide the dirt. On their feet they wore sandals made of old tires strapped on their feet. Finally, they donned their red hats. The hats were large starched scarves that were then folded into the now famous image. The hats served three purposes: 1) protection from construction site accidents since they were very noticeable; 2) blocking the tropical sun; and 3) acting as a place to store cigarettes or money. A folded blue hat usually meant a woman was in mourning. On the job sites the women carried wood , rocks, or sand in baskets hung on shoulder poles, mixed cement, dug trenches and did any other menial job. Their work increased in the 1960's during Singapore's modernization boom; the samsui women continued to work until the 1980's when machines replaced them on construction sites.

Aunt Nee Moi, the "red hat lady," remembers that she is 17 years younger than the interviewer's grandmother who is 102; therefore "Auntie" in 85. However, grandma was born in 1900; so she is actually turning 100, except that "you need to add two years in each person's life, the god gives one year from the sky and the other year granted by the god of the land." Her mother and grandmother always had to remind her of this.

Auntie thought she may have been born in 1917, but her mother did not know exactly when she was born; however, it was the Year of the Ox (1913). She was born at dawn and that meant she would have a rough life because the ox has to start work bright and early in the morning and go to the rice field, just as she did. Auntie worked all her life, but now her nephew and his wife take care of her. Auntie was born in a small village called Sanshui (紅頭巾) in the upper district of Kwangtung Province in China.

Some of Auntie's family moved for marriage, like her older sister, and Grandma, who moved to see her son married. However, Auntie left home at 16 to avoid an arranged marriage. Back then, everyone was anxious to leave the village for the "south sea" (South East Asia), looking for new life and opportunities. It was in 1933 that Auntie left the mainland for Singapore, where she received permanent residence status in 1938. She remembers this because her nephew, her great-niece's father, was born in that year.

Auntie explained why she left the arranged marriage and spoke quite loudly. "Do you know what happened to my sister? Let me tell you! She was married like all the other marriages in China at that time; it was prearranged. She did not like her husband. When she was pregnant, I could feel her pain just by watching her working out there in the rice fields until the last day of her pregnancy. In the end, she died. She suffered serious complications while delivering the baby. I did not want to share her fate. I wanted to be completely in control of my own life, which is why I decided to come to Singapore before they—my parents—could find me a husband!"

When Auntie arrived in Singapore she felt elated. She thought she would now earn her own money and use it as she chose. Nobody could control her. She said, "I felt great that I was able to put some cash in my pocket. I made two dollars a day as a general laborer. By the end of each week, I saved up to fourteen dollars. Then, I had to pay rent as I was sharing a room with three other women that came from our village. We put together $20 a month for the room." The area she lived in was the China Town area, and later she moved to company housing.

Auntie explained that she and the three women from the village all came to Singapore together, a distance of over 1,600 miles. They were helped by "Nan yang" (South Sea) merchants and their wives. The three teenagers traveled for weeks and Auntie felt seasick throughout the entire boat trip. She did not eat a thing, and her three sisters (the other girls) were sick too. They arrived in Kuala Lumpur (Malaysia), where there were many Cantonese people. They rested for two days and got on the train to move south. She borrowed the money to pay for the train fare from one of her relatives in Kuala Lumpur. She paid them back in six months working as a harbor labor assistant or coolie.

In Singapore, during the late 1930s, while other Chinese female immigrants from Kwangtung and Hong Kong worked primarily as servants and prostitutes to the British and Chinese merchants, the Samsui women took the better-paying jobs on construction sites. Between 1934 and 1938 about two hundred thousand Samsui women left China and took construction jobs in Singapore. This continued until it was outlawed in 1949. People could see them in their distinctive big red hats that protected them from the sun. Auntie said, "We were well equipped from our childhood to do such work!" Besides the household duties the Samsui woman had to work alongside the men in the fields to eliminate the necessity of hiring outside workers. Most importantly, in order to work efficiently, they were free from foot binding, a custom once common throughout China. This unconventional attitude toward foot binding gave many of the Samsui women more physical and emotional freedom.

The interviewer asked why her grandmother had her feet bound and Auntie explained that her grandmother was born in Fuzhou, a different province. In Sanshui, most of the women were field laborers. She remembered seeing some women with their feet bound, but most of them were the laboring class; neither her mother nor her sisters had their feet bound.

Life in Singapore was, in some ways, better than in China. She achieved total independence by relying solely on herself to earn a living. She held her head up and was proud of her own achievements. She believes she was "better than men." However, life was still far from a "bed of roses." Many of the women had no promise of long-term work. Each job assignment would last from a few days to weeks, after which she was out of a job and had to seek a new one. She spent all of her youth working as a coolie (manual laborer). Her entire life was devoted to pure hardship. She continued to work at construction sites until she was too old and there was no further demand for that type of labor. Then she turned to other jobs like selling vegetables at the wet market in China Town. The wilted vegetables were laid out on big sheets of brown paper, while other women pushed trolleys collecting recyclable cardboard that they sold for a pittance. Her younger sister arrived at the same time as the interviewer's grandmother came in 1960. She got married and had children. The grandmother promised that her son would take care of Auntie like his own parent. This pleased her very much and she said they were very nice to her.

Auntie did not see marriage as a part of her life. All the Samsui women who came to Singapore stayed single, and all the women shared the same lifestyle. They used to stay in accommodations knows as "coolie houses," two- to three-story colonial-style dwellings with impossibly crowded conditions. Each room was filled with grime and dirt and was shared by six women. That was how they spent their youth. Being single, they depended on each other for support and treated each other like sisters. They never saw marriage as an escape. Marriage was something that would only "put an end to [their] cherished independence." If she had married, her movements would have been restricted and controlled by in-laws. She did not want that to happen. Most of the women preferred independence and did not want to spend their lives looking after in-laws.

Auntie also spoke about her family. Her mother was a great influence in her life. She was widowed when Auntie was ten years old. She was looked down on by many of the villagers in China because she had three daughters and no son. Auntie remembered her telling her oldest sister to be sure to learn to take the role of the man, as there was no son in the family. Her father had been ill all of Auntie's childhood and died when she was ten. Her mother was sold to her husband's family, but he died shortly after the marriage. So her in-laws, Auntie's grandparents, brought in a young man, her father, to the family for the purpose of reproduction. Her mother was obligated to honor the arrangement. Growing up, Auntie did not see her father much because he was always quietly at the back of the house. He did not live very long anyway. Her mother worked in the field independently, and as the girls grew older they helped her some. She took on the financial burdens, including taking care of her in-laws.

Life at home in Sanshui was difficult. Auntie herself had to work from dawn to dusk with the men, but that was not too bad. The worst thing was when Auntie's grandparents wanted her to get married and asked a matchmaker to look for a husband for her. She related to her mother that she did not want this arrangement. Her mother then connected with some overseas Chinese and with the three other young girls they left the village. Before she escaped, her mother let her know that the bad economic condition in China did not promise a future and she was happy to see her looking for a new life. She reminded her to take on the traditional male role of breadwinner, supporting the family back home. Auntie kept her promise to her mother. She sent money to her and later assisted her sister when she came to Singapore.

Auntie thought her independence was her greatest accomplishment. In her generation, not too many women worked hard alongside the men as she and the other Samsui women did. Usually domestic work dominated the lives of women. Auntie felt that her hard work on the construction site was rather unusual, but it all paid back later. Since the late 1960s she saw many of the new generations take on the blue-collar work in society, like working in construction, driving busses, and taking on many other labor-type jobs. She was proud of these women.

Today's women are educated and are able to make a comfortable living. This is quite different than what Auntie remembers; she did not have chance to be in school. She felt that she would have been as good as many of the younger women if she had been given a chance. She did not know how to read a newspaper. She said she could read her name and the word "China" but that was about all. She wanted to learn English because it was impossible to get around without it. Life would probably have been easier, but she would never change her mind about getting married. Why should she? She was a free woman all her life. She did not have to silently put up with a husband like other women. Another reason she mentioned was that traditionally Chinese people rely on their children to care for them when they are old. Unfortunately, many old people still ended their lives abandoned and living alone.

Auntie Nee Mio never thought of going back to China because her mother died and her sister was in Singapore with her. Although she left China willingly, she always regarded that country as her real home. She had a limited income, so visits were considered a luxury, and many could only afford to go back a couple of times throughout their entire life. Some of her friends dreamed of being able to die in their native country. Many of her friends did return to China, but it was not a happy reunion for those who returned. Most of them were already in their twilight years, and by then their close relatives had passed way. The remaining family, due to poverty, did not welcome an extra mouth to feed. In the end, many of her friends lived and died in solitude in China. She closed by saying, "Let's have some more tea!"

CREDIT

Fig. 1.2.1: Copyright © 2019 by Amila Wickramarachchi.

Guadalajara, Mexico (1912)

As told to her granddaughter.

FIGURE 1.3.1   Suburban Residential District, El Paso, 1908

The story of Yasmin Sanchez Morales began on March 13, 1912, in Guadalajara, Mexico. She was one of 12 children born to Victor and Karina Sanchez. Not too long after her birth, she and her family decided to flee the country. At this period in history there was a violent revolution occurring in Mexico. Yasmin's father thought that it would be better and safer if they made the long trip to America. Still a baby, Yasmin and her family crossed the border into Texas and began their lives in the United States.

The Sanchez family settled in El Paso, Texas, for almost six years. During this time, Victor traveled various places for work. Her father worked for five years on the railroads in Illinois. Victor's absence did not affect Yasmin's upbringing. Her mother took care of her and her only living sibling. Even though she was one of twelve children, ten of her siblings died at a very early age. Yasmin and her sister attended a Spanish-speaking school until her father decided that things might be better in California.

Yasmin and her family moved to California in 1919. They settled in a small town, nestled in orange groves, named Burbank. They lived on Front Street, a small street just across from the railroad tracks. It was here that the family built three different homes on a large plot of land. Though having little education, Victor was hired to work for the city of Burbank. Yasmin continued her education but had to overcome a large obstacle to do so. Up to this point in her life the only language she knew was Spanish. However, there was no Spanish-speaking school in the area. Her only option was to attend an English-speaking school. Yasmin found it hard to learn the language but eventually caught on. Her acceptance of the English language would later prove her desire for assimilation into the American culture. With the new skill of speaking the main language of her hometown, one might expect her to have more freedom, although this was not the case.

After having a pretty uneventful childhood, amounting to only school and church, Yasmin wanted to spread her wings. Her free-spirit attitude clashed with her strict, smothering Catholic family. Her father and mother would not allow her to leave the house and have friends. In Yasmin's own words, she was a prisoner. She not only received this treatment from her parents but also from her older sister. Her sister ruled over her like she was her mother. Even with all the pressure, Yasmin's free spirit could not be caged. She found ways to release herself from the shackles put on her by her parents. Yasmin made friends with a neighborhood girl named Ines and together they lived a normal teenage life.

Yasmin and Ines loved to go to the beach and walk the main street. She was not much of a money spender but went window shopping along the main street in town. During this time, Yasmin was continuing her education and graduated from Burbank High School in 1930. After graduation, her life pretty much stayed the same. Unlike most girls at that time, Yasmin did not marry at a young age. For a short period she worked as a seamstress in the garment district of Downtown Los Angeles. Yasmin stopped working when she found the love of her life and finally decided to marry. Yasmin married Pedro Morales on September 18, 1943, at a church in Downtown Los Angeles. For two years, Yasmin and Pedro lived an uneventful life. Pedro worked while Yasmin took care of their household. It was two years before the birth of their first child, Antonio. It did not take them long to add another child to the family. Fourteen months after the birth of Antonio, his brother Alberto was born. The Morales clan made their home in Glendale and started their life.

The marriage between Yasmin and Pedro had its ups and downs. The birth of their two sons brought much happiness but the relationship had its problems.

Pedro seemed to be an honest man. With the education he received at Glendale College he found work at a publishing company in Los Angeles as a graphic artist. At that time it was not possible to print pictures on various materials, so Pedro had to arrange letters to make them into images. This was a very respectable job, but it was not his only job. On the side, Pedro was a driver for a mob family in Los Angeles, and this did not sit well with Yasmin. He also made runs down to Mexico to smuggle in liquor for clients.

Pedro was also an unfaithful and uncaring man. He had a mistress with whom he fathered a child. Yasmin did not know about this, but when she found out she was devastated. In addition to his adultery, Pedro also controlled Yasmin. She was unable to leave the house or have friends. He did not even care for her when she was ill. One case that showed his lack of empathy was when Yasmin was terribly sick and he would not take her to the doctor. Yasmin had to tell her children to go to their parish pastor and get his help. When he came over and saw her state he took her to the doctor. This was the last straw for her. With advice from both the doctor and the priest, she found courage to leave Pedro. Thus, another battle began.

The divorce from Pedro was difficult. Pedro did not want to support his family and refused to pay child support. Pedro thought he did not have to because he had his "new" family to take care of. At one of the court hearings, the uncaring Pedro even brought his mistress and his daughter with him. The court sided with Yasmin and ordered that Pedro pay her $47.50 a month. Though she had a monetary victory, she still felt alone.

Yasmin and her children went to live with her family. She continued to live there until she was into her seventies. Yasmin now had to find a way to support her boys. She took a job as a housecleaner for her parish pastor, Monsignor Singer. This money went to tuition that enabled her son to attend parochial school. She worked for him until he passed. This part of Yasmin's life consisted of mainly raising her sons. However, Yasmin still found time to become an American citizen. For almost all her life she had thought it was very important to assimilate into the American lifestyle. She felt lucky to live in the United States and wanted to become a legal citizen. Though she had suffered so much, she knew that her life was better in America than it would have been in Mexico. She insisted that her sons learn English, which became the only language spoken at home. She felt it was important for her sons to blend in with their American friends. Living at home, Yasmin cared for her elderly parents until they passed. This loss was hard for her to take. Now she had to find something new to fill the void left by her parents' deaths.

Yasmin found her place with a new hobby, traveling. Since she was oppressed in both her childhood and most of her adult life, she wanted to get away. Yasmin joined a travel group and wandered all over the world. She took a cruise to Alaska and Hawaii. She wandered through the Scottish and English countryside. She visited St. Peter's Cathedral in Rome. Yasmin lay on the white sand beaches of Hawaii and saw the lights of Tokyo. She walked the "clean streets" of Singapore where chewing gum is not allowed. She visited the communist country of China and the sights of Istanbul, Turkey. This was a lot of traveling for a woman who spent much of her life "in prison." When she was not traveling, Yasmin spent time at her local senior's center, Tuttle's. She helped serve food and organized various social activities. Though she was elderly herself, she continued helping her friends. Yasmin also loved to take the bus. She traveled all over Los Angeles on the Metro with no particular destination. She still lived in Burbank but decided in 1989 that she wanted to stay with her son Alberto. Once again, Yasmin began another chapter in her life.

The globetrotting life that Yasmin had for many years took a toll on her. She had a pacemaker and was feeling a little less lively. Her son Alberto decided that it might be best if she moved in with him and his family. Alberto wanted a room for his mother and built a studio apartment for her. She had her own entrance, and he encouraged her to continue her bus trips. When Alberto decided to move the family to Hawaii, Yasmin followed them to paradise. She now had a whole island to discover. She hopped on the bus and traveled the island. She enjoyed her time on the island, but when Alberto decided to move back to California she went along. However, she decided not to live with her son. She moved in with her old friend Ines and returned to her old regimen.

Yasmin continued to live on her own for five more years. This changed when she fell down twice and broke both her hips. After nursing her body in an outpatient care facility, Yasmin went home with her son Alberto. She continued to live with her son, his wife, and his daughter. At 93 years old, Yasmin is very healthy and aware for her age. She enjoys the times spent with her family and likes to watch CBS 2 and Judge Judy. Every Sunday she goes to her local church, and she recites the rosary every day. She reads the *Enquirer* religiously and keeps watch over the family pets. Yasmin tries to keep up a normal active lifestyle.

Yasmin is a very smart woman but still has her quirks. Throughout her life she has been adamant that a curse has been cast on her. When she was a young girl, her father invited a cousin to visit. Once he arrived he started to act very strangely. He would just sit and shake. The family was so worried about him that they called for his father to come up from Mexico. Upon his arrival, the family members found a "medicine man" and had him come to the home. He made the boy sit in a chair and placed a pot of hot coals underneath him. He placed a blanket over him and at once the evil spirits started to leave his body. At the end, the cousin was perfectly healthy.

Another spell that was cast on Yasmin was one that made her sick. For most of her life, she was never really sick, but one day she became very ill. No one knew why and no one was able to help her. It was not until she traveled across the country that the illness left her. However, when she came back to California she became sick again. She is convinced that her husband's mistress put this spell on her. The next example of the curse was an incident involving the police. While she was away at the store, the police answered a call involving her house. The police drove up to her house and noticed smoke coming from the windows. Yasmin eventually came home and walked up to the officers. They asked her if there was a fire inside her home, but she said no. There was no reason for smoke to be coming out of the windows. Yasmin decided that this was just another spell of the curse. This is not the end of her experience with the curse.

For most of her life she has been convinced that a flaming rooster has appeared to her. It appeared to her on the step of the studio apartment and has recently appeared in her current residence. She understands that this may seem odd to most people, but she is adamant that it really happens. Yasmin may have her strange visions, but she is still a very strong and courageous woman at 93 years of age.

CREDIT

Fig. 1.3.1: Source: https://commons.wikimedia.org/wiki/File:Suburban_residential_district,_El_Paso,_Texas.jpg.

Estonia (1914)

As told to her granddaughter.

FIGURE 1.4.1   Bombing of city of Tallinn, Estonia, by Soviet Army, March 1944

The following is a delightful story of a woman who was directly touched with the major occurrences in history from the Great Depression to World War II. Despite the many challenges she faced, she always remained strong, determined, and independent. It was very interesting to read and see how historical events affected her life.

Liisi Hughes was born on March 28, 1914, in Sakuvald, a rural province in Estonia, which is located on the Baltic Sea, south of Finland and north of Latvia. The daughter of a sawmill and lumberyard owner, Liisi and her three sisters lived in a farmhouse next to a creek, in which they loved to play during the summer. In winter the girls took carriage rides, after which they would be promptly bundled into blankets and taken inside by their nanny. One of Liisi's happiest memories from her early childhood is of spending Saturday evenings in her grandparents' sauna, after which she and her sisters would eat mashed potatoes together. Liisi's grandfather would wrap the children up in towels and send them into the house, where they would sit down together at the big table. Liisi often found herself sharing her bowl of potatoes with her older sister, who always made a hole in the potatoes to make the melted butter run onto her side of the dish, leaving her sister with none. She and her sisters always had a close relationship, spending many hours playing together at the family's home. After the untimely death of their mother following surgery, Liisi took on the role of surrogate mother to her youngest sister when she was just 21 years old. This loss was her saddest memory of childhood.

Liisi attended a private girls' school in Tallinn, the country's capital city. She knew that education was very important even as a child and always appreciated how lucky she was to be able to attend this private school. The only thing she disliked about school was that some of the students spoke German rather than Estonian, which upset her because the country was just recovering from the occupation by Germany. During the school year, she lived in the city, returning home for summers. She attended this school for 11 years, at which time she graduated high school. She was the only one of all her sisters to do so. Liisi recalled the year she lived at home and rode the train to school every morning, which was 40 miles away. Each morning, her grandfather would meet her at one of the train's stops and give her a sandwich and a cup of coffee for breakfast, with another sandwich for her lunch later that day. She was around ten years old. Reflecting on this, Liisi was amazed of the love her grandparents must have felt for her, to meet her each morning and send her off that way.

After graduating from the girls' school, Liisi continued her education in the city of Tartu at the University of Tartu, a prestigious institution. A student of economics, Liisi explained that all college students at that time were short of money, and that having a car was relatively rare. Although she was on a tight budget herself, Liisi always managed to treat her cousin, also a student at the university and a fraternity member, to a meal now and then. They were such good friends that she could never refuse him, knowing he was even poorer than she.

Following her graduation from the university, Liisi met and married her first husband at the age of 22 in 1936. Two years later, her son was born and her husband was sent to fight in World War II. Liisi learned of her husband's death by reading a posting of the names of casualties of war on a bulletin board in town. She was not sent any letter of condolence from the government. Reading his name among the others killed with her young son by her side was heartbreaking for the young wife and mother, who suddenly found herself quite alone in the world.

With her husband gone, Liisi went to work to support herself and her young son. She worked mainly secretarial and bookkeeping jobs in Tallinn and was paid well. While working in a medical office, Liisi met Gene Hughes. Impressed by his "impeccable manners," she began dating him. They married in 1942. Shortly thereafter, Gene was forced to leave Estonia under the threat of being deported to Siberia by the Russian army, which was occupying the country at the time. Many men were forced to leave their homeland due to their connections with the government. Taking only two suitcases with them, the young family fled under the cover of nightfall to Saaremaa, a small island off the coast of Estonia. There, they took a ship to Germany, where they stayed in a small township with some friends. Liisi did not know where her other sisters and their families were, or when she would see them again. She could only hope that, somehow, escaping the madness of the war would enable them all to find each other again, under safer circumstances.

For seven years, Liisi and her family lived in a displaced persons camp in Germany, where her two daughters were born, in 1946 and 1947. Two families were crowded into one small room, and they were often short on food. It was very difficult, but the families tried to help one another by sharing food and other necessities whenever possible. At this time, Liisi's son began attending German school where he was quite well accepted by his classmates for his blonde hair, blue eyes, and knowledge of the German language. Also at this time, Liisi's eldest daughter became so ill that doctors told Liisi to put her in a hospital, as she was sure to die anyway. Liisi refused to do so, unable to give up any of her children. An uncle who happened to be a physician came to the camp and nursed the girl back to health.

During this difficult time, Gene was working as a translator for the Lutheran World Federation and was able to write to churches in America in an effort to secure sponsorship for his family, which would enable them to immigrate. Liisi's sister and her husband were already living in the United States but were not allowed to sponsor the family. After many letters, a sponsor family was finally found, and the Hughes family was able to leave the camp at last.

In 1952, after a horrible sea voyage that lasted fourteen days instead of seven due to stormy weather, the Hughes arrived in New York harbor. The passengers were not taken through Ellis Island because so many of them were ill. Liisi recalled trying to care for her two small daughters while being seasick herself and separated from her husband and son. Men and women were not allowed to make the journey together, due to the dangers posed to single women on board. By the time they arrived, their food had spoiled, due to the fact that the voyage had lasted twice as long as intended and everyone had been too ill to eat. The family eventually settled in California.

When asked about the most influential woman in her life, Liisi described her mother in a story about a gypsy. According to her mother, whenever someone is in need of help, you should give them as much as you can. At that time in Estonia, gypsies (Roma) were common and would often come to the back door of the house to read palms in exchange for food, a few coins, whatever might be given. The gypsies were shunned by most people, who called them vagrants and thieves, but Liisi's mother was always kind to them. She remembered one gypsy woman in particular, who had two small children. Her mother always made sandwiches for the children when the woman came to see them. One day not long after the death of Liisi's mother, the gypsy woman came to the door and Liisi told her of their loss. The gypsy woman began to cry, saying it was not the food of the money that mattered to her, but the friendship of her mother. She inquired as to where the woman had been buried, and Liisi told her the place. Later, when Liisi went to her mother's grave to water some flowers she had planted there, she was surprised to see that they had already been watered and that a bouquet of wildflowers had been left there as well. She can only guess that the gypsy woman had visited her mother one last time, to say goodbye.

More than any other historical event, World War II affected Liisi Hughes's life. The loss of her first husband, as well as of her home and family, changed her life more than she had ever anticipated. Liisi recalled the day that one-third of her city was destroyed in a bombing. She was making a pot of soup for lunch when the attack began. Grabbing her son, she fled from the building out into the streets below. Later, as she stood in the street in front of her apartment building, Liisi looked up through the side of the destroyed building into her kitchen, where her pot of soup was still sitting on the stove. The side of the structure had been completely demolished, and there was her kitchen, sitting out in the open air. Had she remained in her home, she would have certainly been killed. Since fleeing Estonia with Gene, Liisi never returned; she preferred to leave that part of her life, with all of its painful memories, in her past.

Liisi feels that women have taken on more responsibilities during her lifetime, both at home and in the workplace, and she feels that men too, have taken on more responsibility, with regard to raising children. She sees that as a good thing, but feels that, if possible, women with children should not work in order to stay home and raise them. Of all her accomplishments, Liisi said without hesitating that her children and grandchildren had made her the most proud. Her family was very closely knit and was the most important thing in her life. She had nothing she would change or do differently if she were to live her life over again, but says that she would like more great-grandchildren, if possible. Liisi Hughes is a mother, grandmother, and great-grandmother. She is a portrait of strength and compassion, and much loved and admired by all who know her.

CREDIT

Fig. 1.4.1: Source: https://commons.wikimedia.org/wiki/File:Tallinn_defence1941.jpg.

Indiana, US (1914)

As told to her granddaughter.

FIGURE 1.5.1   KKK Gathering in Muncie, Indiana, 1922

What people decide to do with their lives is often just a reflection of societal norms of the times. Many women follow a prescribed version of their lives as set by family, church, and community. Women who decide to follow their own path demonstrate a remarkable strength and determination that is compelling. Some famous women who exemplify this strength are Eleanor Roosevelt, Susan B. Anthony, and Rosa Parks. However, to find this strength in ordinary women is equally compelling. Beverly McGee Parks is a woman who has always been independent and followed her own path and rarely compromised by conforming to others' ideas about the way in which she should live.

Beverly McGee was born on July 14, 1914, in Mishawaka, Indiana. She joined her mother and father and two-year-old sister, Lois. A couple of years later, Sarah, another girl, was born. Seven years later the family was complete with the birth of a beloved brother, Anthony, who became known as Tony. The girls were responsible for taking care of young Tony, and they all grew very close. A vivid happy memory Beverly has is taking Tony everywhere in a little wagon.

Despite the children being close, Beverly would not consider her family as happy. Her father had a drinking problem that he exercised every weekend. When he drank, he would often be angry as well, and though she does not remember physical abuse, she does remember violent outbursts and verbal abuse directed toward her mother. Whereas this might garner sympathy from some, this caused the very independent and headstrong Beverly to lose respect for her mother. She could not understand why anyone would tolerate such abuse. This is a trait she would carry with her the rest of her life.

The family lived in a three-bedroom home that sat on a hill and had been purchased from Beverly's grandfather. There were a lot of relatives that lived in Mishawaka. The father's father lived right down the street. Beverly does not remember much about her grandmother, except that she was crippled. She may have died when the children were quite young. There were also two uncles and two aunts in town. One aunt, in particular, was very close to Beverly, and she spent much of her adolescence with her. Her mother's side of the family is a mystery as they were Amish and had disowned Beverly's mother for marrying a Catholic man. Beverly also suspects that her older sister was conceived prior to the marriage and that the marriage was never a happy one.

The house had a small garden that produced vegetables for personal use, and sometimes when times were hard for distribution throughout the neighborhood. Beverly remembers this as an unpleasant experience. She did not like it when her mother would load up the wagon and the girls would have to give out food to the families of children they knew from school. The girls found this ritual embarrassing. During the Great Depression, people would sometimes come to the door looking for a meal. Mrs. McGee would provide the meal and then go out to scrub the marking off the tree that the beggars would leave to show other beggars that they received a meal there. Beverly laughs about the irony of this memory.

Other enjoyable recollections include spending time with her family swimming at Eagle Lake in Lower Michigan, which borders Indiana. Sometimes during summer evenings, Mr. McGee would come home from work and load the whole family in the car and drive 16 miles to the lake. Also, in the winter the children were allowed to sled down the snow on the bank by their home. These are some of the times Beverly likes to reminisce about the most. A very scary memory from when she lived in this house is the time the Ku Klux Klan placed a burning cross in their front yard because of their Catholic faith. Beverly was very small and remembers clutching her father's knee as he chased the vandal way a with a shotgun. These are the images that come to mind as she recollects her life in Indiana.

The children attended St. Monica's Catholic School, where nuns were cruel to Beverly. She is not sure why but thinks it is perhaps because they compared her to her older sister Lois. Lois had long curls and was sweet and easy to get along with. Beverly had a mind of her own and did not want anyone telling her what to do. One particular nun did not like Beverly and would beat her regularly until Beverly's father went to school and threatened her. He said, "If you touch her again I will come down here and beat you the same way." It made Beverly feel good that her dad stuck up for her. Beverly, however, never liked school. She was not close to any children except her siblings and did not participate in any extracurricular activities. After eight years at St. Monica's and two years of high school, despite her keen intelligence, Beverly quit school and went to work. She was 14.

Beverly began her working career as a bathroom cleaner for the First National Bank. She did this on weekends while she was still in school. This was not one of her favorite jobs and she quit after about a year. Around the year 1930, Beverly went to work at a dime store called McCrery's as a floor walker. This was a supervisory person who made sure the whole place was running properly. Beverly worked 64 hours per week in the beginning and made $9.99 per week in cash. Even though these were the beginning of the Depression years, Mr. McGee, Beverly's father, had a steady job at Dodge Manufacturing and Beverly did not have to contribute her money to the family income. One of her first purchases was a banjo, which she never learned to play and was broken when her brother sat on it. Another big purchase was bus tickets for her younger sister and herself to visit their older sister in Detroit, where she had moved after marrying. Beverly was 15 and Sarah was 13, and this was a big trip for the young girls. Usually, however, money went for clothes to wear to work and into savings. For years Beverly made sure that at least one dollar went into savings every week.

When the dime store, which was a chain store, closed in Mishawaka, Beverly was transferred to a store in Indianapolis. She received a pay raise to $14.00 per week but now she had to pay for room and board for the first time. She rented a room with the family of another employee for $3.00 per week. The year was 1936 and Beverly was 22 years old and living on her own for the first time. Her mother and her older sister helped her make the move, but they were worried for her. They certainly did not need to be, as Beverly could take care of herself. In 1937 she again was offered a transfer by her boss, who really appreciated Beverly's work ethic and organizational skills. This time she went to Jackson, Michigan. Beverly was very happy with her work and independence. Then her mother fell ill.

Mrs. McGee had breast cancer, and it metastasized to her brain. The family pressured Beverly to come home because they felt that Mrs. McGee worried about her and would be better off with her home. Beverly came home and her mother died in 1939. After her mother's death, Beverly stayed home to care for her father and little brother. Her younger sister Sarah was married by this time and the burden fell to Beverly. Beverly went to work at Dodge Manufacturing where her father worked and became a "Rosie the Riveter" for the war effort. Her job was to grind down scrap metal so it could be used for military purposes. During this time Beverly met and became fond of her future husband Samuel "Bub" North, who also worked at Dodge Automobiles. They met in February and married in September of 1940, during World War II.

At the time Samuel was 36 and no one expected him to be drafted into the war, but he was. He was sent to Scotland for training, then on to France and Belgium. He was an officer's orderly in the signal corps and was right on the front line. He was gone for four years, but Beverly was fine because she was used to being on her own. They were able to correspond by way of "victory memos," which contained preprinted statements that could be checked off if it suited what they wanted to say. Letters were not allowed. Samuel liked to play cards and was good at it, so frequently he was able to send Beverly money he had won. Occasionally he would need to ask for money because of a bad streak. She remembers, with a smile, one memo with the boxes checked, "Thinking of you, love and kisses, send money."

This was a very sad time in Beverly's life as her younger sister Sarah was having a routine operation for a goiter and an enlarged thyroid gland and died on the operating table due to a physician error. Sarah was only 25. In the years between 1939 and 1941, Beverly left her job, lost her mother, got married, sent her husband and brother off to war, and finally buried her sister.

Beverly's brother, Tony, was a remarkable young man and she loved him dearly. He was smart and ambitious. Beverly remembers her mom trying to get him to stop studying when he was younger and go to bed but he would not until he just could not keep his eyes open any longer. He was a pilot in the war and was shot down over Tokyo. He parachuted safely out of the plane only to find himself the target of Japanese artillery men in a line raft. Luckily he escaped certain death or capture when an American plane shot the Japanese raft out of the water. Shortly after, an American submarine surfaced and picked him up, but because they could not maintain any radio contact and did not dock again for six weeks, the only thing Beverly heard was that he was shot down and missing in action. Aside from the anxious six weeks of waiting it was all very exciting with write-ups in the newspaper, and he came home to a hero's welcome. By the end of the war, both Tony and Samuel were home safely.

Tony moved out to California to attend Notre Dame College where he majored in engineering and went on to get a master's degree in aeronautical physics. He got married, and by the time he had two children, Beverly and Samuel moved out to join them in California. After Tony graduated, the whole clan—Tony and his wife, their two children, Beverly, and Samuel—picked up and moved to New York for about nine months until they all got tired of the snow and went back to California. Beverly found a job at Prudential Insurance Company where she worked for the next 19 years in the investment treasury department. Samuel got a job with Aerospace and they were happy. They never had children of their own. Beverly is not sure why but none of the three sisters ever had biological children either. Beverly recalls her mother making the comment that if there had not been "Lydia Pinkham's," an herbal medicine for female "hysteria" popular in the nineteenth century, none of her children would have been born. It was fine with Beverly as she and Samuel never pined for them and they had Tony's children, which came to total four, to help care for and love.

After her mother died, Beverly's father married and divorced two times and eventually succumbed to the disease of alcoholism, after getting an infection in his foot that required amputation. Samuel died in 1971 after a long fight with lung cancer. To demonstrate Beverly's discipline and inner strength, when Samuel was diagnosed with cancer, Beverly, who had been a long-time smoker, threw out her cigarettes and never smoked again.

Beverly went on to retire from Prudential, after which she took her sister Lois, who was now also fighting a terminal illness, on a six-month road trip. Beverly could not stand to be idle, so she went to work for Pacific Telephone Company, where she worked in the directory and long distance. She remained there for 11 years. Again she attempted retirement but failed. She had heard about a job in a parking booth and went down to Executive Parking Company to interview for the job. The owner was so impressed with this 62-year-old woman that he asked her to manage the office. She worked there and helped to make that small little parking company into the largest parking company in southern California. She stayed there for 19 years and was a much loved and respected member of that close-knit group. She left only when the company sold to a larger national corporation.

Beverly is now almost 90. Her mind is still as alert and intelligent as ever. Unfortunately, with the passing of her beloved brother Tony two years ago, she feels completely alone. She has many, many people who love her, but she says that it is just not the same as her immediate family. She is ready for death when it should come. She suffers from arthritis and is in constant pain. But in that indomitable spirit that she has shown throughout her life, she trudges on. She lives alone and keeps an unbelievably immaculate home. She even does her own windows. She still drives. In fact, she just went into the Department of Motor Vehicles where she took her written test and eye exam, and they extended her driver's license for another five years. Of course, she thinks that they are all crazy and will quit driving at the first sign of decreased ability. Nobody needs to tell Beverly what to do.

CREDIT

Tibliz, Russia (1915)

As told to her grandson.

Media Gallery in : www.fouman.com

FIGURE 1.6.1 Armenian Woman in Qajar, 1892

Femi Margarian was born in Tibliz, Russia, in 1915 during the Armenian genocide. Her parents moved to Tabriz (a historical Persian capital) in Iran in 1916 when she was one year old. She had an older sister at the time, and later a younger brother. Her father died when she was very young, and her mother raised her and her siblings by working at the American hospital, sewing curtains and clothing. Femi's hobby, at the time, was sewing and it is still an activity she enjoys today. She attended an American school while her mother worked and took care of the family. Thus, they lived a very poor life.

Femi recalls how the water was distributed to the individual apartments. Of course, there was no running water. Instead, each house had a tank that would be filled for washing, bathing, and so on. Once a month, the doors to the dam would be opened and the water would flow through the gutters to the front of the tenement. The door to the basement would be opened and the water would flow for collection into the tank. Obviously, the water was not clean, so they had screens set up on the faucets to trap debris and parasites (white worms), which were later disposed of. The water was moved through the piping system via a manual pump that induced pressure inside the tank that would force the water through. There was one furnace for the building and only one outhouse. Femi's mother would warm the water on the furnace and then dump it into pails, which she carried up two flights of stairs for her children to use as bath water.

The outhouse was unsanitary. There was no seat to sit on, but instead, two bricks that a person would stand on to squat over the hole in the ground. Persians do not use toilet paper, but instead use a device that was written in the Quran called an *aftafa*. It is like a watering can with a long neck that is used to reach the backside to facilitate washing. Armenians used newspaper that they cut into cubes. They would dispose of them in a bag and frequently burn them because they could not throw them into the hole. Femi recalls the ghastly stench and how, by walking in someone's yard, it was easy to tell what they were doing.

Graduating from school is the happiest memory of Femi's childhood. Mrs. Anderson was her mentor. She was an American missionary who helped Femi with her studies. The American school Femi attended was established by the American missionaries from the Presbyterian Church. The Presbyterian Church also funded the American hospital where Femi's mother worked. The school she attended in Tabriz was an all-girls school and was the largest out of six established at the time.

Femi's future husband Raffi attended the all-boys school that was also established by the missionaries. He graduated at the same time as she did and immediately started working for the American embassy. He was the clerk to the ambassador and was given his job due to his fluency in four languages: English, Farsi, Armenian, and Turkish. Another great asset was his superb handwriting. He was regarded by the embassy as being very active, honest, and punctual. The same was true for Raffi's brother. Raffi's brother lacked any formal education, but he was made the chauffeur of the ambassador and was also commended for his work.

After Femi graduated in 1931, she went to work at the American hospital where she aided poor patients who were suffering from infectious diseases. They were transported to the hospital on donkeys. She worked day and night for three years as a trainee at the hospital before she was given the title of nurse. She then worked under Dr. Armstrong as one of his head nurses. Because her supervisor, Mrs. Lansing, assisted in anesthesia, Femi's relationship with Dr. Armstrong was one of great respect. She viewed him as a second father. A vivid memory was her mother's appendectomy. Dr. Armstrong performed the surgery and Femi assisted. She remembers the doctor asking her if it was all right for him to cut into her mother's abdomen. Without hesitation, she approved, and they performed the surgery.

At the time, everyone contracted typhoid fever from the unsanitary conditions of the buses. When her mother contracted typhoid fever, Dr. Armstrong drove his car to her house and brought her mother to the hospital for treatment rather than leave transportation up to them. Femi worked at the hospital until 1942 when she left to work in the American Army hospital that was established during World War II. She worked at the army hospital for one year until the soldiers went back to the United States.

Femi recalls, at the time, watching over an American captain's children when he went to Beirut for a meeting. There was no one else that he could trust, so he had her watch over his children for two weeks. Muslims did not like Americans because they were afraid that the oil refinery in Abadan would eventually be taken over by the Americans. They regarded Americans as only being interested in taking over the refinery and kept a watchful eye on them. Femi recalls being very frightened at the time, because if the Iranians would have found out about her babysitting job, she could have been sent to jail. An incident happened in post-Iranian revolutionary times (1980), which explained her fear. An Armenian nurse who was a teacher and who had helped the Iranians all of her life was thrown in jail because she had her class write a paper on the Ayatollah's government and how it had double-crossed them. A few of the Persian students had reported her to the authorities and she was thrown in jail for a month. While there, she contracted a massive infection on her side. When the woman was finally released, Femi had to clean the wound and change the dressing regularly. She finally died from the infection and was forgotten. All of her life, she had helped the Iranians in the hospital and for one mistake she had been thrown in a horrid place that eventually caused her death. Femi said that the jails were no different in 1943, and if she were caught and thrown into jail, she would not have survived.

Femi married her husband in 1942 and had her first child in 1943. After her son's birth, Femi formally stopped working at the hospital so that she could raise her child. In 1944, she had a second child and in 1955 she had her third. While taking care of her children, she continued nursing by going to people's homes and administering injections, taking blood pressure, and dressing wounds. Thus, she supplemented her husband's income. From that period on, her life was routine. Femi would wake up at seven in the morning and cook breakfast and help the children get ready for school. Then she would clean the house and do the laundry, all by hand, and cook dinner. When she had time, Femi would help the community with her nursing skills, and frequently people would come over to her house for injections and blood pressure measurements. Her house was regarded as a little clinic.

Femi regarded her husband as an incredible man. He was the most trusted individual at the embassy, he kept the accounts for them. His stack of papers was literally a mountain, yet he managed to keep everything in order. At the time, getting an American education for the children was considered a great thing, and Raffi managed to send his son to the United States, specifically UCLA, where he studied chemistry. This was difficult for them, yet they managed due to Raffi's superb bookkeeping skills. Setting aside money every month for his son was top priority, and even though they made sacrifices, they still managed. When he returned to Iran, he was immediately hired by the Tide Company as their chief chemist. He was given the secret formula (an honor in any nation) and the manufacturing secrets.

In 1979, the Iranian Revolution began. Femi's daughter had married a successful man and had the ability to move to America and escape the impositions that the new government posed. By that time, her son had also married, and the only child left was her youngest. Life changed. No longer could any woman walk on the street without being fully covered, even if they were not Muslim. Everyone was subject to the new ways. Noncompliance was dealt with in a severe manner. Again, Femi found routine in her life until the day her husband died in December 1989. When she discovered him not breathing in bed, Femi did not rush to call her son or ask anyone for help. Instead, she spent the night praying for him. Femi undressed him, bathed him, and put on fresh clothes, and in the morning, she called her son. Two months later, Femi was granted a visa to come to the United States to see her daughter and spend time with her. She managed to stay there and was given citizenship in honor of all the aid she had given during the war.

CREDIT

Fig. 1.6.1: Source: https://commons.wikimedia.org/wiki/File:Qajar_Armenian_Women.jpg.

Pittsburgh, US (1917)

As told to her granddaughter.

FIGURE 1.7.1 14-year-old Italian Child Laborer in Paper Box Facotry, 1913

I was born Anna Maria Marado (Ann Marie) on October 17, 1917, in Pittsburgh, Pennsylvania. My parents, Salvatore and Maria Marado, were immigrants from Italy and both came from the same small town of Pizzoni. My parents decided in 1915 that my father would sail to America with a friend in order to make a new life for the family. The plan was for him to return for my mother in a year's time in order to bring her to the United States once he was settled. Months passed and my father's friend returned and told my mother that if she did not sail herself for America she would lose her husband because he had no intention of returning for her and had been unfaithful. My mother gathered up the family and their belongings and got on a boat to the United States.

My family consisted of my older sisters, Grazia Maria (Mary Grace), Elizabetta Maria (Mary Elizabeth), Italia (Eti), and five brothers of whose names I do not know because they all passed before my birth. (The sisters went by the English versions of their names.) My mother came to America with Grace and Betty and at least one of my brothers; she was pregnant with Eti at the time of the voyage. Upon her arrival my mother took up residence with my father in an Italian barrio in Pittsburgh and soon after had my sister, Eti. Yet right before Eti's birth, tragedy struck the family and my brother passed; my mother gave birth to Eti upstairs in our house while my brother was being laid out downstairs. She was so distraught over her last son's passing that she could not name her baby. The midwife, knowing that our family had come from Italy, named her Italia after it.

When I was born, I was a very sickly child. I caught pneumonia as a baby and was not expected to live to see the age of two. My parents were so convinced of this that they had a family portrait taken with me dressed in what was to become my burial clothes, so that they could remember the family as it was. When I recovered, I continued to have trouble with childhood illnesses and became sick with pleurisy, which had caused fluid to store in my lungs. A doctor came to our house to drain the fluid by inserting a large needle into my lungs through my back and holding me sideways for the fluid to drain out.

When I was a child I rarely saw my father because he was always at work. He worked as a machinist and often had to do dangerous tasks such as fixing machines by climbing into them. One day my father had to wait until his lunch hour to fix one of the machines. He asked a coworker to stand at the bottom of the machine and make sure that no one turned it on because he was going to be inside fixing it. For some reason the man left his post and the machine was turned on with my father still inside. The circumstances surrounding Salvatore's death were unclear and prompted the police to visit my mother and ask if she wanted an investigation put forth in order to know why the machine had been turned on with him inside. She responded that he "got what he had coming to him." Maria knew that her husband upon arrival to the country had taken jobs with the Mafia in addition to his machinist duties. He made the fatal mistake, however, of taking occupations with two families who were considered rivals. It was understood among the older Marado siblings that their father had been killed for double-crossing the families and no one was surprised. My father was also not missed by the older members of the family, due to his horrendous behavior, most notably the abuse of his own daughter, Betty. The machine ripped his arm off, and he died soon after, leaving my mother the sole supporter of our family. I was only three years old when my father passed away; I never got the chance to know him.

After my father's death, my mother quickly found out that he had accumulated a large amount of debt. She went to each of his creditors and asked them to be patient with her and promised to pay off every penny. We were left so poor that there was often little to no food to eat, not that there had been much when my father was alive. During one of the times when we had nothing, our family was surprised in the evening by a large man pounding at our door. At first, no one answered because we were afraid that it was someone who wished to do us harm, but the man continued to knock and eventually the door was opened. The man had brought us a box of food, which included broth and tiny star pasta to cook it in. In order to survive we moved in with my sister Grace and her husband Nick. My mother worked to pay off the debt by picking fruit and vegetables in a field (mostly tomatoes) and selling them door to door in a red wagon. Eventually she paid off all his debts and swore to my sister Eti and I that she would build us our own house one day, and she continued to sell fruits and vegetables to save for her future home.

While we lived with Grace, she taught me how to make my mother's recipe for bread, which had been handed down generation to generation from our family in Italy. I remember one time when I tried to make the bread on my own as a child; my mother was upstairs sick, and I could not remember all the steps, so I would run from the kitchen to the stairs so she could yell down directions to me. Grace also taught me my family's recipe for marinara sauce and other Italian dishes. Grace's husband, Nick, was very much the head of his house. At dinner time, everyone sat around a table with Nick at the head. In front of him would always be a glass of wine and every night he would take a sip of the wine and pass the glass around the table making sure that everyone took a drink and then placed the glass back in front of him. After we were done eating we had to ask his permission before leaving the table, but we were not allowed to leave the room. Instead, we took our chairs to the wall and were to sit quietly until he had finished with the meal and then we were all allowed to leave.

My mother worked hard to keep our family on track to owning our own home. She spent long hours in those fields picking tomatoes and vegetables. There were nights in the summer that she would come home and her back would be so burned from the sun that it would blister, but she always went back because we were the most important things she had and she wanted us to have the best life in America possible. Every time she was paid, she always gave Eti and me a nickel to go get ice cream for ourselves, but never anything for her. Eventually, my mother's savings paid off and she had accumulated enough money to buy her own plot of land, on which she had a house built for her, Eti and myself. We were still very poor but at least we had a place to call our own.

Growing up poor meant that my sister Eti and I often had to help my mother sell her fruit when we were kids. Neither of us finished our schooling with our friends. I finished high school via a night course when I was in my twenties. But I loved school. I remember as a child, if our teacher forgot to hand out homework I would always raise my hand to remind her. This did not go well with the other kids, but I wanted to learn! For the few years I went to high school I participated in chorus and performed in a play where I got the most laughs by playing a boy and singing the song "Smoke Gets in Your Eyes." Even though I loved to sing and could have had a career as an opera singer, if I could afford to do so, what I wanted more than anything was to become a nun. I was unable to follow my dream as my family needed me to go to work to help support us, so I got a job with Italia at Mine Safety Company, a company that manufactured first aid supplies where it was my job to fill little glass vials with laudanum (opium) and mercurochrome (antiseptic).

My mother worried excessively about my sister and me. She was always afraid that something would happen to us and was especially concerned about my well-being. There was one day that Eti and I wanted to take the ferry to an island off the Pennsylvania coast. My mother was adamant that we not go because she was afraid we would miss the ferry back and become stuck on the island, so she decided to come with us. My mom had such a good time that she lost track of time and caused us to miss the ferry! Luckily, we met a gentleman who drove a hearse and was kind enough to take us and our mother home from the island by sitting in the back.

When the war broke out, I was already working to support my family, so I did not have the option of choosing to work for the war effort. During the war I wrote to many fellows who were stationed overseas. My favorite was a young man, Robert, to whom I wrote often. He would send me trinkets and even arranged for me to meet his family. Whatever he did during the war had to be kept quiet, and he was not allowed to tell anyone where he was in the world, but because he cared so much for me he always wanted me to know his location. We developed a system with the help of his sister so he could divulge his location without the army catching on. He gave his sister a list of countries where he might possibly be going and matched each country name with a different closing that he would use to end his letters to me. I knew, based on how he signed his letters, where he was writing from. (For example, if he signed, "Love" then he was in Germany, if the letter closed with "All my best" then his location was Poland, etc.)

He promised to return for me after the war, but that was not to be. He was killed in a foxhole, and I was notified of his passing via a letter from his sister.

I also wrote to my future husband, Paolo Bellisima, during the war, and after it was over we were formally introduced by mutual friends. We were married not too long after in Pittsburgh and moved into the house with my mother. My sister Italia had also gotten married and gave birth to her first daughter, Norma, and moved to California, as well as my sister Betty. Not too long after Eti moved out west, Paul and I followed with my mother, whose health had started to fail her. We did not think that my mom would make the long car ride across the country, so after we drove our belongings out, I returned to Pittsburgh to try to get her on a plane. My mother, who never complained about anything, refused to get on the plane. It took much convincing, but she finally boarded and calmed down enough to sleep for most of the flight. She was petrified that we were taking her to put her in a home, which I promised her I would never do. Mom passed soon after we moved. I remember the day she died clearly. I was sitting on the bed with her when she looked up suddenly at me and said, "Maria, get off the bed." I did not move, because I could see no reason for me to need to, but she told me again, "Mary, get off the bed," this time adding, "Your brothers are here for me." I explained to mom that there was no one there but she and I, yet she insisted that my brothers had come for her and minutes later she was gone.

My life in California with my husband started in Los Angeles. We lived in a duplex neighborhood with Italia, Betty, and their families. I got a job as a teller for the Bank of Italy (which later became the Bank of America) and eventually moved on to work at Lambert Kay in their office for the owner Mr. Kay. We eventually moved from our duplex to our own place in Los Angeles. It was there that I became pregnant with my first child, Gerald Frank Bellisima, and gave birth to him on November 7, 1947. My second child, Maria Regina Bellisima, was born April 28, 1950. (Of the four sisters Mary and Betty had the fewest children, having two each. Grace had over ten children, and Italia had four.) After Maria was born, it was clear that we would need to move again, this time to Sixth Avenue, also in Los Angeles, from 1950–1959, when we were robbed. The burglars took the only trinkets I had from my mother, including her watch. The thief was eventually caught because he had stolen my husband's matchbook collection. One day a policeman noticed the books in the thief's trunk and questioned him about Paul Bellisima, whose name was on the books. Though the thief was caught, my mother's items were never returned. I no longer felt safe in that house, so I moved the family to Westchester where we lived for only six months because the house was so small. From there we moved to Inglewood, where we stayed until Maria was married and decided to move to the suburbs. Shortly after she moved, my husband and I, along with Gerald and his family, moved as well.

My health has always been delicate, and throughout my life I have often been sick, suffering from various stomach ailments, but nothing too serious. Then, when my children were young adults, I was diagnosed with breast cancer and underwent a mastectomy in order to survive. I remained cancer free for decades until the cancer was found again, this time in my colon; it was removed, and I am again cancer free.

As I reflect on my life I have decided that, if I had the chance to do it all over again, there would be very little that I would change. I would have liked if my mother would not have had to work so hard, so I would have gotten to spend more time with her. I feel that, overall, I have lived my life as best I could and will continue to do so until the Lord takes me.

CREDIT

Afghanistan (1918)

As told to her grandson.

FIGURE 1.8.1   Afghan Women in 1927

When Arminah Karim was born on June 6, 1918, it was the time when Afghanistan was ruled by the British Empire. She was born into the Karim family of Kabul, which was a powerful, wealthy, and conservative Muslim family well known in Afghanistan. Her mother's name was Nilam Mirza but was named Nilam Karim after her wedding because of the patriarchal system in Afghanistan, which expects a girl to take the name of her husband. Her father's name was Ali-Naqib Karim, and he was a scholar of Islam.

The Karim family has its original roots in Saudi Arabia, and after several generations, they ended up in Afghanistan. It was a tradition in Afghanistan that the sons ought to study Islam and immerse themselves in the subject. People pushed their sons to immerse themselves in Islam because Afghanistan had many illiterate people, and since Afghanistan was under the British Empire, the British introduced many rules and everyday products that were not allowed under Islamic law.

Arminah was the first-born child in her family, and she was born a year after her parents' marriage. Her father gave her the name Arminah. In Afghanistan during the 1900s, the first born child was a big thing, and over 90 percent of the population wanted to have a son as their first-born child. It was not because they did not like girls, but since most of the people were farmers, they wanted to have sons so that their sons could help them with farming. On August 19, 1919, Afghanistan got its independence from Great Britain. For some it was a happy day, but for some a sad day because thousands of young men died to give Afghans their freedoms. Afghanistan in the 1900s was not a well-developed country, and the majority of the people lived in the villages. The schools were very limited, and most of the schools of that time were just for boys; there were very few schools for girls. Arminah's father was a kind man, and he loved her very much. He never treated her the way other Afghan families treated their daughters. When she was five years old, her mother gave birth to another daughter. For him, daughter or son did not matter because he was a scholar of Islam, and Islam teaches that men and women are equal. Although he would have loved to have a son, he never treated Arminah and her sister as less than a son. He gave them everything they wanted and loved them even more than their mother. He was not a father to the girls, but a friend. After nine years of marriage, her mother gave birth to a son. Her father was very happy, and she could still remember the big smile on his face when the midwife told him about her brother. Her father gave her new brother the name Aamir. It was one of her happiest days because there was a little brother and now she could brag about him in the neighborhood.

After her brother's birth, her mother's health condition became very serious, and on February 25, 1928, after several months of illness, her mother died. Arminah was almost ten years old, and it was the saddest day of her life. Every family member cried and even she cried. After her mother's death, she was dedicated to her siblings. Her father was very busy with his work and her grandmother took care of the three children. Her father's family often pushed him to remarry, but he always refused. But after a few months he realized that the children needed a mother who could take care of them since their grandmother had poor health. On July 5, 1928, her father married Zubaida. She was only 22 years old. Zubaida was very sweet lady, and she never let them realize that she was their stepmother. She helped Arminah with her homework and did most of the housework, even when they had a servant.

The family members were very close to each other. Her three uncles lived in their own homes with their own families. Her grandfather had died before her father got married. Her father had no sisters, and he was the oldest of all his siblings. He had married her mother when he was 36 years old. Since he was the oldest of all the siblings, he was responsible for taking care of Arminah's grandmother. There is a tradition in Afghanistan that the eldest son take care of both his mother and father. Grandmother was a great lady. She told stories every night before bedtime. In the morning, she woke up her grandchildren for school because she always woke up early to pray the morning prayer. She taught them how to read the holy book or Quran. She used to teach them how to behave with their elders. Arminah remembered that all of her siblings were good friends with one other. They used to play together in the garden, where her brother tended always to cheat. It was good times.

When Arminah was ten years old, she liked to play with her friends. She helped her stepmother with housework and enjoyed listening to stories that her grandmother used to tell. When she grew up, her grandmother's stories started to change. Sometimes she would tell about the children's mother and how she lived. She used to tell Arminah that she would marry one day just like her mother did with her father. One day when she was 15 years old, Grandmother called her over to her room. Arminah went to her room and she started the conversation by saying that Arminah had grown up, and sooner or later she would get married and move in with her husband. Then she said that Arminah's mother had gone through a lot in her life. Her father died when she was only two years old and her mother died a few months later because of an illness. Her father's family took care of her and brought her up. She was illiterate and could not read and write, but she could read the Quran and had a great memory. She was very good in the households such as cooking and cleaning. She was a very kind and innocent lady. She married my father when she was only 16 years old. During these days, it was tradition to marry a girl who had recently become a "woman" (*onset menarche*). Her father's family was not rich, but they were highly esteemed. Then she concluded by saying that Arminah had a better life than her mother had. Her grandmother said, "You have all the freedom in the world. You have a loving family, you go to school, you have great siblings, and you have a good stepmother that takes care of you just like a real mother tends to do. You should always be very grateful for what you have." Arminah asked her why she told her all this, and she responded by saying, "I see your mother in you, and I wanted you to know everything because you will be the one who will tell about your mother to your siblings when they grow up." That day Arminah felt that her life had a meaning and reason.

Arminah started school when she was seven years old. At this time there were very few schools for the girls, and boys and girls were not allowed to attend the same school. It was not normal that a girl went to school because most families knew their daughter would marry as soon as she became a woman; instead, they learned household skills so that they could have a good married life with their husband and his family. Fortunately, her father was not from those kinds of people. He was a man who believed that a person must go to school to learn social norms and rules. He used to say that by denying girls from going to school, we are making a big mistake because these girls will one day be mothers and when they get their own children, what will they teach their children about Afghan society, religion, and traditions? Arminah really loved going to school because she liked to learn.

During her school years she had many good and reliable friends, and they used to have much fun when they all were together. A specialty that the friends had was that they were there when someone needed them. They never said no when asked for help. They always supported each other in all aspects, and Arminah wondered if that is why she never had a best friend, because every single one of them was a best friend. The best thing she liked about school was that she met her friends every day and the thing she liked least about school was the punishment. The teachers used to beat the students every time they did something wrong or when they did not do their homework. But when Arminah thinks of it now, she thinks they used to beat them because they wanted the girls on the right path so that they could study hard and do something in life.

When Arminah turned 17, people from the families of young men began to come to her father for her hand. It was this way since the marriages were typically arranged by the male relatives of the two young people. He refused them all by saying that she was still too young and not quite ready for marriage. She used to love when he was caring enough to say no. But when Arminah turned 20, her father finally decided that she had to get married soon because he wanted to see his grandchildren before he died. One day a good family came for her hand and her father said yes. They were merchants and their son Najir had studied law in Paris. Her father agreed to the proposal. Her father was very happy that she had found such a good proposal. They represented the Hakim family who were great merchants in Afghanistan.

Arminah got married six months later with Najir and moved to her new home. Now she was a wife, a daughter-in-law, and soon a mother. Najir and his family were very nice and sweet. They treated her not like a daughter-in-law, but as a daughter because they did not have one. Najir had a large family. He had four brothers, two uncles, his mother and father, and his grandmother and grandfather. They lived together in a big house. Now Arminah was a part of their family as well. Her husband was the oldest of all the brothers and was the first to get married. She said her husband was a very nice, handsome, sweet, and caring man. Often people fall in love before they marry, but she fell in love after she married. Her husband took very good care of her. He gave her all the happiness and never let a single drop of tears come into her eyes. Arminah thought the reason behind his behavior was, since he studied in Paris, he knew how to respect people and their choices. Najir was a very liberal man. He never said no to a single thing. Their first child was born one year after their marriage. It was a boy, and she gave him the name Budail. He looked exactly like her husband. Her husband was so happy that he began to cry. He gave money to the poor, and when Arminah came home from the hospital, they sacrificed a sheep. The very next week they had a circumcision of *Khitan* ceremony for their new son. Circumcision is a religious tradition in Islam, and every boy must be circumcised. Being a mother felt very good, and after having her first child she said it was "one of the happiest days in [her] life. It was a different feeling that cannot be described." Her in-laws were also very happy when her son was born. They had their first grandchild!

Being a wife and mother was better than Arminah expected. She had three children after Budail, a boy and two daughters who were called Saliha, Sozan, and Muzaffar. Her husband loved her daughters more than her sons. Najir used to say that daughters were God's gift to humanity. Being a wife was one of the best things in her life. She enjoyed every single day of her marriage and all the credit goes to her husband. Being a mother and a wife was a big responsibility. As a mother she took good care of the children. Arminah sent her children to the best schools so that they could have a bright future. She taught them how to talk to the elders, how to respect people, and all the other little things that are necessary for a child to learn. She used to help the children with their homework as well. It was quite a job because she had never actually "worked out" since she finished school. As a wife, she took good care of her husband. As a wife and a daughter-in-law, she fulfilled all of her duties. She worked at home and took good care of her father- and moth-er-in-law. They always used to say that God gave them a daughter in the form of adaughter-in-law. She used to cook too, even though they had a servant. She never let her servants cook food because she wanted to cook for the family herself. The whole family used to praise her cooking!

Sometimes her husband teased for fun. Arminah never minded because she knew he was joking with her. Her husband was a very busy man. He used to travel a lot because of his work, and wherever he went, she was with him, and in their absence her in-laws took care of the children. She proudly said that she fulfilled all the duties of a mother, daughter, daughter-in-law, and wife. She never had to work outside the home because she had enough responsibilities in the house, and also because her husband and his family were very rich. It was against their honor that Arminah work outside the house. They sometimes refused to let her work inside the house too, but she insisted, and they understood the reason behind it. They knew she was only fulfilling her responsibilities and were happy because of that. Arminah was proud to carry the title of a good daughter, wife, mother, and daughter-in-law. Her sons graduated with great results and went to London to study medicine and business. Her daughters both studied politics, married, and live good lives full of joy with their husbands and Arminah's grandchildren.

The biggest problem in her life was when Afghanistan was invaded by the Soviet Union in December 1979. Millions of people had to move away because of the invasion. When the Soviet Union invaded Afghanistan, in the same night, thousands of people were arrested and imprisoned. Her brothers-in-law were among these people. They were arrested and a few days later she received information from Pul-e-Charkhi prison that they were executed. Pul-e-Charkhi was a prison known for performing executions under the Soviet regime. Every political prisoner was sent to the Pul-e-Charkhi, and over 90 percent of inmates never came back. Arminah's family was among those who had to leave their country and migrate to neighboring countries. Her whole family moved to Pakistan. They had to go through the mountains for days to come near the Pakistani border. The roads were closed and the Soviet army did not let anyone leave. Fortunately, during that time her sons lived in Paris and her daughters lived in London and Sydney with their husbands. Yet when she thinks about 1979, she becomes depressed because many of her family members were executed during the communist regime and her lovely country was in ruins after several years of war. This incident was perhaps one of the major historical events that had a strong influence in her life. This event created a great hatred in her heart for communism and for every person who supported it and its ideals.

Arminah says that women's ideas and roles have not changed significantly during her eighty years. She said she might be wrong since she lived all of her life in Afghanistan and Pakistan, but as far as she has seen it, the women's roles in these countries have not changed so much. They are still housewives, and over half of them do not even work. There has been a little change in the society, because even though the roles are the same, women's rights have been changed a lot. They are now more than just wives. A decade ago, a husband could say anything and the wife had to obey it with closed eyes. Now this does not happen. Both husband and wife make decisions together, and men have started to appreciate the effort that a woman puts in her work and house. Men still have higher rank than women because they are superior and have better physical abilities than women, but women are being respected for what they do and that is what matters the most. Girls go to the same schools as boys and get the same education. They are offered good jobs such as doctors, nurses, and politicians. Arminah can see a big change in society and hopefully the gap between men and women will vanish and they both will be equally treated. She closed saying she lived a perfect life.

Children and grandchildren may live far from her now but still are close to her heart. Several times her sons have told her to come to Paris, but Arminah has always refused because she does not want to leave her homeland. Her wish is to spend her last days in Kabul in her old house where she was born and where she spent some precious years of her life. And when she is dead, she wants to be buried beside her mother and father. She always thinks that if she lived her life over again she would have lived her childhood to the fullest. The change that she would have made would be to never let Soviets take over her country. These two things are her dream and if she gets a new life she will definitely make sure that these two things happen.

CREDIT

Fig. 1.8.1: Source: https://commons.wikimedia.org/wiki/File:Afghan_women_in_1927.jpg.

Things to Think About

1. The time period between 1910 and 1920 witnessed many revolutions. Looking back at the oral histories, which ones refer to political or national violence? How do you account for this cluster of problems around the world?

2. Religion plays a large part in the lives of many of these women. Cite some examples of the positive aspects of their religious beliefs and then cite how others reacted to these belief systems.

3. The use of statistics in the discipline of history is called cliometrics, named for the Greek muse of history, Clio. Make a list of the marriage ages of the women who married and plot them on a graph. Despite the stories being geographically spread out, do you see commonalities in marriage ages? Pushing it further, count how many women worked outside the home after they married.

4. In the early twenty-first century migration and the movement of peoples remains a prominent subject. Reread the oral histories and take notes on the movements of peoples. Note where they began and where they ended up. How many moved across the borders of nations? How many moved within their country? Would you say that human migration in the early twentieth century was common?

5. All of the women in the oral histories had hopes and dreams. What were they? How do they differ from your hopes and dreams, or do they? What common themes do you see between people and their hopes for a better tomorrow?

For Further Reading

Mexican Revolution

The Years with Laura Diaz: A Novel (2002) by Carlos Fuentes

Singapore

The Indomitable Florence Finch: The Untold Story of a War Widow Turned Resistance Fighter and Savior of American POWs (2020) by Robert J. Mraze

Mexico

Across the Great River (1989) (novel) by Irene B. Hernandez

Catholics in America

Communion of Immigrants: A History of Catholics in America (2007) by James T. Fisher

Estonia

Walking Since Daybreak: A Story of Eastern Europe, World War II, and the Heart of Our Century (2000) by Modris Eksteins

Russia

The Russian Revolution: A New History (2017) by Sean McMeekin

Immigration

The Transplanted: A History of Immigrants in Urban America (1987) by John Bodnar

Afghanistan

Little Women of Baghlan: The Story of a Nursing School for Girls in Afghanistan, the Peace Corps, and Life Before the Taliban (2018) by Susan Fox

TIMELINE

- **1919**

  Spanish Flu begins. It wil ultimately kill 50 million worldwide

  Ho Chi Minh attends Versailles Treaty to request end to French presence in French Indochina, League of Nationas Founded

  First Red Scare in United States (through 1920)

- **1927**

  Kellogg-Briand Pact "outlaws war"

- **1929-1940**

  Great Depression begins. It lasts through 1940.

- **1930**

  Mohandas Gandhi leads Salt March in movement to decolonize India

- **1933**

  Hitler and FDR elected to lead Germany and USA

- **1935**

  Antibiotics—Sulfa in 1935 and Penicillin in 1938

- **1936-1939**

  Spanish Revolution led by Francisco Franco

- **1937**

  Nanjing Massacre

- **1938**

  Munich Conference and Kristallnacht in Germany

- **1927**

  Hitler begins World War II by initiating the blitzkrieg in Poland

1918–1930

Introduction

Despite the fact that entire nations wage war, the onus of the crisis tends to fall on one generation, becoming the responsibility of only a portion of the children born within the span of a few years. For World War I this set of years lasted from 1895 to 1900. For World War II, the bulk of this new set of soldiers were the children born after the First World War, between 1918 and 1924. They formed the group now called the "greatest generation." But what made them so great?

It is easy to offer that it was their grit and determination as they collectively survived the Great Depression and World War II, but it goes beyond that. After they returned to civilian life, they had to rebuild a stable world order since the old one had clearly failed, colonial empires had collapsed, and millions of world citizens then tried valiantly to build and design new state structures. Historiography of the period demonstrates that the nineteenth century gave birth to strident nationalism. This nationalism did not die with the world wars; one could argue it was reinvigorated with the world settling into "spheres of influences" organized during the war and leaving its indelible footprint in the clash between the world economic systems of communism and capitalism. Whereas the war lasted less than a decade, the ensuing Cold War lasted until 1991, and, as some would argue, beyond.

Despite what hindsight suggests, the decade of the 1920s opened with the new United States president, Warren G. Harding, calling for a return to "normalcy." That return included an exuberant youth culture that often resented the restrictions of its parents as the youth moved to cities, watched the skylines light up with electric lights, danced to the new jazz tunes at the New York Cotton Club, watched the "Sultan of Swat" Babe Ruth elevate baseball to the national pastime, and bought "off-the-rack" clothes that were accented with short hair, cloche hats, and new sayings like "23 Skidoo." From the farms, young men and women took up housing in "furnished rooms districts," some moved to either white- or pink-collar jobs, and others listened to the hopeful ideas of men like W.E.B. DuBois and Marcus Garvey, early civil rights leaders. The economy boomed, Europe was rebuilt, and the world, freed from the empires of old, embraced a new standard of fun and frolic typified by places like Coney Island that displayed the inventions of a world literally burgeoning with new ideas and new wealth.

Despite the laughter and the ragtime music ushering from radios that stood over three feet tall, there was a darker side to the 20s. Around the globe the old empires might have died, from Austria-Hungary to the Ottomans and from Britain to China, but the absence of organization led to disquiet. The Versailles Treaty that ended World War I was based in large part on the Fourteen Points of President Woodrow Wilson. He and the leaders of Britain, Italy, and France redrew the boundaries of Europe, set up a League of Nations to police the new order, and largely ignored the issues of the former Ottoman Empire, the incursions of Japan into the lands of its Asian neighbors, the Irish cries for independence from Britain, and the dominance of strong-arm dictators in the former Spanish and Portuguese colonies. Theoretically, the "war to end all wars" had brought "peace in our time" as the British prime minister assured the world in 1938, following the Munich Conference.

Some observers feared all was not as perfect as it seemed. In order to rebuild France and Britain harsh reparations were levied on the only member of the Central Powers still standing, Germany. This policy left Germany prostrate and its citizens, who strongly believed they had not started the war but backed their ally, Austria-Hungary, angry and impoverished. It was fertile ground for radicalism to grow and one young veteran, Adolf Hitler, was prepared to upend the status quo with his nationalist rhetoric by 1923 in the Beer

Hall Putsch. He needed a scapegoat and by the time he became German chancellor in 1933, he found one in the Jewish citizens of Germany.

Across the Atlantic, the United States faced its own set of problems with a Red Scare and a series of "terrorist" bombings between 1918 and 1922. Often these radical beliefs, including communism, socialism, and anarchism, led to increased xenophobia and the deportation of immigrants who were seen as a threat to the American culture. The older generation of Grant Wood's *American Gothic* painting saw the young Americans as a threat to the American culture. As the young "intelligentsia" decried American norms, they moved to Paris to see the world wrought by war and sample new drugs, edgier ways of life, and philosophies that often found their way into the writings of men like Ernest Hemingway and F. Scott Fitzgerald. This group of discontented young people were called the "lost generation" by their den mother, Gertrude Stein.

At home, the ideas of Darwin and evolution filtered into schools and resulted in the Scopes Monkey Trial. Progressive women like Margaret Sanger openly called for birth control, while also endorsing the notion of Nietzsche's "superman" and eugenics. The Ku Klux Klan reinvigorated itself in 1915 just as the movie *Birth of a Nation* began showing in movie theaters and the issues of segregation for African Americans remained largely unresolved. This new, powerful Klan was not just a southern phenomenon but one that spawned "whisper" campaigns against divorcees, Jews, Catholics, African Americans, and Hispanics. Reform efforts seemed to fail as the 18th Amendment to "prohibit" alcohol only served to create a new underground culture of speakeasies, risqué dances, "petting parties," and organized crime. It seemed to many people that morals were fading as "flappers" and their gentlemen friends embraced a life of frivolity. However, underlying problems, including overproduction by farmers, unrestricted buying on the stock market, and economic nationalism, caused the stock market to collapse in October 1929, heralding the beginning of the Great Depression that lasted until World War II began.

Across the Pacific, Japan quietly built the structure of its Greater East Asia Co-Prosperity Sphere. The first Asian nation to industrialize, Japan embraced the leadership of its fellows on the continent, filling the void left by both the fall of the Qing emperor in China and the withdrawal of many European colonizers after World War I. Japan's power depended on both markets and raw materials, all of which could be garnered from increased hegemony in the Pacific region. That goal ran directly afoul of both the British holdings in the area and the American movement inexorably across the Pacific from land holdings obtained at the end of the Spanish-American war, including the Philippines. The United States already had a strong Pacific presence that dated back to the 1860s in both the Aleutian Islands and the Hawaiian archipelago. Japan's ambitions set the stage for later confrontation.

Before turning its attention East, Japan worked throughout the 20s to terrorize and intimidate the citizens of Korea, Manchuria, and China by either outright domination or the creation of client governments. Chiang Kai-shek and Mao Zedong, two former leaders of the Kuomintang party who vaulted to power after the 1912 coup, vied for control of China. Chiang Kai-shek was favored by Western powers and led the nationalists. His adversary Mao was communist and viewed as a threat to Western power. While Chiang Kai-shek holed up in Chungking throughout the war with Japan, Mao Zedong led the peasant Long March from 1934–35 over more than 4,000 miles. This action, which broke through nationalist lines, secured his leadership of the Chinese Communist Party and later the victory in the 1949 revolution.

Nowhere was the impact of decolonization more evident than in the countries bordering the Indian Ocean, from French Indo-China to the British Raj in India, and into the Persian Gulf where the end of the Ottoman Empire left a power void. Beginning in 1915 Mohandas Gandhi began to organize the peasants in India to protest the inequities in British-ruled India. Although many soldiers from India supported Britain during the war, by 1947 India was an independent nation. Similarly, in 1919 Ho Chi Minh participated in a petition to the Versailles Conference asking for Vietnam's independence from France. Like India, Vietnam fought with the Allies during World War II, but the lack of resolution to their plea for self-determination resulted in two Vietnam wars. Similarly, the United Kingdom, France, and Russia divided up portions of the former Ottoman Empire with the Sykes–Picot Agreement in 1917, which was followed in 1917 with the Balfour Declaration recognizing the concept of a Jewish homeland in Palestine.

By 1930 the heyday of the Roaring 20s ended. Hems dropped down, urban workers found themselves in soup lines rather than speakeasies, and the inability of the League of Nations to control either the Irish rebels or the Japanese empire became clear. Despite the fact the Kellogg–Briand Pact outlawed war in 1927, it became obvious that the postwar concept of using relative ratios for disarmament and ship tonnage had failed. Despite US efforts to halt reparation payments during the Great Depression, Germany simply withdrew from the League and the new chancellor began to rearm. Although Hitler's use of youth groups, technology, and work projects seemed similar to his American counterpart, Franklin Delano Roosevelt, Hitler's idea was to unite the German-speaking world in the Third Reich under the aegis of his National Socialist German Workers Party (NADSP). Unlike the previous two reichs this one was based on scapegoating "undesirables," including Jews, homosexuals, Romani, dissidents, and the disabled. His alliance with Benito Mussolini in Italy led to the support of Generalissimo Franco's right-wing government in Spain, immortalized by Picasso's painting of *Guernica*. In an effort to recapture the glory that was Rome, Italy attacked Ethiopia in 1935, sending the Ethiopian emperor, Haile Selassie, into exile in England until the defeat of the Axis Powers in 1945, further destabilizing the region.

Although Europe regained prominence after World War One, the rise of Germany by the 30s leads some historians to call the combined world wars the Thirty Years War with Germany. Divided up by the Versailles Treaty, all of the Austria-Hungarian empire became a series of small states in which many languages and ethnicities vied for dominance. In some cases, German speakers found themselves in either Poland or Czechoslovakia because of border changes. Russians also found themselves displaced, as did many smaller ethnic groups who had fought for self-determination prior to 1915. Some of the Slavic countries looked to Russia for guidance, but Lenin's leadership, followed by Josef Stalin's rigid authoritarianism, left the Soviet Union fairly isolated from the western countries on its border. In 1939, Hitler reached out to Stalin with the Non-Aggression Pact, despite the fact the National Socialist German Workers' Party (NSDAP or Nazi) and its predecessor, the German Worker's Party (DAP), consistently persecuted communists in Germany. With Stalin occupied with eradicating the *cordon sanitaire* and absorbing the eastern portion of Poland and Finland, Hitler was poised to invade Poland in September 1939 with his *blitzkrieg* or "lightening war."

The reaction to these aggressions in the United States remained limited. Americans, convinced by the Nye Committee report that they had been hoodwinked into involvement in World War I for the profit of wealthy investors, hunkered down and embraced isolationism. Evidence suggests that Roosevelt was well aware of Hitler's actions, but Congress passed a series of neutrality acts forbidding US support of any of the combatants. These laws hurt Spain and Ethiopia far more than they hurt the Axis Powers. Only after Hitler's invasion of France and the aerial Battle of Britain in 1940 did the United States reverse its neutrality policy and aid the Allies. Roosevelt authorized both the founding of the United Nations in a meeting with British Prime Minister Winston Churchill in August of 1941 and had American ships shepherding British supply boats across the Atlantic that autumn. However, it was only when Japan attacked Pearl Harbor on December 7, 194,1 that the United States entered World War II.

As the oral histories demonstrate, the war was the most significant factor in the lives of many women. The stories are from Afghanistan and India, as well as South America and Europe. They illustrate the contrast been the ways of life of Indigenous peoples as well as minorities around the globe, from Jewish refugees to African Americans at home in the United States. For many, life in the first third of the twentieth century was often not so different from life in the nineteenth century. For that reason, the twentieth century is often discussed in two periods: before and after the war. For Europe it meant the destruction of a thousand years of history. For the Asian continent it meant an entire reversal of previous power structures. For decolonized nations, a

Maryland, US (1922)

As told to a family friend.

FIGURE 2.1.1   Henryton State Hospital and Sanitarium, Maryland, 2013

My name is Birdie Fleet. I was born in a little town called Henderson, Maryland. It was so small that the sign on one side of the street said, "You are now entering Henderson" and the sign on the other side said, "You are now leaving Henderson." That was on March 12, 1920, and my mom tells me I arrived in the biggest snowstorm of the year, in time for breakfast. Actually, I wasn't born in the town. We lived on a farm but our post office was Henderson.

My father's name was Ezra Harley Lawton and my mother's name was Iona Mary Waters. My grandfather was Prescott Lawton. I have his dog tags from the Civil War, but the name on them and some of his military papers is Prescott Lawson. His pension was in the name of Prescott Lawson, too. We never figured out how it happened, but my grandfather enlisted in Lancaster, Pennsylvania, as a freeman. My mother's mother was Virginia Ann Clark, called Virgie. I knew a little because sometimes she would stay with us, but most of the time worked as a servant in Philadelphia,

I had seven sisters and brothers. I am the second. There were five girls and three boys. We had the usual relationship. Some days we were the best of friends. Other days we screamed at one another. Fourteen years separated the oldest and the youngest of us. My mother was very busy.

I liked to read. I liked to play games. We were isolated because there were not too many Black children in the area within walking distance. We were able to play with White children only until we were eight or nine years old, so after that we interacted mostly within our family group. Of course, we had friends in school, but there again, the distance to their house was not walking distance, so the only way we could see one another was if our parents or their parents drove us.

I started going to school at four years old for the simple reason that my elder sister had no one to accompany her on the walk, so I went along as a companion. We attended Engleside, Maryland Elementary School, two and a half miles away. It was a one-room school that went to seventh grade. Of course, they would not let me just sit there while my sister was in class, so I started in primer (which they now call kindergarten), and then of course I advanced on and finished school early.

High school, which was in Denton, was called Lockerman High School. That was all told about 17 miles away, but by that time we had a bus that would pick us up and take us to school. Where we lived, there was a school about three-quarters of a mile from us, but we could not go there because it was only for White children. Then they closed that school and there was a school bus that passed our gate every morning, but the same situation remained, even though my father was a landowner and taxpayer. We had to walk two miles to the place where the school bus would pick us up and take us to Denton. At the time that was the situation. You may resent it but that was the way it was. If you wanted an education you walked and my parents were very very "gung ho" on us being educated. Both my father and mother had only gone through the sixth grade. That was all.

I've always enjoyed learning about different things—new places and ideas. I was an avid reader from when I was about six years old. In elementary school, our teacher was a man named Mr. Singer. I have very good memories of him. Up until last year, my brothers and sisters still had contact with him, He still lives in Maryland. He was someone who was truly concerned about your learning and about being able to deal with life. He did not discuss segregation as such, but he focused on us as we had to deal with it.

Of course, I had a good grounding in the segregation issue because my father and my uncles used to discuss it freely and openly. Especially, there were people like Marcus Garvey trying to bring about some sort of end to segregation or at least loosen the bonds, and of course there were others doing things like the NAACP. My father used to subscribe to the *Baltimore News* and the *Afro-American* (a Black paper that was published in Baltimore and mailed to us.) He was somewhat active in the very early days of the civil rights movement and had an old truck with magazines and papers that discussed what was going on at the time.

My father was a truck farmer. We had 26 acres of farmland and nine acres of woodland. I will never forget that. He grew vegetables. Of course we had our own chickens and turkeys and pigs and cows, which we used for food and sold some surplus. My grandfather purchased the farm with his pension from being injured in the Civil War. When he died my aunts and uncles did not want to stay in the country, so my father put up money for their interests and they moved to Philadelphia and areas around there.

When I was ten years old, a typical day meant we worked. In the summertime, during the harvest season, we would have to help harvest our own crops and then we would go on different days to other nearby farms to help with their harvests. If, for example, we were picking beans, for each 5/8-bushel basket of beans we would pick we would get so much money. Most of the money went to the family, but our parents let us keep a small percentage for ourselves. We did not grow wheat on our farm because it was not large enough, but we did grow corn for the stock and needed extra help during harvest. Our chores included watering and feeding the livestock during the winter and watering and putting the animals out to pasture in the summer. We milked the cows morning and night (we had two or three cows most of the time) and brought in the wood for cooking in the wood stove and for heat, too. That's where the nine acres of woodland came in handy.

After our morning chores we would eat breakfast and then take off for school between 7:30 and 7:40. School started at nine a.m., and if we were late the teacher would keep us after school. If we were late getting home in the evening, of course, we would have to answer to our mother. If I had been on a track team like my great-granddaughter, I would have been a star because we did an awful lot of running to keep up with these times. After school there were more chores and homework.

Each of us had different chores to do. Mine were mostly outside chores until I became sickly when I was eight years old. I began to swell up a lot and my parents took me to doctors, but they could not figure out what was wrong. Once I had to stay in bed for three months and was only allowed up to go to the bathroom. That did not solve the problem, but it did cause some friction with my brothers and sister who did not understand why I would lay around and not do my share of chores. Only years later did a doctor diagnose that I had had rheumatic fever.

Life wasn't all work. When our chores were done or on Sundays we could play. On Sundays no work was done. We did not go to church on a regular basis but maybe once a month. We were not allowed to play ball or cards on Sunday because we were Methodists, but we did play games like hopscotch or hide-and-seek. We couldn't dance either, so the first time I danced was not until I was 15 years old.

I turned 15 in March and I was supposed to graduate from high school in May. In February of that year they found spots on my lungs from TB, so I was put out of school. I went to a sanitarium in Western Maryland in the mountains. I was in a children's building and there were a lot of children there. It was close to Baltimore and there were a lot of children there from the city. I was able to learn a lot from them about urban Black culture. The name of the place was the Maryland Tuberculosis Sanitarium and its address was Henryton, Maryland. I was there over a year. It was a segregated facility.

I did not came back in time to start class in the fall, but because I had already gone through that portion of it, I was permitted to start at the second semester and finish at 17 years old in 1937. After I graduated, I applied to Howard University. We did not have the money for tuition and board, and I thought I could work my way through, but they did not allow freshmen to work. I stayed at home for the summer and in the fall I went to Philadelphia and started working. Just about all that was available was housework. To be able to go out and get a job in a store or business, forget it. I did try after a bit but was given "Well, we'll call you." I got fired from one job because I wanted to go to night school. I wanted to take foreign language and other subjects that would help me get into college, but my employers wanted me to take only classes that would enhance my domestic skills.

After I got married and moved to New York, even in Harlem in such places as five- and ten-cent stores you could not get a job. Practically all the clientele was Black, but they couldn't have Black clerks. It was during the war that I got a job making life jackets at Charles Bloom. They used to make bedspreads and drapes, but during the war they started making war supplies. I was living in the Bronx and one morning in 1943 I got up and took the train to work. Everyone was surprised to see me and asked what I was doing there. That's when I found out there had been a great riot in Harlem over the policy of not hiring Black people in the stores that served Black people.

My husband was Jamaican. His name was Aloysius Jerome Grey. I met him at the Democratic Club or the Republican Club; I'm not sure which it was. My aunt and I used to go there on our nights off to dance and socialize. There was a little hitch with a portion of his family when we decided to get married. Some of them thought I was too Black. They were all very fair. Some were blonde. My husband's grandmother was Scotch Irish and his grandfather was Black and East Indian. They were not too pleased to have too much Black in the family. Over the years they relented a little and granted me a lukewarm reception. My husband was a long-distance truck driver who used to travel to the South frequently. He told me a story about one time when he and his partner got a flat fire and an old gentleman walking by remarked, "By God, I bet you wish you were a n-g-r too. I bet this one has not had to wash his face since he left home." That's how light-skinned my husband was.

We got married in 1940 and moved to New York in 1943. Aloysius got a deferment from the draft for family reasons, although I cannot remember exactly why. At that time, people of different cultures grouped together. My first place in New

York was on Kelly Street. General Colin Powell grew up on Kelly Street. I was the 800 block and he was the 900 block. That was the Jamaican neighborhood. It was a good life. During that time I had three more children. We had five children all told. The eldest, Marion and Royston Jr., were born in Philadelphia. Belva, Phoebe, and Helen were born in New York. Phoebe was "slow," and a friend told me about the Brooklyn Hebrew School for Special Children. The rabbi there agreed to take Phoebe according to what I was able to pay. There she was able to learn some letters and numbers and eventually was able to become fairly independent.

In 1953, my husband was deported to Jamaica for being an illegal alien. He had gotten into some legal difficulties, and that's when they discovered he had entered the country illegally. I could have gone with him but that was not what I wanted to do. I was left to support my five children on only my income, and I could not make it on that. My job closed down every summer and we lived on unemployment during those months. I did not know what I was going to do when the children returned to school in the fall and finally had to sign up for AFDC (Aid to families with Dependent Children). I told the caseworker of my problem and she helped my situation along. I had taken the civil service exam in 1951 but had not heard anything. In December of 1953, the City of New York called and offered me a job as a transit worker selling subway tokens. I was probationary for six months and then the job became permanent. It started at $1.50 and hour. When I retired from that job 25 years later I was making a little over $7 an hour.

In 1976, a few years before I retired, I went back to school to earn a bachelor's degree at York College. I was nearly sixty years old and was very scared that I would not be able to make it. After three semesters, I found that I could succeed without too much effort. I decided to switch over to nursing because I had always wanted to be a nurse, even when I was a little girl. Of course, I had to go back and take some science classes over again because when I took science as a girl, the atom had not even been split. In 1978 I got into the nursing program at City College of New York, finished in February 1980, and got my registered nurse's license in May 1980.

By then, all of my children except Phoebe were living in Southern California. I had planned to retire to New Mexico as I owned two lots there on which I planned to build. They used to advertise lots there, and I decided to pretend that I smoked and put the money that I would have spent on cigarettes toward the lands. Eventually, I paid off the land just outside Albuquerque. But by the time I was ready to retire, my children all protested my moving so far away from them as I was not getting any younger. I put in applications in California for nursing positions and moved to Los Angeles in July. My first nursing job was at Northridge Hospital and the next February I moved to Valley Medical to the wound care unit. In December 1981 I bought a house in Simi Valley and moved there. In 1985 I came out of hospital work entirely and started doing homecare. I retired in 1991 to take care of my great-grandchildren whose mother had died.

For all the years that I worked, I feel I was fairly paid. I had enough to pay my bills and live a comfortable life. Even when I quit working in the hospital as an RN and started doing home are at a lower LVN rate, it was enough. Now that I'm raising great-granddaughters I say that I am soon going to retire for the third time. There are two accomplishments in my life that I am particularly proud of. My self-esteem was not extremely high until I had to take care of my family on my own and was able to do it in a good manner. The other thing was that I was able to go to nursing school, graduate, and get a license. There was only one section of the exam that I did not score in the 500s and that score was in the 490s, even though I was the grandma of the class. Three women had profound influence on my life. There was one teacher named Miss Steuben who I had in high school. Her example and the things she said convinced me that I could decide the way my life would go. She was a music teacher, but she did not just teach music. She would talk to me and inspire me to do the best I could. Another woman I remember is Mrs. Van Buren, the charge nurse at the sanitarium when I was a patient there. She would let me assist in patient care and taught me a lot about the nursing profession and the medical field. She helped refuel the desire in me to get into nursing that I finally realized more than 45 years later. Of course, my mother was important. She urged me to get an education and do the best I could. She saw to it that I had the things I needed. She sat at the sewing machine many days and nights, reworking old used clothing for us because we did not have very much money. Even during the Great Depression we always had food to eat.

One of the major problems I have had to overcome in my life is public stupidity. It's just the way people look at things. For example, I remember once when I was trying to find a place to live. I'd call and they would say the place was still available When I arrived, I would be told the place was just rented. Once I asked if they rented to Negroes, a lady told me, "Why no, but why do you ask?" I said, "Because I'm a Negro." She then said, "Well you don't sound like a Negro." The one thing I can't stand is people who are fake. They pretend be one way when everything they do points in a different direction.

Over my lifetime, a very beneficial change came about in women's roles. I can remember back in the days when I would hear my parents or friends. Women had no say in what went on. A man decided anything that was to be decided and the women were expected to accept those decisions, Also, women have gained the ability to earn their own living and to have a say in the laws that affect them. Today, women can hold public office. One day we might even have a woman president.

CREDIT

San Francisco, US (1922)

As told to her granddaughter.

FIGURE 2.2.1 "Pipe City" by Paul Schmitt, 1930, Oakland Museum of California On Fifth Avenue on the pier in Oakland, CA, a city of 200 homeless men spread out in a warren of large unused sewer pipes during the winter of 1932–33. The town was called "Pipe City" or Miseryville. A combination of the 1929 Stock Market Crash and a nation-wide drought left almost 20% of California's population unemployed. The pipes belonged to the American Concrete and Steel Pipe Company and homeless men hauled their clothing, blankets, musical instruments, and pets to the large pipes and made them into tiny apartments where they were protected from wind and rain. The "housing" had strict rules insisting men be able to contribute to the success of "Pipe City" and a mayor named Dutch Jensen was elected to distribute food, approve the squatters rights, and maintain order. In order to provide their contribution to "city" life, some men helped store food or do laundry , while others founded the Unemployed Exchange Association (UXA). Led by a musician named Carl Rhodehamel men from Pipe City and other nearby Hoovervilles exchanged work for food to feed others. When spring came the company sold the pipes and the men moved on.

Lizzie Miller was born Elizabeth Adele Miller on November 28, 1922 at the General Hospital in San Francisco, California. The only child of Laurence and Agnes Miller, Lizzie grew up spending most of her time with her parents, who took her everywhere with them, including camping to the Sierra Nevada Mountains, movie theaters such as the Paramount theater in Oakland, and the World's Fair at Treasure Island in 1939. On camping trips to the Sierra Nevada Mountains, east of Sacramento, Lizzie and her parents often had to put the car in reverse and back up the steep hills in order to make it safely to the campsites. On trips to the theater, Lizzie loved to listen to the large pipe organ that played before the movie, a leftover from days before "talking pictures" were invented when an organist would accompany the silent films. Lizzie, who played the piano as a child and had piano practice every day, marveled at the enormous sound produced by the organs. As a teenager, she accompanied her parents by ferry to Treasure Island to visit the Golden Gate International Exposition, a World's Fair held to showcase the newly finished bridges, and the Golden Gate and the San Francisco–Oakland Bay Bridges in 1939 and 1940. Her favorite memory from the fair is the vaudeville-style shows, which were a fantastic, different image of the life led daily by Americans in the early twentieth century.

On a daily basis, Lizzie led a fairly normal, "uninteresting" life that was typical to most girls her age at that time. Most days she woke up at 6:30 a.m., did her ablutions (washed), tidied her room, dressed for school, and had breakfast. After school, she had a piano lesson and playtime, did her homework after dinner, and listened to the radio with her family before she read in her room before bedtime. Most of her friends lived in her neighborhood, and her best friend in elementary school was several years older. Playtime consisted of dolls, roller skating, playing hide-and-seek, tennis, making scrapbooks, reading books, and playing cards. Her father and mother both loved to play cards. Agnes continued to love to play cards with her daughter and son-in-law and their children. Lizzie's parents treated her like an adult and included her in most every aspect of their lives, both happy and sad.

Some of the happiest memories of her childhood were spent with her father, Laurence, who was an only child as well. They had a close relationship, even though he had said he wanted a boy; he nicknamed her "Jack" and lovingly called her that throughout her life. Lizzie's father taught her many things, including the very real, very sad aspects of the Great Depression, one of the biggest historical events that influenced her life. While she learned to be "frugal, pay cash, consume only what was needed, make do with what you have and never assume that whatever you have today will be here tomorrow," her family was lucky enough to not suffer greatly during this difficult time in American history. Some of the things she and her father did together were related to the Great Depression. On weekends, Lizzie's father took her to the transcontinental railroad tracks just before they reached the Port of Oakland, the very last stop on that line. They sat and watched the "hobos," who jumped off the trains just before the final station to avoid getting caught by the railroad police. Another place her father took her was Pipe City, or "Miseryville," in Oakland. Pipe City was a community of mostly jobless, homeless men who made large concrete pipes their homes and created a city of sorts that even had its own mayor and laws. These outings drove home the fact that "the many people in need were real," and Lizzie learned to appreciate the things she had and never take her comfort or happiness for granted.

Lizzie's mother, Agnes Ferguson, was one of the most influential women in her life, along with Eleanor Roosevelt and several lifelong friends. Her mother was not only an active participant in Lizzie's childhood but lived with Lizzie and her family until her death from cancer in the 1970s. Agnes's upbringing was also one of the reasons Lizzie learned to work hard and appreciate her good fortune; she came from a hard-working, poor, farming family in a small town in southern Utah. The family had settled in the area that had been the Church of the Latter Day Saints "empire" called Deseret. The nearest railroad was 40 miles away by horse, there was no local doctor, and they shared the land with the native Paiute Indians. Agnes was one of seven children, two of whom died from smallpox during the outbreak that swept the state between 1900 and 1925, when fifteen thousand residents of Utah died from the disease. Lizzie's mother, and her surviving siblings, lived through the epidemic with help from the Paiute medicine woman who lived nearby and used medicinal herbs to treat the symptoms.

Agnes firmly believed that her opportunities and education were inadequate, and when she was a teenager she ran away from home several times in hopes that she would find an easier and better life elsewhere. She did not want to "work herself to death" as her mother eventually did. Both times she ran away, however, she returned home voluntarily. She finally started her "better life" when she married Laurence Miller and moved to California. Laurence was not a Latter Day Saint and Agnes did not raise her three children in that faith; she wanted each to participate in a self-chosen religion or none at all.

As a teenager, Lizzie worked at Sears Roebuck, a company that continued to expand even during the Great Depression. She focused on school during her first years at the University of California at Berkeley, but when her father died, she quit school to help support her mother and worked several jobs in Oakland, one in purchasing for the Board of Education of Oakland, the other at a cement factory in Oakland, also in purchasing. When World War II broke out in 1941, Lizzie took a job with the War Price and Rationing Board until she met and married Jasper Brown in 1943 at a hospital in Oakland so that Jasper's terminally ill father, and only remaining parent, could attend. Jasper enlisted as a combat infantry officer in WWII in the early years of the war. After they married, Jasper had training at Ft. Benning, Georgia, so the newly married couple relocated and lived with two other young couples with similar stories. All three men sneaked off of the base at night to spend time with their wives, as soldiers were not allowed to sleep off base during training. While Jasper was away at training, Lizzie worked for Kaiser Engineering in accounting. She started as a secretary and quickly became an executive assistant to one of the company's vice presidents, the highest position allowed to a woman. In 1944, the husbands of the two couples who lived with Lizzie and Jasper in Georgia were sent to the European front a few weeks ahead of Jasper and both died soon after their arrival at the Battle of the Bulge in December 1944. When her husband was sent to Europe, Lizzie transferred back to Oakland and lived with her mother, who was driving a jeep for the US government and knitting at Capwell's department store. Shortly after being shipped out, Jasper was discharged when he was wounded, shot in the neck during the invasion of Normandy on June 6, 1944. After his wound healed, Lizzie quit her job at Kaiser and the couple continued their lives in Oakland, where Jasper took advantage of the GI Bill and spent ten years getting his MA and PhD, eventually doing research for the military in San Francisco near the Presidio Army Base.

Throughout these first years after Jasper returned from the war, he and Lizzie mutually decided they wanted a big family in contrast to their own, somewhat lonely, only-childhoods. They began their family with the birth of a daughter, Maria, in January of 1947. Their second child, Derrick, was born in June of 1952 and was shortly followed by Richard in May of 1954. Lizzie recalled that they considered having more children but decided to stop "after meeting Richard." One of Lizzie's main goals was to be a good wife and mother, and she felt that she was successful on both counts. Lizzie and Jasper enjoyed backpacking, boating, fishing, traveling, dancing, and camping together and took their children with them, often with their lifelong friends. Lizzie remembered time spent with her female friends fondly and believed that she had so much fun with them because their personalities were so different from her own—very direct, outgoing, and likely to speak up about what they wanted. As a wife, Lizzie considered herself a good complement to Jasper. They were often mistaken by strangers as siblings because "they seemed so similar and were so peaceful together." She was very happy with married life, and both she and her husband recognized how important it was to have someone to share your life with. Jasper had lost both parents by 1945 and Lizzie had lost her father early in life, so they appreciated each other and shared everything. Being a mother was "entertaining and busy," and Lizzie was most proud of her children when she looked back on her life. In order to be a good wife and mother, she became an excellent cook, sewed and knitted clothing and blankets for her children and grandchildren, maintained a beautiful garden well into her senior years, and did volunteer work with Boy and Girl Scouts and for her children's schools. She kept busy as a mother and wife and felt involved, interested, satisfied, and happy but missed the "busy" aspects of having a career.

When her children were old enough to "handle themselves" in high school, she went back to school at San Jose State University and earned her bachelor's degree with straight A's. She then continued on at Santa Clara University and received her master's degree in social work. She remembered her time at school fondly and enjoyed both the academic aspects and being able to spend time with women and friends her age; many women in her program returned to school after their husbands got jobs following the war. She used her degrees to go to work for the Redwood City School District and worked in the Special Education program. She worked for the job, not the money, as Jasper made enough to support the family, but recognized that the men and women who worked in in that department did not get paid enough for how hard they worked and the importance of the job itself. Along with traditional jobs, Lizzie assumed complete responsibility for her mother, who lived with the family until her death. While it was a job that was performed out of love, it was also Lizzie's sense of duty that drove her to care for her mother without open complaint or negativity. After her mother's death, Lizzie and Jasper enjoyed having their home to themselves but missed Agnes's notable presence and witty anecdotes, especially when all three kids had moved out.

Lizzie's first grandchild was born in 1984 to her son Derrick. The switch from mother to grandmother was anything but difficult, and Lizzie's greatest joy in her later life was spending time with her children's families. By 1996, Lizzie had four grandsons and two granddaughters ranging from newborn to 12 years old, each their own special person but all of whom reminded her of her own children in some way. Her stories about their parents entertained and delighted her grandchildren up into their young adult years. She happily stated that "she spent her life taking care of others" and considered that her greatest contribution to her family and friends. Her daughter said Lizzie was a "woman who could be put down anywhere and would busy herself with improving the situation of those around her." Her best traits were complemented by her husband, and his death in 2001 was a huge change to her lifestyle.

The house that they had bought in Menlo Park, California in the late 40s was too large without her husband and children in it for Lizzie to handle on her own. When Jasper died and after more than 35 years of living in the same home, she sold it and moved to an independent living community where she was visited frequently by her children and grandchildren and continued to travel for the first few years of her stay there. In her later years, Lizzie enjoyed volunteering at the care center in her retirement community and was awarded "Person of the Year" in 2005. She kept busy volunteering and helping others around her and enjoyed being part of a group of friends and peers but missed her husband, Jasper, every day. Change was something Lizzie learned from an early age to adapt to and used this skill throughout her life. When asked about how she felt about women of her time and those of today, she responded, "Although women during my lifetime have gone from being nurses, teachers and office workers into being anything from lawyers, pilots, engineers, and politicians to industry tycoons, I often see and consider them to be overloaded, stressed out and juggling too much with full time jobs and raising families. I had the joy and pleasure of having a husband who shared all family responsibilities with me, but every woman was not as lucky as I was."

CREDIT

Fig 2.2.1: Copyright © 1930 by Paul Schmitt.

Utah, US (1923)

As told to her granddaughter.

FIGURE 2.3.1   Flapper on a Ship, 1929

R uth Gramm Bates was born on September 29, 1923. She can remember some of what was going on in the world when she was a little girl. It was the 1920s, the roaring 20s. People drove roadster cars. People lived in two-bedroom homes with a one-car garage, and those were the nicer homes. Ruth's father went to work, and her mother had to walk to the store to buy groceries because the family only had one car and it was unacceptable in those days for a woman to drive. People had iceboxes because refrigerators were not around yet. The iceman would come two or three times a week and bring a 50-pound ice block to put on top of the icebox. Dancing was the thing to do back then. Ruth had one sister who was four years younger than she named Emma. They lived in Salt Lake City and would go to a place called Lagoon. It was an amusement park with rides and concessions. They also liked to go to a place called Saratoga, which was on Lake Utah. They only had radio, as television had not been invented yet. Some popular programs were *Inner Sanctum, Amos and Andy,* and *Betty and Bob.* Ruth and her family would just sit around the radio and listen to those programs. Ruth enjoyed the radio as it allowed her to imagine whatever she wanted as the story unfolded.

The most fun Ruth remembers as a little girl came from roller skating. They had the kind of skates that had clamps on the toes with a key that went around their necks. When those clamps got loose, Ruth would just bend over and tighten them to her shoes with the key. Ruth skated everywhere. There were sidewalks, and Ruth skated to her friends' houses and then back to her house every day. After school, the children would go inside and get a slice of bread and peanut butter, and after they finished eating they would go skating.

Ruth was seven years old when the stock market crashed in 1929, so most of her memories are not of the Roaring 20s but rather the years of the Great Depression. Ruth's father was a mechanical engineer who was educated in England and had a good job. He had a savings and owned a home, but then came the Great Depression. Many people lost their homes and their jobs. Only federal workers and those involved with important things like trains, railroads, and buses maintained their jobs. At that time, Ruth's father was continually looking for work. He would get a week's worth of work at one place and a week's worth somewhere else, taking whatever kind of job he could get. There was no construction going on at the time, so he had to take menial jobs. One job he was able to get was at the Utah Poultry Association. He was highly educated and professional, yet his task was to load trucks with big bags of feed. It did not pay very much, but it was enough to put food on the table and pay the mortgage.

Money was not spent on anything that was not absolutely necessary. Ruth had one set of clothes for school and one set of clothes to play in. As soon as she got home from school, she had to take off her school clothes because they had to last all week. They did not have washers or dryers at that time. Everyone, including her mother, would wash clothes on Monday and hang their clothes outside and then iron on Tuesday.

As a child, Ruth was never sick despite the fact that there were no immunizations for measles and whooping cough. Ruth's sister was not so fortunate. She caught chicken pox, measles, mumps, and whooping cough. One time, Emma had scarlet fever and the whole house had to be quarantined. People even had to put big signs in their window saying "quarantined." No one would go into a quarantined home because no one wanted to catch such serious diseases because penicillin was not available for complications. When a person got scarlet fever, no one could leave the house unless they lived in a part of the house that the sick person did not occupy. Most houses had two bedrooms at the time, and Ruth and Emma shared a room while her parents had the other. Ruth's father had to just live in the kitchen and the bedroom so he could go to work, and Emma would have to stay in the front room and her bedroom. Ruth and Emma slept in the same bedroom, but Ruth never caught anything.

The only major illness she had was pneumonia, which she caught in the third grade. She was extremely ill, but in those days hospital visits were rare. Instead, doctors made house calls. Ruth remembered the doctor coming to the house rather than the hospital because people did not have insurance. People did the best they could at home. Most homes were not centrally heated at the time, and the only heat source in the house came from a big stove in the kitchen. Ruth's family put two easy chairs together in the kitchen and that is where Ruth stayed for weeks. She was so ill that she missed half a year of school. Ruth remembers the doctor coming into the house and the only medicine they gave her was a spoon full of whiskey one hour and a spoon full of castor oil the next. The whiskey was believed to cut down all the phlegm that was in a person's throat and lungs, and the castor oil was supposed to act as a laxative to take it through a person's system. Ruth just remembers being very, very sick.

Her illness took the majority of her hearing, which was devastating to her when she finally returned to school. At the time, no allowances were made for children with disabilities like the one Ruth had. She could still hear, but she could not hear well. The way in which her teachers dealt with her problem was to seat her in the front of the classroom. This would work only if the teacher remained in the front of the classroom, which the teacher did not normally do, especially when giving spelling tests. Ruth was a good speller, and her hearing was such that she could hear the words but did not know whether they were plural. If she did not write down the plural form of the word because she did not hear the "s," her teachers would mark the word wrong. She never received a hundred percent in spelling.

Ruth's trouble with hearing also affected her playtime after school where the children would play street games. They were not gang games, but just the neighborhood gathered to play a game of kick-the-can or run-sheep-run. They divided their neighborhood into three or four smaller groups. There was a group of reds, a group of greens, and so on. One person from the group was the sheep leader and hid the whole group. That person gave the other group a code word like a color or number and when that person called the other group's word, the other group had to run back to their base without getting caught. Everyone could hear the codes except Ruth, and the game would be over and she still would be hiding. She hated to play that game, but her mother insisted that she join in.

The relief society to which Ruth's mother belonged would go to the hospital and they would mend sheets. Ruth was about 12 when, on one such occasion after her mother had left for the relief society, Ruth decided she would go into the kitchen and cook herself an egg for lunch. Their kitchen had an electric stove and Ruth put some oil in a pan and turned her back to it for a moment. When she turned back around, the skillet was on fire, spreading up the wall and the side of the refrigerator. She was so scared that she hopped on top of the stove and put the fire out with her hands. She yelled for her sister Emma who came into the house. Emma got a bowl full of water from the sink and threw the whole thing at Ruth, the bowl and the water. Then the neighbors came and called the fire department. Ruth severely burned her hands. She later described that they peeled, just like a hot dog does when cooked. Ruth was taken to the hospital where they scraped all the skin off of her burnt hand. After that, she had to wear big white mitts on her hand, which turned out to be fun because everyone helped her as she could not use her hands. There had been damage to the wallpaper in the kitchen where the fire and smoke were, so the man who hung wallpaper came and cleaned it and then re-hung it. Ruth's home was insured, and the man said that Ruth deserved something because she saved the insurance company money by putting out the fire. He said to Ruth's father that he was going to charge her father more money than what it cost for the repairs and that her father was to take her out and buy her a new dress. Ruth's father followed the advice, and Ruth got a new dress for putting out the fire.

High school for Ruth was very similar to elementary school. In those days, the neighborhood groups were very close friends and for the most part stayed in their own groups at school. No one had a car or drove, so going to visit anyone outside the neighborhood was very difficult. Only one person in the whole Granite High School in Salt Lake had wheels, and those wheels were on a motorbike, not a car.

Ruth had some goals for herself, one of which was to be a stewardess. She had the right build for it as stewardesses could only weigh a certain amount and be a certain height. It was also required to have a nursing degree to be a stewardess at the time. With her problematic hearing, there was no possibility for Ruth to be able to be a stewardess. Another goal she had was to be a schoolteacher. She could not become one at the time for the same reason of not being able to hear well.

Ruth met her future husband Amos Bates when she was a teenager. Despite the fact that they attended the same school, he was not from her neighborhood, so they did not know each other. They met when he got a job delivering papers. In those days, the paperboy had to collect as well as deliver the newspapers. Ruth remembers answering the door and there was Amos Bates out in the front. She would say to herself that she would never marry him because he was too short for her tastes, and she was the smallest girl in her class. Amos grew, though, in his senior year of high school, and the next time Ruth saw Amos he was tall. She got acquainted with him at a church dance. His sister Eva raised him. She used to say, "Now you dance or don't come home." Amos did not dare go home without a dance. He would stand at the wall and watch all night. During the last song, he would hurry and get a girl and dance with her so that he could tell Eva that he had danced. Amos danced with Ruth early that night and they danced all night.

When they started going out together, Amos had a little red Plymouth and was going to the University of Utah. He was very serious. He knew what he wanted, but things in Europe were starting to escalate. He knew he was lucky to be in school. He studied all week and only went out on Saturday nights. He always took Ruth out on Saturday nights, and they would come back to her house where she had a special dessert waiting for them. Most of the time, they went to the movies or to a dance. Those Saturday night dates went on for a few weeks. When Ruth and her girlfriends got together, they talked about their boyfriends. They would say, "Are you still going with Amos Bates?" Ruth would reply that she was. Then they would say, "Has he kissed you yet?" Ruth would reply no, and every week they would ask her the same thing and every week she would have the same answer. Ruth's girlfriends teased her by saying that Amos must not like her that much because boys kiss girls. Ruth decided that she could not stand the teasing anymore and that if on the next Saturday night Amos did not kiss her, she was going to kiss him. The next Saturday they went to a movie and then back to her house. He parked his little red Plymouth out front and they walked up to the house. Ruth's parents lived in a house with a high front porch, about three or 4 feet high. Amos was in the process of saying goodnight and was just about to turn to leave when Ruth reached up and kissed him right on the lips. It startled him so badly that he jumped off the porch and ran down the street, leaving his car still parked out in front of Ruth's house. Ruth went into the house and her father, who was always awake when she came home, asked her if she had a nice time. Ruth told him that she did have a good time with Amos, but that he would not be back again. Amos did come back, the next day in fact, the first time he ever came over on a Sunday. He kept coming back.

Amos and Ruth married in 1942. Amos was in his third year of accounting school and they talked seriously about getting married. The war was going on at the time, and the United States was getting nervous. People were getting drafted and the students at the universities were joining a group called the Reserves, which promised to let students finish school without being drafted. Amos joined that group, and they expected he would be able to finish school. Then Pearl Harbor happened, and the Reserves group no longer existed. Everyone was called up early in January of 1942. Ruth and Amos wanted to get married before he left, so they set a date for January 22, 1942. They only had a couple of weeks to get ready for the wedding. When they married, they had the reception at their house, and in order to serve refreshments the neighbors gave them their sugar rations so that Ruth and Amos could make punch. Amos left for the service in March and was gone for two and a half years.

When Amos left for the war, it was awful. He joined the Air Force and was an officer. Amos was stationed in Santa Ana, California, for basic training, and Ruth got a job at the base. They had enough ration cards to buy two pairs of shoes a year. Ruth would wear paper shoes and walk miles to catch the bus to see Amos on Saturday nights. She got horrible blisters from those shoes. When he finished with basic training, Amos got reassigned to Texas, and Ruth went on a train to visit him.

Ruth would go down to visit him for a week and then come home. They did that for about the first six months and then Amos went overseas. Ruth was pregnant when he left and had her oldest daughter Faye when he was still away.

During the war, the government sent home some of Amos's pay and he saved the other half. When the war was over, they built a small house and Amos finished his schooling. Ruth and Amos had missed their newlywed years, so when Amos got home from the war, they just jumped into family life. It was hard getting used to everything, but they loved each other so much that they made it through. Divorce was not a big thing back then, and Ruth believed that many people struggled with their marriages. Amos finished school and Ruth stayed home to raise the children. It was just a customary thing at that time for women to be in the home. Most of the employment line was made up of men and a few professional women.

Ruth experienced many changes in her life, including the fight for equal rights. Ruth remembers one time getting on a bus and the White people sat in the front and the Negroes had to get on in the back of the bus and sit in the back. Both women and Negroes were fighting for equal rights during those years. Careers for women were changing. Ruth remembered that one time their telephone was not working and they sent for a repairman to fix it. When the repairman arrived, it was a woman. She climbed right up the pole and fixed the phone lines. Ruth's father had something similar happen to him as well when a female was sent to repair the lines, and he would not let her climb up the pole. He believed that women should not do things like that.

Ruth went to the University of Utah with her eldest daughter Faye. She graduated four years later and taught school for twenty-two years. When she went to university, she was the oldest woman in her classes at forty. She earned excellent grades and maintained an A average. Ruth was nearing the end of her schooling, and in order to graduate she needed to complete two quarters of student teaching. In order to begin she had to pass a physical without her hearing aide. At the time, her father was a teacher at the University of Utah, and he was furious. He went to the head to the Education Department, but nothing came of it. Ruth was upset so Amos made an appointment with President Fletcher, who was the president of the university. In fact, Fletcher became the head of NASA after being president of the university. Amos showed him Ruth's records and told him what had happened. President Fletcher was appalled. Fletcher was a man who was living in the future and Ruth's professors were living in the past. President Fletcher said he had never heard of such a thing and as long as Ruth passed the physical with her hearing aide, everything would be okay. The experience really showed Ruth how backward some people still lived in those days. Part of her student teaching was to teach and be observed to see if she could function in the classroom. Her professors would come and observe her, an experience she described as being like a fish in a fishbowl. Ruth did really well, and the university could see no reason to keep her from teaching.

In the years that Ruth spent teaching, the difference of working with students in the classroom was great. When she first started teaching, it was everything she thought it would be. Teachers could teach what they wanted, the classrooms were small, and the children wanted to learn and were respectful. Toward the end of her tenure, classrooms were so big that the majority of time was spent on discipline and there was not much time left for teaching.

During her senior years, Ruth moved to a little town called Boulder in Colorado. Life there was paced a little slower and the atmosphere was very reminiscent of years past. When Ruth and Amos first arrived, the school was in need of another part-time teacher, so Ruth came out of retirement and taught for a couple more years. Teaching there was like going back in time for Ruth when teaching was fun and everything that Ruth thought it would be. The class was small and the children all respected learning and wanted to absorb all that Ruth could teach them.

Ruth noted that people must determine what things a person must accept and what things you can change. Change just for the fact of change does not make things better. A person has to determine for themselves those things that are worth changing and things that are not. If things are going to change and a person cannot stop them from changing, that person better change with them. When a person looks back over the years, there are a lot of changes that are just fads, but there are a lot of changes that are for the good and people must just accept them. If people do not, then when they get older they will be bitter. Happiness lies inside of them, so they must accept what they can and do what they must.

CREDIT

Peru (1925)

As told to her granddaughter.

FIGURE 2.4.1   Carretera a Junin, Peru 2014

Beyond the noisy city streets and its chaos, there are several small villages throughout the world of which we know little. Some of these unknown and lost cities have never reached the geographical map until now. In the past, there was little or no information on the small territories that were once occupied by a few Indigenous families. For instance, apart from the famous Nazca lines, Incan trail, and busy city atmospheres of Peru, there lay a remarkable village named Parpacocha. In the 1920s, the small rural land of Parpacocha was populated with about five families, each living within a twenty- to thirty-minute-walk radius. Among the few families that lived in the isolated village, one of them is known as the Flores family, Marco Flores Sanchez and his wife, Bonita Perez Nuño de Flores. Through the union of their love, the Flores's had eight children. Their second-oldest child, born on May 17, 1925, is Ora Flores Perez. She was born and raised in the beautiful rural village of Parpacocha, Peru. Unlike most babies who are born in a hospital, Ora was delivered in her parent's home by a midwife, at the beginning of winter. As she got older, those who loved her and carried a strong affection toward her called her "Or" for short.

Although time has passed, the way Ora remembers her past is quite astonishing. It seems as if she were describing yesterday, but in fact it has been over seventy years since the last time she recalls playing in the fields with her seven siblings. The smile and graceful gaze as she remembers her childhood years is extremely overwhelming. For her, Parpacocha is not her past, but instead lives within her, in the present. Ora describes her hometown as a small piece of land filled with clean open air and a gorgeous lake filled with trout. The fields and mountains surrounding her home grow a soft green grass that never goes above the knee. There are no clear gravel roads, like in the modern world, but instead only rocks that pave the way to neighboring homes. Ora's home was also made completely out of rocks and roofed with dried pasture. Her home did not have several rooms, bathrooms, or even walls that separated the rooms from each other. Instead, her home was divided and unattached into three single huts, one that was seven by three meters and two that were four by three meters. The biggest hut was used to sleep in, while one of the small huts was used for storage and the other as a kitchen. Since there were no bathrooms or indoor plumbing, everyone had to go in the open field, and if they wanted to bathe they soaked themselves in the nearby river. As for water that was needed for drinking and cooking, they used the fresh lake water that was only a few steps away from their home. In addition, there was no electricity and therefore no television or radio. The only sort of entertainment available was singing, dancing, or playing an instrument, if there was one. As for cooking, Ora's parents used an elevated stove made of dirt and within the dirt they used sheep, llama, or cow manure for heat. The kitchen was made of dirt and was not only used for cooking but also to keep warm in the winter. At first, Ora's parents were the ones who went to buy other food necessities in the neighboring village, but as the children got older, they would be sent to buy the food such as sugar, bread, and flour. To this day, Ora remembers the long entertaining walks to the nearest village, San Pedro de Cajas, which was done about every other week and took her siblings and her almost an hour and a half to reach their destination. During the joyful walks, she recalls storytelling, singing, and playing tag with her siblings.

Ora grew up with four sisters and three brothers. The names of her sisters are Nina, Azucena, Carmen, and Fonda Flores. Her brothers go by the names of Jamie, Javier, and Nardo Flores. Sadly, Ora set to rest two of her loving sisters, Nina and Carmen Flores. The relationship between her brothers and sisters is quite remarkable because they always got along. Ora never had a problem with her siblings because she loved them dearly and always felt united. The one she was most attached to was Nina, her older sister. Ora saw Nina as another mother figure since she was the oldest. There was no moment in her life that she recalls where she argued, complained, or fought with her siblings and parents. Both of her parents worked in some form or another, just to make ends meet. Ora and her siblings were not obligated to work for money somewhere else, but instead they worked by helping out their parents on the farm or by weaving crafts. Her father, Marco Flores, worked his entire life as a weaver and farmer. Her mother, Bonita Perez de Flores, was responsible for managing the household activities, such as cleaning, cooking, and raising the children. However, Ora's parents never had a fixed income; instead, when they needed money to buy the necessities such as food, her parents would sell their livestock meat or the blankets and clothing that they wove. Both of her parents worked equally together by sharing tasks around their home. Her father not only attended his farming duties, he also managed to work wonders with a yarn of wool. To make all the handmade crafts such as blankets, socks, sweaters, hats, and mittens, they started by obtaining the wool from their sheep. Then, once threaded into yarn and dyed for color, Ora's parents wove and knitted the essentials to keep warm in the winter. In addition, her mother was not only in charge of the household chores but was also involved in taking care of the animals, growing her own remedies, and harvesting the only agricultural product that could be planted, *maca*, a Peruvian vegetable rather like a radish. Ora's family had numerous livestock, and, at times, it was hard to pinpoint the actual number. For instance, her family had about two hundred sheep at one time. The animals on her farm, which her family depended on, included sheep, cows, horses, pigs, chickens, llamas, and guinea pigs. The sheep and llamas were used for wool. The cows were used for their milk. The chickens were used for their eggs. The horses were used for transportation. Finally, all the animals other than the horses were used for selling meat or for their own consumption. Furthermore, Ora's duties as a child were to knit, wash clothing in the river, and take care of the sheep. Ora began to weave and knit by the age of five. The only way she learned was by looking at her elders and seeing how they did it, the same way she learned to cook. Ora learned by the age of eight just by watching her mother and older sister, Nina. As Ora got older, her duties for taking care of the sheep grew. At times, she was set off to travel with the herd of about 150 sheep for three to four months, along with another girl to keep her company. During the months she was not home, she would stay in empty huts, making her own food and fire. Although the work seems unbearable, for Ora it was like an adventure waiting to happen.

The fact that Ora's family lived in such a secluded place gave it more reason to visit other families nearby. Then there were times where it was a must to visit family such as on holidays or days of festivities. Ora and her family celebrated birthdays and Christmas. For birthdays, family from nearby villages came together to sing and dance and enjoy a typical birthday dinner. The food served at most *cumpleanos* dinners included roast guinea pig and *ponche*, which is a hot beverage made of egg whites. As for a regular family dinner, the food included soup, sheep meat, potatoes, toasted corn nuts, and hot herbal tea to drink. During Christmas

Eve, Ora and her family traveled to San Pedro de Cajas for the traditional Mass service at the church. Unlike the American tradition where it is about presents and a Christmas tree, in San Pedro de Cajas it is just a time for the whole village and small neighboring towns to come together and enjoy each other's company as villagers performed dances for viewers. Other than the performances, there was always live music in the background, and people danced the night away to Christmas morning. Another traditional celebration for Ora and her family was the annual festivities for anyone who grew livestock. During the month of February, her family celebrated the day of the sheep. In May, her family celebrated the day of the llama. Then in July they celebrated the day of the cow. During each of these months, the celebration lasted two days, and it was tradition to decorate the live animal being celebrated. During that time, family and friends came together to sing and dance and ate the traditional *pachamanca*, which is sheep meat, cooked underground with the help of hot rocks. To this day, Ora remembers her family gatherings, which she holds dear to her heart.

Growing up Ora had several happy childhood memories. She loved playing with her siblings, even though they had no actual toys to play with. Since her family was not economically stable, having a toy was a luxury that they just did not have. Instead, Ora and her brothers and sisters had to imagine or build their own toys. For instance, to make a doll Ora and her sisters would roll up blankets into a small bundle, and then they would imagine it was a real doll. In addition, she and her siblings would take cow bones and pretend they were cows roaming on the empty lands. Although Ora had joyous memories as a child, she still has some sad memories that are in her thoughts still. For example, when she was about 12 years old her sister, Nina, got married and for the first time her family felt incomplete. Ora recalls the day she left with sadness in her eyes. Nina left her family, hand and hand with the man whom she married. Ora could not believe what was happening the day her sister walked out with her new husband and a bag filled with all her belongings. Unlike her other siblings, Ora suffered the loss of her sister more, because for her, Nina was her best friend and a second mother. As time went on, Ora's parents insisted she attend school, but she always refused. Her parents gave her an opportunity, along with unconditional support, but she just let it fade away. Ora neglected to attend school in San Pedro de Cajas because she was afraid of having contact with other people. She grew up with the fear of people because she had always lived in an isolated village away from any human contact, besides her family. In Parpacocha, Ora had no childhood friends, only companions she was paired up with during the long months of traveling with the sheep. Her only true friends were her siblings. Attending school was not the only issue. Ora was also always afraid of going into San Pedro de Cajas when doing small errands such as buying food, clothing, and even when attending Mass. Although Ora is a devoted Catholic today, when she was a young she barely went to church twice a year, for Easter Sunday and Christmas Eve. Eventually, by the time she got married, her fear of people diminished.

Ora married her true love, Santos Hernandez Moreno, on September 8, 1951. The two met in 1947 after their fathers decided to buy a piece of land together. However, at the time Santos Hernandez was her junior by four years. Luckily, for both of them age did not matter. The two got to know each other for about five years before they actually got married. Back then dating did not include dinner or a movie; instead, it was getting together to talk or take walks around the village. After a year of dating, Santos proposed, one month prior to their wedding day. Eventually, the two had a small and simple wedding in a nearby village by the name of Acobamba, then after they moved to Ocucancha, which is about an hour and half away by foot from Parpacocha. Ora describes her husband as charming, caring, and an amazing father to their children. For her, the key to a successful marriage that lasted more than fifty years is to live in harmony and honesty. The marriage that they have conserved throughout the years not only overcame obstacles, but it taught them to live their lives one day at a time. Ora and Santos Hernandez had ten children, two of whom died at a young age. They had six daughters named Isi, Reina, Irena, Jara, Flor, and Aracely. Flor died at the age of 12 because of *susto*, which is known as a folk illness where the soul leaves the body after a frightening event. Aracely died at only two months after a severe cold. In addition, Ora and Santos have four sons named Ernesto, Felipe, Xavier, and Sancho, who is Jara's twin. Overall, Ora and Santos have sixteen grandchildren and five great-grandchildren. All of her children were delivered by midwives and all but Reina were born in Ocucancha. Once in Ocucancha, Ora's husband dedicated himself to weaving, harvesting potatoes, and raising livestock such as cows, horses, and chickens. Ora, on the other hand, spent her time raising her children and managing the household duties such as cooking and cleaning. Ora and her husband did exactly what her parents did to make money. There was no other choice but to sell meat, potatoes, and handmade crafts. In addition, in the case where someone in her family became ill, she would use herbal medicine just as her mother used on her family. There were no doctors to rely on. Therefore, everyone depended on herbal remedies. Furthermore, as the children got older, Ora and her husband decided to move to San Pedro de Cajas in 1968 for their children's education. Once in the bigger village they dedicated themselves to making blankets, hats, gloves, leggings, and eventually beautiful tapestries. Today, San Pedro de Cajas is known for its villagers' remarkable tapestries, who still occupy the rural town. San Pedro de Cajas is quite similar to Parpacocha; although it has more people, they both share similarities in climate temperature. During winter, there are heavy storms, light snow, and cold breezy air at all times. Then, during the summer, the temperature is only a bit warmer. In 1978, Ora and her husband were held responsible for passing the annual weeklong tradition in honor of the Saint Peter. Every year, they honor the saint by having Mass in late June, followed by a procession in the town's plaza. The whole celebration is for the village and welcomes all visitors. During the festivities, there is a live orchestra, fireworks, bullfight, and dancing until late hours of the night. To this day, this long-lived tradition still exists in San Pedro de Cajas, Peru.

American Sector, Berlin (1926)

As told to her grandson.

FIGURE 2.5.1   Berlin Demolished by Bombs, 1945

My entire life I had not known much about my grandmother. No one in our family spoke much of her other than to let me know that she was alive. A few years ago my grandma moved into our town and, since then, I have learned a lot about her. I sat down to do this interview thinking I knew most of her life story already. I found out that I had only begun to know the amazing ride that was my grandmother's life.

Maitilde Schneider was born in Berlin, Germany, on March 30, 1926. Soon after her birth a great depression (not as large as that in the United States, but still significant) hit her homeland and people suddenly found it difficult to get work and pay the bills. Her father was a chef, baker, and gardener, among many other things. His first love was baking, and he owned a bakery in Berlin that he loved. Maitilde said that she loved going to the bakery and was in constant supply of "junk" food. The Schneider family also sold fruits and vegetables that they gathered from their own garden. When the items in their garden were not enough, my grandmother and her friends would climb local trees (whether they were supposed to or not) to feed their supply. From an early age, this woman did what she could to help out her family.

As a child, Maitilde Schneider had many friends. These kids would play in abandoned houses for fun, sometimes pretending there was treasure inside that was theirs for the taking. My grandmother actually recalled climbing into the chimneys of these vacant houses to get in. This little girl was quite the tomboy. My grandmother and her friends never really understood why so many houses in their neighborhood were abandoned at the time. Looking back now, she knows that it was because she lived in a predominately Jewish area and that a lot of the Jewish families there had moved away so that they would not be put into work camps. As it turned out, many of the friends my grandmother had were Jewish. At this time (1932–33) there was not a lot of publicity about what Adolf Hitler was planning on doing with the Jews, and many people went on living their regular lives without fear. Within the next couple of years, those who were able moved out of town, and Maitilde had only a small group of friends left.

My grandma would jump on the back of the milk wagon in her neighborhood for a free ride to school every day (otherwise it was about a half-hour walk). She found that school was tough, and the teachers were even tougher. If a student got "out of line," a teacher would whip them with a willow. Overall, Maitilde liked school, but it was not her favorite thing in the world.

By the mid 1930s, Hitler was in full power. The common greeting of "Hello" had changed to "Heil Hitler" no matter what situation that a person was in. Maitilde remembers thinking that it was weird going into a store or to school and addressing other people in this way, but she did it because that was what she was taught to do. In 1939, World War II began and life in Berlin changed a lot. The town was evacuated of almost all children, and it began to get bombed by the Allied nations.

At 15 years old, my grandma was working in an orphanage during the day and went to night school all of the way through college. Her mother had heart problems, and life was beginning to get even rougher. Maitilde began working at the Red Cross in 1943 to gather wounded soldiers from the battlefields in Russian and Poland. Days were long and the Red Cross workers often had 26- to 28-hour shifts. They began to learn how to sleep standing up so that they were ready at a moment's notice to do whatever job they were assigned next. These workers were always running low on supplies and would have trouble getting drugs and bandages for their injured.

In 1945, my grandmother can remember a specific moment when her family went outside because they thought that the shooting had stopped. When they got to their porch they looked up to see Russian planes flying overhead and soon after heard explosions of bombs that those same planes were dropping on Berlin. This was one of the scariest times and places in history, and my grandmother was there.

When the bombing stopped, Russian soldiers began raiding Berlin. They were drunk because they were not able to get enough food, and they would go through town stealing, raping, and killing "Nazis" (all Germans, even though the majority of them had been forced to follow Hitler). A lot of the German people did not know about the Jewish death camps, only that Jews were being sent to work camps. My grandma can remember hiding out from these soldiers in the attic of her house. The neighbors who were hiding with her had two dogs that would not stop barking. The owner had no choice but to shoot them both so that the Russians would not find their hiding spot. Had the Russian captains found out what was going on, they would have killed them, but most of these horrible things were done out of their view.

Foreign radio stations had been blocked, making it very difficult to get information about what was going on with the war. Berlin was eventually separated into four sections: one American, one French, one English, and one Russian. My grandmother felt that she was lucky to end up in the American quarter because they were slightly more human toward Germans than the Russians or English. People in each section were forced to eat what their new government rationed out. Depending on where you lived, this meant bread, chocolate, cereal, beans, or tea. There was not much deviation from these staple foods, but people felt fortunate to be eating at all.

In 1943, Maitilde met a French prisoner of war (POW) and fell in love. They were married in somewhat of a secret ceremony, and she became pregnant soon after. When the German government found out about the marriage, they had it annulled, and shortly after Maitilde's husband was killed. Three months later she had her first child, a baby girl named Adali Schneider.

The Americans turned a majority of the restaurants in their section into clubs where military persons and locals could hang out and drink. By 1946, Maitilde worked in one of these clubs at night and worked in a hospital during the day, cleaning and cooking for the most part. People at this time were so poor and hungry that they would take any work they could get and trade anything that they could get their hands on (usually rugs or jewelry) to farmers for food.

In the late 1940s, Maitilde's daughter developed polio (a common disease of the time) and got to the point where breathing was very difficult. Living in the American section of Berlin was a lifesaver because that was one of the only places in Berlin where one could be put on an iron lung. Through rehabilitation, Adali was able to get back on her feet and go back to living a healthy life. In 1948 Maitilde was transferred to Frankfurt and had to leave her daughter with her godmother in Berlin. Without having moved to Frankfurt, Maitilde would not have been able to support herself and her daughter. She would get to see Adali in summer and on winter vacations. In 1953, Maitilde met her future second husband in Frankfurt, a soldier in the US Army. They moved to Manheim, Germany, shortly afterward. The two got married in 1954, and he adopted Adali so that she could be with them.

In 1957, with her daughter and husband, Maitilde moved to the United States. They came over on a boat to New York and took a train all the way to Fort Louis, Washington, where they were stationed. They lived there for about nine years until they were transferred again to Panama in 1962. Adali had fallen in love at this point and refused to leave Washington. She became pregnant with her first child at the age of 18 and was married soon after. Maitilde was not too happy with this, but she believed it useless to argue with her daughter, so she stayed for the wedding and then went to Panama to start her new life.

In 1966 Maitilde's husband retired from the US Army and began working for the Panama Canal Company supervising cleaning crews. In 1978 he retired from the Panama Canal Company and bought a house on the Pacific Ocean side of Panama. These 1.5 acres started out empty and over the years filled up with gardens, people, and pets. Maitilde never had any more children, and she instead surrounded herself with animals. There were geese, dogs, cats, birds, rabbits, and many other creatures that found their home with her in Panama. Maitilde loved animals and with a group of friends she began the Humane Society in Panama. Streets were crowded with animals that people would let loose, and the Humane Society saved many of them from being poisoned by police in the area, as was custom at the time. One could say that Maitilde was a heroine to animals in Panama.

Maitilde enjoyed living in Panama because there was a wide range of peoples living there. She taught English to a few Indian groups while at the same time learning Spanish. In 1989, the Berlin Wall fell, and in August of 1990 Maitilde went back to Berlin to see what life was like there. She found that it was nothing like it had been as a child. Everything had become much more expensive and the people were not very friendly to each other (there were grudges between the people of the former East and West Berlin). Seeing these changes was somewhat of a disappointment to Maitilde.

Maitilde returned to the United States, and in 1994, her husband was hospitalized with several Army-related injuries as well as heart problems. He was sent back to the United States to a veteran's hospital where he died during heart surgery. He was buried in 1995 in Louisiana where most of his family resided. After his death, Maitilde went back to Panama and sold their property for $56,000. Maitilde believed that she would have gotten a larger amount of money for the property had it not been for the Panama Treaty of 1978 that President Jimmy Carter signed. This went into effect in December of 1999 and, according to Maitilde, scared many people from buying property in the area. After selling this property, Maitilde moved to Panama City for 16 months and then moved in with a friend from Germany in California in 1999. Daughter Adali had three children and also lived in California for a large portion of the last thirty years.

Maitilde says that she feels lucky to still be alive and doing interviews like this one today. She believes that life in America is not as easy as Panama (where she admits to having been spoiled), but that she has seen worse places in her life. Maitilde says that in certain ways she misses Germany and the life that she had there when she was a child. She still has relatives in Germany and Canada but has not kept in close contact with any of them.

Maitilde Schneider feels that a few of her greatest accomplishments in life include learning multiple languages (German, English, Spanish, and French), learning how to get along with all types of people, teaching Panamanian Indians how to speak English, and helping found the Humane Society of Panama. There are things that she admits to wishing she could go back and change, but she believes that overall she has lived a good life. At 77 years old, Maitilde Schneider looks forward to spending time with her family and seeing how the rest of her story unfolds.

CREDIT

Pomerania (1927)

As told to her grandson.

FIGURE 2.6.1 League of German Girls, Potsdam, Germany, 1935

My name is Elke Weber Rodgers. I was born on December 9, 1927, in Pomerania, a former province of Northeast Germany that, since the Second World War, is now mostly Northwest Poland. I was the fifth child born to Josef and Wilma Weber. Dad was a city administrator and Mom was a housewife. I had three brothers and three sisters. Coming from a large family was the best thing in the world, and I had a wonderful childhood. My family was very close, and we had a great relationship. I remember there was always music in the house and we always had fun. Everything we did we enjoyed—even work.

We were brought up in a Lutheran home, and it was part of our growing up to go to church every Sunday morning. Though we were raised in a political machine, no matter what the political agenda said, Mom and Dad always said church came first. After that we could do whatever we wanted to do, so long as any other chores and responsibilities were finished. Often our free time was spent among friends and family, playing games or taking part in various youth organizations.

I still have vivid memories of my childhood. Some of my happiest memories are playing sports and various other games with my brothers and sisters. Though we did not have organized sports, we did play games like handball and *schlacbal* (a game similar to American baseball). Since we lived only 1 mile from the Baltic Sea, we spent our summers swimming and canoeing, and winters ice skating and tobogganing. We finished school at 1:30 in the afternoon (we went from 7:30 in the morning to 1:30). My parents would let us go swimming or ice skating for an hour after school, and then my father would help us with our schoolwork. I am not sure what the other children did. Basically, we organized our own activities and met in the afternoons. We kept ourselves entertained, and it did not cost anything. You could not really do anything wrong because the news would have spread quickly.

My grandfather was a baker. He owned his own bakery. He lived to be one hundred years old. I remember my grandmother always carried money under her two long skirts, and she would always lift them and give us money. My relatives were all hard-working people, and they had a great influence on my life. Often, the whole family—uncles, aunts, and cousins—would all get together and go hiking. We would ride into the woods on a horse-drawn carriage with benches on the side so we could sit down. Since our whole family was so close, Christmas time and other holidays, with all the ceremonies, were always special.

Amid the households of my friends, relatives, and other people I knew, the mothers always stayed home and took care of the house, children, and husband. The husband was the wage earner, and the wife was to support him as much as she could. Whenever we ate, my mother always served Dad first. He had the first choice of food. He was bringing in the money. After Dad had been served, the food went around the table, and Mother was the last to help herself. My mother really shaped our lives—not just the girls, but the boys as well. She was very important to us all. She and my father gave us a stable home, and there was never any doubt about our roles. We always knew where we stood with our parents. We knew our place in society and had confidence in all we did. As I said, we all had a wonderful relationship with our parents.

Since the area where I grew up was mainly agricultural and there was no industry and no defense contracts or anything like that, we were kind of bypassed by the actual war. Once in a while, there were times when a Russian plane came over the Baltic and we had to keep everything in darkness. But, apart from not having any tropical food, we had plenty of milk, we had a garden, and we raised our own chickens. So, we did not really suffer much like the rest of West Germany. Often they transferred whole schools of children to our part of Germany in order that they might avoid the disruptions of constantly going into the air raid cellar. I was in the Hitler Youth as a young girl, but it was like being in the Campfire Girls or Girl Scouts. We would hike and camp and play sports. Sometimes we would bake cookies to raise money or write letters for the troops. We did not do anything bad. I did not know anything bad was taking place. As I said earlier, the war really did not affect us much where we lived.

When I was 16 years old, my two older sisters, my little brother, and I got diphtheria. I remember we had to be quarantined. All our belongings were burned. My brother, who was the first to contract the disease, got the worst case, and because he became so sick, was hospitalized after ten days of quarantine. He died three days later. He was only six years old—so very young. His passing remains my saddest memory.

I would say that until about three months before we had to leave East Germany, we did not know too much about the war machine. When the first refugees coming from East Prussia heading west came to our town, we did all we could to help them. They came in horse and wagon like the old settlers in the United States, with only a few belongings. They wanted to be with the Americans and English and not the Russians. I remember hearing so many bad stories about the Russians.

After the war when the Russians came to Pomerania, there was no longer any law and order. Being the conquering nation, they thought they could get any woman they wanted. My parents' primary concern was to get us girls out because of the rapes and other actions of the Russians. Two of my sisters and I were forced to leave for West Germany. The people of West Germany had to give one part of their house for refugees and their families.

My mom packed a feather bed, a pillow, a cup and bowl, and silverware for each of us. We were the last three people to get aboard on a cargo ship. It was absolutely loaded in the cargo hull, but they let us board because earlier we had done so much to help the trucks of refugees coming from East Prussia. They said, "These girls worked so hard, let's get them on the boat." So we were the last ones to escape. We were very lucky we could get out. We arrived in the harbor of Lubeck and moved into a home with a West German woman. All three of us shared one bedroom in the house. The West Germans did not like the East German immigrants because they had to give us a room to live. My sisters were my closest friends. My older sister and her son were already out of Pomerania, living in Norway. Since my dad was a city official, he felt that he could not leave unless everybody could, so he and my mother and my younger brother stayed behind.

The end of the war had a major influence on my life. I was sad when we left East Germany because we had to leave our belongings behind. We lost everything we owned. But I know if we had not left East Germany, I would have never met and married Mike. I often forget about the sad times in life, because they always seem to open the door to happy times. My older sisters were raised the old-fashioned way. When they graduated, they went to "housekeeping school," where they learned everything they needed to know, like how to run a household, how to can, slaughter a pig, weave, and do needlework. They stayed in school for a year and learned all that they needed to know. Then they, more or less, went out to look for a husband. My younger sister and I were raised under the ideals of the later generation. Upon graduation, we then continued our education in order to get a degree and get a job. Nevertheless, the aim was still to one day get married and have a family.

One of my older sisters went to Berlin to go to school and the other stayed in our hometown because they eventually opened up a house school there. I went to school for 12 years in my hometown (from age six to eighteen). Then I went to three years of photography school, which the state partially financed. I worked in photography for three years, and as I recall, I received good pay for those times. I also was an au pair (nanny) in England for four years. The pay was very little, but I also got room and board, so I did not really need much more in pay. For a short time, I was an X-ray technician for an internist. During this time, I lived with my parents (who had now moved out to West Germany) because the pay was not much. I worked for the federal government as an executive secretary for four years. My rent was subsidized, medical was paid for, and I received very good pay. It was during this time that I met Mike.

In the summer of 1960, I met Mike at the Rijksmuseum of Amsterdam. I was there on holiday and he was there after finishing his work in England. I fell in love with him almost immediately. Some things just happen very unexpectedly and instinctively. It sort of hits you and that was it. I just knew Mike was the right person. We talked for quite a while, having coffee in the Rijksmuseum cafeteria, and I just thought he was such a nice guy.

I later learned that Mike had recently bought a 40 foot yacht, and having taken some time off from his job in England, began to teach himself how to sail. He sailed across the North Sea to Holland. He felt that if he could sail around in the close quarters of the Netherlands, then he would be skilled enough to take on most any expedition. We spent some time together until my vacation ended and Mike had to return to England, doing so aboard his yacht, the *Peregrine*, amid stormy conditions. We corresponded through letters for the next few months, and in October of the same year, I journeyed to England to spend time with him. We were in London and Mike had booked theater tickets to *Irma La Duce*. Before the show we walked along Oxford Street, and he pulled me into a jewelry shop and he said, "Let's get engaged!" The jeweler brought out a tray of typical American/English diamond engagement rings and I said, "I don't want a diamond; I just want a plain gold wedding band." And that's how it happened.

Mike returned to the States to meet with various magazine, journal, and news-paper editors in order to sell his idea of writing a travel log, which would chronicle his planned adventures of sailing throughout Europe and across the Atlantic. His proposal was met with approval and his journey was subsidized. In December, just before Christmas, Mike came back to Germany, where I was still working for the government. We went up to see my family and spent Christmas of 1960 with them.

In August of 1961 we left the yacht in Holland, took the Ostend ferry across to Dover, and went to Scotland by train. We married in Scotland. I never thought I would get married because I was already 33 and there were nine women to each man because of the postwar situations. During the war, so many men throughout Europe lost their lives. After staying for three weeks while the paperwork went through, we returned to Holland and began our honeymoon aboard the *Peregrine*. The plan was to sail around France and Spain and into the Mediterranean. I remember sailing through the English Channel was extremely rough and Mike, sensing my anxiety, decided to stop along the coast of France and get a license to cross the French county via slower-moving rivers and canals in order to reach the Mediterranean.

We then sailed through the Mediterranean, making a number of stops until we reached Barcelona, where we stayed a couple of days before going down to the island of Ibiza. At the end of the summer of 1962, Mike set course for the United States. We sailed down the coast, stopping over in different towns along the way whenever provisions were needed. We spent about two and a half months in the Canary Islands. On December 23, we left the Canary Islands to cross the Atlantic. In January 1963, we set sail for the Caribbean and finally docked at one of the small islands of Grenadine, where Mike wrote his articles for publishing. After my visa came we arrived in Miami in September and went up the inland waterway until we reached Cape Canaveral, where Mike got a job as a chief launching engineer. Our son James was born aboard the *Peregrine* in 1964. At the end of the year and three months, Douglas Company hired Mike to be the chief test conductor at their California headquarters.

I think our time on the *Peregrine* was a wonderful experience. It taught both of us so much. As with most things, you tend to remember only the good parts of it. But I know that sometimes there were situations where I thought to myself, "Why are we doing this?" We could have been on land and not have so many of the worries that we had living a life at sea. But looking back now, I think it was such an extraordinarily amazing experience. It taught us how little one needs to live, as far as material things. People so often get carried away with things that really are not necessary.

When I first came to the United States, I did not see any clotheslines or wash hanging out to dry. In Florida, I remember seeing a one sign that read, "Don't fry your clothes." In other words, use the dryer. It was "consumption, consumption" all the time. I was also impressed by a lot of things. I remember being in awe of supermarkets. One day I will try to find some letters that I wrote to my parents at the very beginning because you forget so quickly, and the first impressions are the very ones that one needs to treasure.

The biggest thing I had to overcome in my life was being told that I had bladder cancer in 1967. The tumor was removed, and they inserted cobalt spirals into my bladder (this treatment was somewhat the predecessor to chemotherapy). In 1991,

I had a relapse, and they gave me a treatment of the tuberculosis bacillus to activate my antibodies. I have been well since.

Some years ago, Mike convinced me to return to my homeland and visit my parents. Upon returning, I found that in some ways it was nice to see my homeland, but in other ways it was quite disturbing. The country is still as beautiful as it was when I was a child—the trees, the fields, the woods, and so on, none of that has changed. But I was really struck by how much time stood still there, while other countries, like both West Germany and the United States, made such big leaps. It was quite disturbing to see how run down everything was. Society and industry are just now beginning to come back to life.

CREDIT

Calcutta (1927)

As told to her grandson.

FIGURE 2.7.1   Chowringhee Square, Calcutta now (Kolkata) India, 1945

My maternal grandmother, Delilah Elkana, was born in Calcutta (now Kolkata), India, on June 17, 1927. Her parents had come to India as immigrants from Baghdad, Iraq, in the early 1900s to flee persecution and to seek a better life for themselves and their children. Delilah's mother, Lily Sheba, had been married at the age of 12 to Silas Elkana, a man more than ten years her senior who was chosen by her parents. She recalled crying at having to leave school to get married. Delilah was a member of a Jewish community that was started at the end of the eighteenth century, after India had become part of the British Empire, by a young Orthodox Jew named Shalom Aaron Obadiah Cohen, an ancestor of my grandfather, who came to Calcutta from Aleppo in Syria. A descendant of exiles in Spain, he became a rich court jeweler, after which Jews came to join the community he was founding. There was no persecution of Jews living in India. The Jews of Calcutta, a very small minority of the population, lived in the midst of many religious groups. Eighty percent of the population was Hindu, Muslims made up thirteen percent, and the rest were Buddhists, Jains, Parsis, Sikhs, Bahai, and Christians. Each group lived separate lives and respected each other's differences. The Calcutta Jewish population reached its peak of five hundred in 1942, after Burma fell into Japanese hands and more people were seeking safety. One of four girls born to Lily and Silas, Delilah had one older sister and two younger ones. Two baby brothers died in childbirth. Diana and her sisters had the usual sibling tiffs, but they loved each other. She very much enjoyed spending time with her family. Delilah's grandmother, her mother's mother, had several children and was sometimes pregnant at the same time as her mother, so Diana had aunts and uncles younger than she was. Her primary language was English, but she also spoke Hindustani.

Although she had a happy childhood, Delilah's saddest memory was when she saw her father crying as he read a letter. He told her it was from his family in Baghdad and that it reported that Jews were being killed and raped in pogroms and that their property was being looted and destroyed. This was especially heartbreaking because it was the last letter he received from his family, and he never found out what happened to them. The Farhud pogrom, in which much of the family was killed, took place in Baghdad in 1941. It was a very brutal time of violence, during which babies were slaughtered before their parents' eyes and thousands of Jewish shops were plundered.

Delilah attended the Jewish girl's school in Calcutta, a small boarding school under auspices of the British Education Authority. Hebrew and Jewish scripture and Torah cantillation were added to the curriculum. Delilah loved and respected all her teachers, who, along with her headmistress, were all Jewish. Her school had the best academic record in the Province of Bengal. The schoolgirls were divided into four houses, each named after a poet or playwright, and each house had its own color. Delilah's house was Tennyson and her color was blue. There was competition between the houses to be the best in sports and academic standing. Delilah won the spelling bees that they had every year, even against more senior girls. In fact, she was known as a bookworm who had the highest grades in the class. But she struggled with mathematics, and she did not shine at sports because she had asthma until the age of 13. Delilah loved to win prizes at school, which were books recently published in England, given out at the annual awards assembly at the end of each school year. She pounced on having something new to read.

Discipline at the school was strict. Students were not allowed to speak in class unless the teacher had asked a question. Punishment was writing a hundred lines for homework, such as, "I must not talk in class" or, "I must not run in the halls." The matron had to see and initial each of these assignments. If behavior was really bad, students had to report to the headmistress, at which time she struck a slender rod on a girl's open palm five to ten times. Sometimes misbehaving students would have to wear a "dunce" cap. There were also detentions during the morning, afternoon, and recess. Parents supported the teachers and the headmistress 100 percent, never questioning a school's decision. At that time, it was believed that adults knew best. Children were supposed to obey elders and to show respect at all times, and they were not allowed to make their own choices.

In her spare time, Delilah enjoyed a number of different activities. She played games, chatted with her friends, knitted, read books, and sang in a choir. She did not have a radio in the dormitory, and television had not been invented yet. On Sunday mornings, the matron would take students for long walks in the park or to see ships in the harbor. At home during school holidays Delilah would go on outings with her sisters, go to parties, and visit friends. On Jewish holidays she would dress in her best clothes and go to the synagogue.

Diana had a best friend named Sally, who slept in the same dormitory at boarding school. She and Sally used to tell each other secrets, talk about their feelings, borrow each other's clothes, and help each other with their homework. They would visit each other's homes during the holidays. Their friendship was very strong. It lasted all through the years of school and for many years after. They still write to one another, even though Sally now lives in Australia. As Delilah became a teenager, World War II impacted her life. For her, the war was a lesson in how an evil man like Hitler could damage the world with his insane hatred for Jews and with his desire for power. In the 1930s in the prequel to the war, the community took in European Jews fleeing from Hitler's grasp. When war broke out, the British government wanted to intern them as enemy aliens, but the Jewish community said that these people were actually victims of Hitler, Britain's enemy. The community stood as a guarantee for them and they were not interned. Many of the men Delilah knew went off to fight, and soldiers from other countries were seen in the streets of Calcutta. India supported the war effort. Two million Indians served in the army and twenty-four thousand were killed. Everyone listened to the news on the radio to find out what was happening in the battle. Calcutta was bombed by Japanese warplanes, requiring everyone to take shelter whenever an air raid siren sounded. They could come out of their shelter when the "all clear" sounded. All schools held air raid drills and the children had to carry air raid kits.

Delilah's family escaped death during the war, although they came very close to personal tragedy. She remembers a particular Christmas Eve when she was among 25 to 30 neighbors huddled in a ground-floor apartment of a young Jewish family. Delilah, along with her parents and her three sisters, had had to leave their apartment next door in order to shelter there. Like other men, women, and children waiting out the air raid on the chairs beds and floor, they had converged on that place by prior arrangement at the first sound of the air raid siren. Among them were some Jewish refugees from Burma (now Myanmar); survivors of Japanese aerial bombardments that were carried out, in part, because the British were building up their supplies in Burma. Planes buzzed angrily. Bombs exploded, some far away, one too close for comfort. In the darkness of the apartment, Delilah held her littlest sister close. Then she heard her mother sobbing uncontrollably. She was shocked. Adults, she believed, should be more courageous than children. Yet somewhere in that darkened room, her mother was crying, and her deep, wrenching sobs were tearing at Delilah's heart. It was some time before the "all clear" sounded and someone snapped on the overhead lights. Now she could see the others, and she learned what had happened. It seemed that her father, impatient with another "false alarm," had left to go back to their second-floor apartment down the street scant minutes before the bombs had started falling. Delilah was stricken with horror, contemplating her father's tragic end. When she, her mother, and her sisters returned to their severely bomb-damaged apartment, they found him waiting there for them. Luckily he had been standing in the only part of the apartment where the ceiling had not fallen down.

It was not until 1945 that the Japanese finally surrendered, four horrific months after the war ended in Europe. All over the city of Calcutta on V-J Day (victory over Japan) the lights glittered in defiant glory, dazzling after the gloom and doom of the past years, reminding everyone that there would be no more bombs over the city. They were relieved that Japanese enemy forces were no longer poised to attack Calcutta from neighboring Burma, and that the street signs exhorting "All together, get that Jap" would soon be taken down.

Years after the war, India's struggle for independence from Britain greatly affected Delilah and her family. She witnessed riots in Calcutta, the burning of streetcars, and attacks on British companies as they made it clear they wanted the British Raj to end. There were calls of "India for Indians" and "Quit India." Finally the British negotiated their withdrawal in 1949, but first they divided the country into India and Pakistan. The independence movement's roots existed before World War II, but the war itself put economic pressure on Britain. All over India, in the newly partitioned areas, Hindus and Muslims were setting fires, killing each other, and committing terrible atrocities. There were also instances when, at great personal risk, Muslims protected Hindus and vice versa. One million people died and thirteen million were dispossessed. At this time, Delilah's husband (then fiancé) saw a Hindu man lying bleeding in the street and crying out weakly for water. A Muslim with a large knife came over to my grandfather and said, "If you help my enemy, you become my enemy," so he had to walk away.

Three years after the end of the war, at the age of twenty, Delilah married my grandfather, Aaron Milgain. In the spring of 1954, along with her children Harry, aged four, and two-year-old Rachelle, she immigrated to Canada on a cargo ship. They were part of a large wave of Jews who left India for England, Australia, the United States, or Canada after India gained its independence. In fact, there are now only about thirty Jews left in Calcutta. Once in Toronto, she faced each new day with blind faith and the optimism of youth. If she could be said to be adapting to all the changes, she was doing so without conscious strategy, working her way through homesickness, a suddenly limited budget, climate shock, and culture shock and was trying to get through the days without her trusty *ayah*, cook, sweeper, and *dhobi*. Back in her Calcutta home, the *ayah*, or nanny, used to come to them at 6:30 each morning. She would get the kids out of bed, wash, feed, dress, and amuse them until she put them down for their afternoon naps, when she would go home for a couple hours. When she returned, this loving, childless woman looked after the children until she bedded them down for the night. All Delilah had to do was sing with them, play with them, and read to them. The cook, or *borchi*, was indispensable. He would do the marketing early in the morning and then report for duty. He prepared and served porridge and eggs, soups, roasts, curries, and Iraqi-style *pilaus* and *koobas*, and he washed the dishes. The *dhobi* came once a week to take away their accumulation of soiled clothing and household linens. Exactly a week later he brought it all back, clean, starched, and pressed. The sweeper came twice a day to chase the dust off the floors with a soft broom called a *jharoo*. Then he washed the floors, cleaned the bathroom, polished the shoes, and salaamed (saluted) as he departed.

Once in Canada, however, Delilah had no servants to depend on. Suddenly she had to take charge—to bathe, clothe, feed, amuse, watch over her two preschoolers, shop, cook, clean, and do the laundry. Learning to do all of those chores that she had never performed before was a laborious and painful process. Her kind landlady came down to the basement apartment of her suburban Toronto bungalow to show Delilah how to dust and mop the floor. Delilah took her first trip to the supermarket with this woman. Talk about culture shock! Where, Delilah wondered, were the squatting Indian vendors with their live chickens that the *shoquet* (ritual slaughterer) would efficiently dispatch? Where were the colorful heaps of exotic fruits and vegetables, the odorous fish market, the Muslim butchers presiding over joints of beef and mutton? Strolling the Toronto supermarket aisles, making choices from a bewildering array on display, she was thankful for the fixed price tags. In India, she had been the oddity who did not enjoy the custom of haggling.

Although Delilah and her family were making some progress, money was becoming a pressing problem. With the accommodation question settled, Delilah's husband Aaron went job hunting. They were in straitened financial circumstances because the Reserve Bank of India had frozen their savings, permitting them to bring to Canada a little over $2,000, stating that they would send them the same allowance once each year until the funds were exhausted. Delilah adapted by learning how to scrimp and save, questioning every purchase, buying secondhand furniture, and storing their clothes in orange crates, which she prettied with colorful plastic covers. After a desperate search for employment, in which his Judaism and the fact that he was from India were held against him, my engineer grandfather was relieved to get his first job, even though it was only as a draftsman. He went off to Branford, about an hour or so outside Toronto, to become one of several temporary employees, keeping expenses down by sharing a room at the YMCA with a nightshift worker, living only on bread and ketchup, and looking forward to spending weekends back with the family.

Ultimately, Delilah did adapt, but along the way she made the sort of mistakes Lucille Ball was paid big bucks to perpetrate on television—only she was not laughing.

Quite often she cried into her pillow at night. Yet, her learning experiences began to move forward, both on the domestic front and beyond. In time, she added her own earnings to her family budget, saw her husband's job opportunities improve, made new friends, brought another baby (my mother) into the world, and kept everyone in her family reasonably healthy and well fed, with only an occasional wistful memory of those long-ago days when she had an *ayah*, a cook, a sweeper, and a *dhobi*.

Through the move to Canada and as progress was made in the area of civil rights, Delilah saw changes in ideas about women and in women's roles over her lifetime. She was happy to witness the arrival of more freedom for more women inside and outside of marriage, and to see them gain more control over their lives, their children, and their money. To this day she is very pleased with these changes. In fact, one of the talks she gives as a lecturer is called, "Canadian Women's Struggle for Political and Professional Rights," in which she chronicles the fact that women used to not have the right to vote or to own their own money; it was managed by either their husbands or fathers. They could not attend college, so they could not get a professional education. If they did manage to train to be doctors or lawyers, the actual field was barred to them. Their husbands had complete control over their children's lives. Women could not get a divorce unless they could prove that the husband had brought a mistress into the home. In a 1929 landmark case in the province of Alberta called The Person's Case, women were finally defined as "persons" in the British North America Act. The victory symbolized the right of women to participate in all aspects of life.

Coming to Canada enabled Delilah to learn more about equality. In India she had grown up in a class-conscious society, and she had taken her role as wife and mother for granted because it was the same for her friends in the community. Women there had only two fields of work available to them: secretarial or nursing. She became a secretary. In Canada, however, more doors were open to her. She worked as an editorial assistant for a nonprofit quarterly magazine and, most recently, became a lecturer and historian. Delilah believes that she owes her success and tenacity to her mother, a loving woman who taught her to be honest and to achieve to the best of her ability. Golda Meir, the former Israeli prime minister, also influenced her. Delilah still lives in Toronto with my grandfather. In 2002 she had a heart attack from which she recovered. At age 82, Delilah is going strong, but she acknowledges that she gets more easily fatigued than she used to. In addition to hitting the lecture circuit, she is part of a group that writes and performs plays to bring attention to the issue of elder abuse. As well, she is part of a writer's collective and a soprano in the choir at Temple Emmanuel in Toronto. Judaism continues to be a huge part of Diana's life, although she is now part of a reform, rather than orthodox movement. Diana is happy with the way her life has played out. Her only wish is that her three children and six grandchildren lived in the same city as she.

CREDIT

Austria (1928)

As told to her granddaughter.

FIGURE 2.8.1 Jewish Women Wearing Star of David, Paris, France, 1942

Born on the border between Bavaria and Austria, Rachel Grosch was the descendent of prominent Germans and was born to an affluent family, who enjoyed the privileges of its rank. On June 6, 1928, when she was born, it was still the custom for men and women to have prearranged marriages. Ruth's mother had a prearranged marriage to her father and accepted it as "the right thing to do" as required by her Jewish faith. It was also done to preserve and enhance the family finances and ensure the preservation of the "family lines." Both of the parents were well-to-do, well educated, and well. traveled. Religion was not practiced in Rachel's generation, and she attributes this to her mother and a lack of respect for it due to Rachel's grandmother, who was very committed to the religion.

Traditions were not generally followed except when Grandmother arrived for visitations. Habits die slowly, and Rachel admits having felt a loss for not practicing these traditions and admits their influence and concern during the Holy Days. Rachel was the only child in her family and that situation was simply one of choice. Her mother had done "her womanly duty" and then decided no more. It was not expected for a woman to work at this time in their station of life, and her mother was indulged in most whims, just as when she decided that motherhood was not for her.

Rachel was raised by nannies, teachers, and babysitters. She enjoyed her father's company most of the time, and he was the parental figure while her mother was off somewhere enjoying herself and traveling the world. However, when World War II and Adolf Hitler arrived, and with the events that followed, her mother soon took over the responsibilities needed to ensure her family's survival. As the only child, Rachel was the object of her father's attention as if she were a male child. Her father wanted her to achieve, do the family respect and justice and become educated. She went to grade school in Paris, France. However, a desire to go home interrupted her travels in Paris. Labor or work of any kind was neither required nor expected and, in fact, considered inappropriate. Since there was not a strong female figure in her life, Rachel admits to not adopting female hobbies such as crocheting and sewing. Cooking was done by the hired help. Foods in her time represented her heritage as well as her land. Meals ranged from matzo ball soup and corned beef to rich delicacies such as crafted desserts designed with her name on them and fresh baked fruits with chicken and duck. Since she felt she identified with her father so much, she wanted to go to school and enjoyed it tremendously. Rachel said that in school she enjoyed and participated in soccer. During her early teens, when she was at home, she dated only a few interested suitors and admits that during her youth she had only one best friend. She described feeling lonely most of the time and having to entertain herself quite often. Ultimately, these habits saved her life.

By the time Rachel was ten her father had read a book entitled *Mein Kampf* by Adolf Hitler. The description of the superior race in the book, and the takeover and eradication of the inferior race (the Jews; her!), caused her father to decide to move his family from Austria to other parts of Europe that were at that time safe. However, the decision was not soon enough. Rachel's grandparents, aunts, and uncles were arrested for "permanent relocation." It was asserted that Adolf Hitler first went for the Jewish aristocracy to undermine any leadership to ensure the success of Hitler's master plan. Rachel was warned about this, but plans for her safety were not set up soon enough. One day in 1939 she came home from school and found no one there. Neighbors came and told Rachel to "come quickly and quietly." In the streets, people, including those she knew, were dressed in shirts with yellow stars pinned on them. They would say nothing and refused to acknowledge anyone. Rachel followed her neighbors and was told to hide, keep her head low, and not look at anyone. There was a silence in the city that was deafening, yet the takeover and the destruction were a representation of the time that was passing her and still the noise did not let her sleep. Preservation of her life overrode any desire for food and the need to reconnect herself to anyone or to know anything. She stayed in an upstairs bedroom and was told not to go near the windows, not to turn on the lights, and not to turn on the water. Soon others joined her. They did not say anything to each other. They did not need to; everyone knew why they were there and the need to keep quiet for survival. Finally, food came, and it was soup and a piece of meat. Some water was there in bottles but not much. This is the time when everyday life was in a dream along with trust and a nightmare became reality.

Two hundred and seventy-four days had passed since the disruption of Ruth's life and still no word had come as to her family and where they had moved under the "relocation." It was still cautioned, "Do not talk, do not look out the windows, do not walk as if to be seen in the windows, do not turn on the lights and do not turn on the water. Any sound will attract attention." In an attempt to keep warm in the devastating cold, three to four people were in a bed, as heating was kept to a minimum and/or turned off completely. Rachel remembers that one time her neighbor walked into the bedroom, saw her and another woman in bed and said, "Don't do that." And Rachel said, "We aren't doing anything." She found this fact disturbing in such a time of desperate measures.

It was always a tradition for Rachel's birthday to be given a celebration and this year one of her friends gave her lipstick. It was a treasured day for her. It meant that she was moving into womanhood and she was still important in a world that was turning upside down. She treasured this moment in this silent corner of hell. In 1941 Rachel was 15 years old. Shortly after her birthday a letter arrived and told her that her father was in Auschwitz and that her grandmother had been sent to the "kilns." There was no word regarding her mother yet. Her uncles were still to be found. Writing in these letters needed to be done carefully. Later she learned that her grandmother went to the fires without resistance at all. This fact disturbed Rachel to such a point that she decided she would never give up so easily, a decision that would become crucial after this historical set of events.

Then there was a break in the silence that kept everyone alive. The troops were coming, and everyone needed to get out. In the interim, Rachel had developed a cough and a fever. She was smuggled to a local facility that still could see Jews for health care, and she was hospitalized under the name, "Sandra White." For the first time in over nine months Rachel was able to shower daily in the hospital, and she felt as though she had finally moved into heaven.

Time and again Rachel recalled hiding under stairs and in neighbor's homes as she bided her time for the nightmare to pass. Finally she heard the "Liberation" had come (March 1945) and Austria was free. She heard it from her protectors, from the people on the street and in the newspapers. Rachel admitted that for a short time of approximately one week she was afraid to come out of hiding and that she was convinced it was a plot from the German Reich to find her. She thought that possibly her neighbors gave in to the pressure of the war and they wanted to be rid of her. Finally, it was her uncle who came and told her it was okay to come home. She quickly removed herself from their presence and went home with her uncle to her family. Only her father was there, and he was looking for her mother. Finally, Rachel's mother was found in France and returned home.

Life as Rachel knew it was completely destroyed. The home she knew was in rubble, the school she went to was functioning on bare essentials, and Ruth was held back in school as a result of absence during the war, though she could pass the test with high grades. At least Rachel's family was together. Many friends, neighbors, and relatives did not know where their family was. A traumatic assault on the family unit had severe repercussions for many years as a result of the German occupation.

Rachel remembers that when visiting her uncle in his home someone asked, "How was it for you during the war?" Such questions were "not done." No one talked about the war: what happened, the occupation, the war, the resistance, and the fear. Soon Rachel's family referred her to a psychotherapist as a result of her introverted tendencies. She remembers the psychotherapist. She remembers visiting the psychotherapists and still facilities were not functioning normally as the therapist had not bathed either. For a long period of time Rachel still could not talk about what had happened and discontinued seeing the therapist.

Rachel remembers that her next choice in a man was that of an American soldier who was there after the liberation and they became involved. She fell in love with him, but he went back home to his wife. From that point on Rachel decided that her next choice would be only those who were not committed elsewhere. Rachel admits that contraception was condoms and diaphragms, and she believed that unmarried sex was permitted and had no problem with it.

Rachel's decision to move to America was unhindered by any reservations at all. She had no expectations. She decided that she would take anything as it happened. Rachel mentioned that this was the day she celebrated her true birthday, January 30. Her next step was to get a job. She was hired as a secretary because of her ability to speak four languages. An interpretive skill was highly desirable after the war. After crossing the Atlantic she lived in Michigan.

She still had an innate drive to get married and have children as if it were an integral part of her makeup. She says that she is glad to see the present generation of women questioning whether they want to marry and have children. This questioning was simply not done in her generation, and she is happy to see the change. Rachel then met and married Ezra from her workplace and they had two children, Nathan and Hannah. She admits that control in the family became almost a compulsive effort, and she wondered what was happening. She says that motherhood was an overwhelming responsibility and admits to wishing she was never there. However, later in life she was happy that she did. Rachel stated that she persistently pressed her mother asking, "Did you really want to be a mother?" and at her mother's deathbed, her mother finally said no. Rachel noted that most in her family lived long lives, for as far back as she remembers (seventy years or more), which she believes contributed to a low stress level in their lives and not having to work too hard.

Rachel's viewpoint, lifestyle, and direction became altruistic after this event. She prevented two children from going to an orphanage by adopting them. Vivian and Vance were mulatto, and they were rejected by society because of their mixed race. Rachel sympathized with being judged for your race and/or ethnicity. Her efforts to help them gave her life meaning. Her family was one of the first Jewish families in their neighborhood, and she and her husband pushed for open housing on a legislative basis. She admits to moving into a conservative neighborhood such as Gross Pointe where egalitarian issues were not practiced.

Rachel's marriage to Ezra at that time was under stress. Ezra was arrested for "lewd conduct" with a man. Rachel and Ezra decided to keep up appearances for the family and were able to make it "go away," along with any other issues from his work life. Rachel again found herself living one life and knowing another. This event affected Ezra's daughter significantly after her own marriage when she decided to live with a woman.

In an effort to assume direction for her children, Rachel decided that a choice of religion was necessary. However, the only one she knew of was the Unitarian Universalist Church that was not decidedly against any kind of ethnic or religious background. Since that time her efforts have been concentrated there, and that was where her second marriage took place twenty years later. Shortly after that, significant events took place that changed Rachel's life permanently.

Rachel was diagnosed with ovarian cancer and had to receive treatments, have a hysterectomy, and admits having total breakdown with the anger around the war and the persecution of the Jews. She felt her life went into a tailspin. She was again dealing with life and death issues and decided once again not to give up. She agreed to the hysterectomy, the radiation, and the chemotherapy, as well as therapy for herself. Shortly after this Ezra had a heart attack, was hospitalized, and died. Life and death still dominated, and yet Rachel did not give up. Her natural-born children were out of the house and away at school and her two adopted children were at home. That situation changed as her adopted children were moved to an aunt's house. Rachel entered into her own psychotherapy and chose a women's-only group because of the lack of female figures in her life. She says that at this time her life changed significantly, and she owes this to these women in this group. The Nazi occupation and the war years left her with low self-esteem, anxiety attacks, and a constant feeling of being persecuted. At age 42, in 1970, she decided this had gone on long enough and she wanted to turn it around. Ultimately, she decided to become a therapist and help others as she had been helped.

CREDIT

Things to Think About

1. Throughout the oral histories there are numerous descriptions of how children were raised and what they did for fun. How would you describe the parent-child relationships in the stories? Do you notice differences in how genders were treated? What type of discipline was used in the decades before World War II? How does it compare to your own experiences growing up?

2. The stories highlight multiple health issues. Look through the oral histories and make a list of the diseases described. Are these diseases that you might have? Why or why not? What has changed in the early twenty-first century in terms of contagious diseases?

3. Decolonization efforts began in the early twentieth century and the push was exacerbated by the war itself. Which nations in these oral histories were colonized and by whom? How did the war change these relationships?

4. It stands to reason that no one wanted another world war after the first one ended. How do you account for the fact that peace only lasted for two decades? In your opinion, what were the main factors on the road to war? Was it the economics of the Great Depression, the nationalism of the combatants, or the political factors of the Versailles Treaty?

5. Both the Balfour Declaration and the Holocaust contributed to the success of the Zionist movement and the creation of the State of Israel in 1948. The legacies of these events persist into the twenty-first century. Which factors do you feel are most important and why has settlement of the strife been so difficult?

For Further Reading

World War I
A World Undone: The Story of the Great War, 1914 to 1918 (2007) by G. J. Meyer

Russian Revolution
Red Winter: One Woman's Struggle to Survive the Russian Revolution (2016) by Kaptzan Robino

Radicalism
The Day Wall Street Exploded: A Story of America in Its First Age of Terror (2009) by Beverly Gage

Roaring Twenties
One Summer: America, 1927 (2014) by Bill Bryson

India
The Splendor of Silence (2006) by Indu Sundaresan

Native Americans
Killers of the Flower Moon: The Osage Murders and the Birth of the FBI (2018) by David Grann

Harlem Renaissance
Not Without Laughter (novel) (1930) by Langston Hughes

Spanish Civil War
A Long Petal of the Sea: A Novel (2020) by Isabel Allende

TIMELINE

- **1932**

  FDR elected president for first of four terms: 1932, 1936, 1940, 1944A

- **1935**

  Italy invades Ethiopia

- **1939**

  Franco's dictatorship begins in Spain, lasts until 1975.

  World War II begins with German invasion of Poland

- **1941**

  United Nations founded; Japanese bomb Pearl Harbor

- **1945**

  World War II. First use of nuclear weapons

- **1946**

  British Prime Minister Churchill delivers the Iron Curtain Speech

- **1947**

  The India Independence Act granted India independence and began the end
  of political empire building.

- **1948**

  State of Israel founded and Zionism (1897 by Theodor Herzl)

  Berlin Airlift

- **1949**

  Mao Wins in China–Taiwan

  Mao wins Chinese Civil War, NATO founded

1931–1944

Introduction

The women born after 1929 grew up during the worst parts of the Great Depression that began with the stock market crash in October 1929 and continued up until the United States entered World War II in 1941. Although the stock market crash was considered the turning point in the economy, the economic problems began in the 1920s with an agricultural depression, speculation and marginal buying on the stock market, and the overproduction of manufactured goods since the industrial might of the United States failed to adjust for a world without the war. The women born in the 30s grew up with shortages, limited funds, and a worldview that required them to endorse the oft cited adage, "Use it up, wear it out, make it do, or do without." The concept lasted until the end of the war and contributed to a phenomenon called "Depression psychosis" that impacted voting, buying, and even whether one ripped open the presents with gusto or pealed them open, folded them carefully, and reused them for the next birthday.

The two most well-known people America during the 1930s were President Franklin D. Roosevelt (FDR) and his wife, Eleanor. In his inaugural address on March 4, 1933, the president stated that Americans "should fear nothing but fear." His optimism allowed him to lead the country successfully through the 1930s and into World War II. It is somewhat hard to imagine, but during his "fireside chats" the country drew up their settees and armchairs to listen with rapt attention to the radio program. Children who interrupted to talk found themselves quickly chastised.

The atmosphere of the time period was defined by the Depression. The New Deal programs offered relief, recovery, and reform, often by funding large-scale projects like the Tennessee Valley Authority's dam project that employed many and delivered hydroelectric power to poor farmers in the South. A different set of projects paved the way for Dorothea Lange to photograph the migrants in the agricultural camps, while still others funded by the WPA recorded labor history through large public art murals by such luminaries as Diego Rivera. The success, or the hope, of the New Deal led to FDR being elected to four terms as president before the 22nd Amendment to the US Constitution limiting a president to two elected terms was ratified in 1951.

The Depression was a worldwide crisis that hit countries tasked with paying reparations for World War I particularly hard. Germany's new leader, Adolf Hitler, used the Depression as an excuse to rally his people to his nationalistic views and to rearm, putting men back to work. By 1936 the civil war in Spain between the Generalissimo Franco and the Spanish Republicans allowed Hitler and his allies to "test" their new weapons and in September 1939, Hitler began the Polish invasion. In the Soviet Union (USSR) Josef Stalin initiated the first of his Five-Year Plans to industrialize the USSR and in China the Japanese attacks multiplied to the extent that the Chinese requested intervention from the League of Nations. The Japanese stormed out of the League meeting and by 1937 the Second Sino-Japanese war rained bombs on coastal China and attacks on their large port cities of Nanking and Shanghai, with the loss of over three hundred thousand civilian Chinese lives. Despite these military invasions, the United States took a position of economic nationalism and passed a series of neutrality acts that unintentionally aided the aggressors.

In September 1938 the powers of Europe met in Munch, Germany, to discuss Hitler's annexation of Austria and his push into Czechoslovakia over the Sudetenland that bordered Germany. The conservative European powers felt that Hitler's aims were limited to uniting German-speaking populations under his rule and allowed his expansion. This Munich Agreement is often referred to as the Munich Betrayal as the "appeasement" treaty only served to embolden Hitler and his demands. In less than a year, Europe would be at war only two decades after singing the Versailles Treaty.

Unlike the women of the earlier era, who were adults when the war broke out, the women born in 1931 were children, and the reality of their young lives was fear of the Japanese on the west coast, fear of German U-boats on the east coast, and later the fear of atomic warfare. For children born in Asia in 1931 war was a constant factor of their lives until they were in their teens. For many the fighting would last throughout their young adult lives. For children born in British territories they would find their fathers and mothers called into the world war far from their homes in places like India and Australia. Even children in Africa found themselves fighting the war on their own lands in both northern and eastern Africa.

Children in Europe lived through six years of war with Germany, while children in Eastern Europe faced first the Germans and then further aggression from Soviet troops. The USSR lost over twenty million citizens in the Second World War and Stalin vowed to create a "buffer zone," or spheres of influence, by making all of Eastern Europe satellite states of the USSR. Although both the British and Americans nominally agreed to Stalin's demand, they would have to rethink that decision as the "Iron Curtain" spread across Eastern Europe by 1949, creating two opposing economic systems of capitalism versus communism. For the leaders of the United States the need for free markets and free trade was fundamental to avoiding a return to the Depression. For the Soviets, the need for protection, workers, and industrial goods was integrally tied to their system of communism that remained very repressive. Historians to this day debate where and why the Cold War started. "Traditional" historians, generally born before 1931, blamed the Soviets for their coercive tactics in Eastern Europe and for stealing atomic secrets. Revisionist historians born during the war period blamed the United States for not finding a way to compromise with our ally, Stalin, and post-revisionists of the baby boom tend to say opportunities were missed on both sides. Either way, World War II was barely over on September 2, 1945, when the 45-year Cold War between the "free world" and the "communist world" began.

Although the usage of medications like penicillin and sulfa drugs emerged from the world wars and more lives could be saved, humankind also killed more people, more quickly, than at any other time in history. It is estimated that approximately three percent of the world's population of 2.3 billion in 1940 perished in the war. In actual numbers that is between 70 and 85 million people. The number included not only battle casualties, but civilians, from the Holocaust victims to the civilian victims of the atomic bombs dropped on Japan in August 1945. The death toll greatly impacted the next generation of workers and the ability for Europe and Asia to recover from the war. By

1947 the United States would initiate the Marshall Plan in order to rebuild Europe and deal with the large number of refugees. The Soviet Union would implement a similar plan for its satellite states.

By 1949 the world was clearly divided into the "red" communist states, including Eastern Europe, the Soviet Union, and the People's Republic of China, and "democratic" states, including the United States and its allies. The US and its allies rebuilt West Germany, and "Checkpoint Charlie" between East and West Berlin became a symbol of the world's division. Although a conflict between superpowers is often discussed in regard to the Cold War, at the end of the war the United States was actually the sole nation capable of rebuilding the world and the only one with nuclear weapons. Nuclear parity between the US and the USSR would take another 25 years to achieve and bankrupt the Soviet Union in the process. Unfortunately, the role as the world's "policeman" would cost the US billions of dollars and require a large standing military at bases around the world. It would also enmesh the country in a series of proxy wars in places as far-flung as Korea, Cuba, the Congo, and Vietnam.

For the girls born in the period between 1931 and 1944 a specific set of expectations existed. First, the years before the war witnessed a depression in the national birthrate as couples married later and avoided having children when possible. Although many children were poor, most would say they did not realize it as everyone else was relatively poor also. Children expected to run beside trains as they chugged across the heartland and pick up coal that bounced out of the coal car. At least 25 percent of men left their families looking for work or from just being depressed by their inability to support their families. Hobos became commonplace, and children even had hobo-themed birthday parties during the war years. Girls were taught to work hard, particularly on household chores, although many of their mothers would be working industrial jobs for the war effort by 1942.

The role of mother often fell to the older female children as they cared for their younger siblings and made sure they were clean and fed. Children whose mothers were not home wore their door keys around their necks on a string and were called "door key" kids, a name that became "dorks." Children also contributed to the war effort by working in Victory Gardens, collecting nylon hose, fat, and tin cans, and selling war bonds. Despite not being "minded" by adults, juvenile crime remained very low. As the war ended and men were based around the world, their families often traveled with them, so children saw the results of the war on a personal level.

For children directly impacted by the theater of war, many had lost relatives and/or their homes. They found themselves refugees without a home as national lines were redrawn. Others, including death camp survivors, vigorously endorsed the founding of a Jewish homeland in what was then Palestine, but was portioned off to create Israel in 1948. Many Jewish families migrated there or to the United States. Another group impacted by the war was those individuals held in wartime internment camps other than the German concentration camps, both POWs and civilians. In the western hemisphere, persons of Japanese ancestry were interned throughout the war. These families were sent from not only states like California, but from American allies in South America, including Peru and Panama. In addition to the Japanese, Italians and Germans were interned as enemy aliens and some of the latter were exchanged after the war for American POWs.

The tenor of the 20s had been one of freedom, and, some might argue, "acting out" with new dances and drug use. That trend was rolled back by the Depression. While women attended college in significant numbers in the 1920s, the oral histories will show that women born in this period either skipped college to marry young or in their teens or went to college to get their Mrs. degree by marrying a returning GI. The GI bill granted returning military tuition aid, and that meant there were fewer spaces for female students. Having a man to care for the family was paramount, and marriages were quick and fertile, highlighted by the birth of 15 million more babies in the years after the war than in the same time before it. Although some women did retain their employment in industry, many more married and moved to the suburbs with their new husbands. Marriage begun in the delight over the war's end often ended in divorce by 1970.

Women's rights made significant gains with the 19th Amendment, but the idea that men needed jobs more than women in the Depression meant women often lost their jobs. The shorter hemlines of the 20s gave way to longer skirts, often sewed at home from flour sacks during the Depression or parachute material during the war. The 20s also witnessed movements for African American rights with the Harlem Renaissance. This movement would be reinvigorated after the war as Black GIs, who had fought in a segregated army, came home and endorsed the "Double V" campaign. The "V" stood for victory in the war and victory in civil rights at home. Within the next two decades, the Army (and baseball) would be integrated and the modern civil rights movement, led by Martin Luther King, Jr., would become part of postwar America. The emphasis on diversity also became a theme for the Soviet Union and, therefore, the Cold War. Despite these gains, Japanese internees returned to their homes to face discrimination and, often, a loss of goods. Hispanics were deported during the Depression to give their jobs to Dust Bowl survivors from Oklahoma and Arkansas. During the war years the Hispanics workers returned only to face "Pachuco" riots in places like Los Angeles.

One of the greatest impacts of the war was the idea that a "woman's place was in the home" and she should make "home better than he [returning GI] remembered it." Girls who went to college often majored in home economics, learning to care for a family, to sew, and to cook. The oral histories contain many examples of this trend. Women were to keep the children quiet and clean, greet their husband at the door with a martini, and let him lie down and rest before dinner. Needless to say, not all women enjoyed this role, and prescription tranquilizers called "Mommy's little helpers" filled many medicine cabinets. The men who returned were "company men" with wartime training, a tendency to work as a unit, and the expectation of having to "commute" to work, something no other generation had anticipated. The period after the war in the 1950s is sometimes viewed as a period of conformity.

With large bank accounts from wartime savings by both men and women, metal to build big cars, and material for women to sew big skirts with large petticoats, the years after the war seemed unusually wonderful and blessed. Men and women returned to church in large numbers, happy to be home after the war. Within a few years vaccines for diseases that maimed, including polio, would change how children played and lived. Suburbs called for new station wagons, new schools, new kitchens, and new styles of mid-century modern decor. This new world was often defined as one of consumerism with the "invention" of the credit card and the strip mall. Televisions arrived on this wave and brought nationwide cultural norms in music, dance, and dress. Although the specter of nuclear war lingered, most people embraced the world of juke boxes, drive-in movies, carhops, and the shared idea that the greatest generation, born before 1935, had made the world a better place.

Reading the oral histories you can watch these changes unfold, told by those who lived through the times. Despite the halcyon postwar days, there were problems with equal rights and equal access to jobs. The suburban builders often had restrictive racial clauses or anti-Semitic clauses in the sales contracts. The Ku Klux Klan experienced a resurgence, often directed toward African Americans in the South. The conflict between communism and capitalism colored much of the era, both at home and abroad. For some parts of the globe, the war's end opened opportunity; for others their lives were limited by new military forces, and you will read three oral histories dealing with those experiences. In general this generation's success in World War II meant any problem could be solved, and they set out to do just that!

US Territory Hawaii (1929)

As told to her granddaughter.

FIGURE 3.1.1 Japanese Attack on Pearl Harbor, Hawaii, Decewmber 7, 1941

My name is Rene Chikoyo Koyoi, and I was born in Honolulu, Hawaii, on October 28, 1929. I am Japanese and was of the first generation of my family in America. My parents emigrated from Japan to find work. I was raised Buddhist; however, I do not go to Buddhist temples, although I still live a Buddhist lifestyle. I am not sure if I believe in the afterlife. I had five siblings: one older brother, one older sister, two younger brothers, and one younger sister. My oldest brother passed away 15 years ago. They were all born in Honolulu as well. We were really close growing up. I was especially close to my younger brothers and sister because I had to take care of them when my parents were working. My father's oldest brother is the oldest person I can remember because my grandparents and great-grandparents lived in Japan or died before I was born. He was very easy going, and he had a huge family—thirteen children, but three died very young.

My father was a cement contractor. My mother was a dressmaker; she worked from home. We were never comfortable financially, but we always had enough food to eat. We grew our own vegetables and raised chickens for meat and eggs. My father loved to fish. My mother took our extra vegetables and eggs to the store and exchanged them for canned goods. I hated feeding the chickens growing up. It was so different then. We have more conveniences now with technology advancements. We did not have a washing machine. I remember how dreadful it was when we had to wash all our clothes by hand. We did not have a water heater. If we wanted to take a warm bath we had to boil the water outside on a fire pit.

I am not a very political person. I can remember three wars that were fought in my lifetime: World War II, the Vietnam War, and the Iraq War. The only war that really affected me was World War II. When I was 12 years old I personally witnessed the attack on Pearl Harbor on December 7, 1941. My family and I were in our car heading for a family friend's beach home. We were on the highway in front of Pearl Harbor when we started seeing Japanese planes hovering above us. Then we started hearing explosions. We saw sailors jumping off the burning ships. We were very worried about my older brother because he decided to stay home by himself and there was no way for us to reach him to see if he was all right. We were evacuated to a nearby hill for about five to six hours. We were allowed to go home after that. My brother was safe.

I do not remember ever feeling scared during the war. I just remember feeling very restricted. The day after the bombing of Pearl Harbor, the islands were put under martial law and remained under martial law until 1945.[1] There were curfews, and movement on the island was limited. We had to turn the lights off after a certain time. I also remember feeling intimidated by the military personnel. We were not treated badly. I was just intimidated to see them carrying big rifles patrolling the area around our house. They would come to our area once a week to make sure everything was under control. They were not friendly at first, but my mother gave them cold water and soda to drink anyway. They became very friendly after that. We later found out that our friend's beach house was hit by one of the bombs. The whole place was destroyed. Our original plan was to leave the night before, but my father said it was too windy to drive, so our departure was delayed until the next morning. We felt it was a premonition because our whole family would have been killed if we had arrived at the beach home the night before.

During the war, I went to Roosevelt High School in Honolulu. It was the only public English standard school in the area. My mother wanted all of her children to

---

1   Approximately one-third of the islands' population was of Japanese origin. The actions on Hawaii, then a US territory, did not mirror the actions on the mainland following Executive Order 9066 in 1941 under the Western Defense Command. Initially four internment camps were set up for persons perceived to be sympathetic to the Axis powers. Eventually a larger camp was constructed called Honouuli on O'ahu. Altogether approximately 367 persons of Japanese heritage were detained, 93 persons of German heritage, and 13 of Italian heritage.

read, write, and speak English very well. I do not remember how far away it was, but I remember taking the bus for a half an hour and walking uphill quite far. Science was fascinating; it was my favorite subject. Math was very easy. History was my least favorite subject because it was boring. I did not participate in school activities because I did not have any free time. I had to go to Japanese language class every day after school. I did not have time to hang out with friends after school because I had to take care of my younger siblings and help my mother with chores. My happiest childhood memories would have to be spending summer days at the beach and not having to go to school. I am too old to remember any sad childhood memories.

I was 18 years old when I went on my first date. It was a picnic on the beach with a bunch of friends. We never went anywhere alone. I did not marry that date; I got married after I moved to California. I lived in Honolulu until 1951 when I moved to California. I have been here ever since. My husband and I met in a dance class when I was 29. I have two sons. I had the first one when I was 32. Raising children and working full-time was very difficult. I was lenient because my sons were good boys. Now, my oldest son lives with me. My younger son just moved away for better career opportunities. I am still very sad about the move because I rarely get to see my only granddaughter now. She just turned four a couple weeks ago.

Living with my husband was the most stressful experience of my life. World War II was easier to live through. My children gave me the strength to get through it. My husband and I owned a business together; I was the bookkeeper for the business when the boys were young. I had worked before I got married and then went back to work when my youngest was in first grade. Before I got married I was also a bookkeeper, and I was not paid fairly. I only received $125 per month. Most of my jobs were clerical. It was hard for me to get a job after World War II due to discrimination. I was discriminated against because I was Japanese. Even in 1951 the memories of the war were very strong. For the last quarter of a century I have worked for a prominent pharmaceutical company. I will retire when I cannot work anymore. Outside of work, I like to read. I love bowling, but I am too old to bowl now.

My mother had the most positive influence on my life. She was very strong and resourceful. She would always find ways to buy gifts for all her children, even though money was very tight. My granddaughter being born was the most amazing thing that has ever happened to me. The most beautiful place I ever visited was Quebec, Canada; I was there in the fall and the leaves just started turning colors. I do not like to go on long trips. The longest trip I have ever gone on was 17 days. I went to Australia and New Zealand. I always wanted to skydive and go in a hot air balloon, but I am too old to do those things now.

CREDIT

Fig. 3.1.1: Source: https://www.goodfreephotos.com/united-states/hawaii/other-hawaii/pearl-harbor-bombing-hawaii.jpg.php.

Lompoc, California (1931)

As told by the interviewer's grandmother.

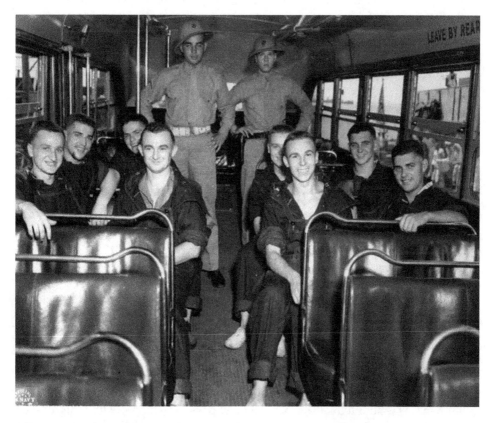

FIGURE 3.2.1   Crew of German Submarine POW's in Lompoc, California, 1943

I walk into my Nana's house to talk to her and find the house saturated in the scents of chili soaking through tender *carne asada*. "You want to learn how to make pozole?" she asks me as she begins heating a *comal* for tortillas. "Of course," I reply, watching her slice holes in an onion and slide it into the spicy Mexican soup whole. This seems appropriate because most of the things I have learned from my grandmother I learned in this kitchen, elbow deep in flour, New Mexico chile powder never far from reach. "What do you want to know?" she asks, to which I reply, "Everything."

My grandmother, Beatriz Camacho, was born near San Gabriel, California, July 22, 1931. A second-generation Mexican American, she lived with her grandmother until she was five, spending her days with her cousins Anna and Claudia. "My mother's family came up from Durango, Mexico, in 1895 for the sugar beets," she tells me, "and my real father's side came to Arizona in 1892 for the silver mines. They came by train, I think. I think everyone came by train in those days."

Until she started school in Lompoc, she spoke nothing but Spanish, and when she started school she began to learn English. In those early school days, she remembers that she would hide behind buildings to eat the burritos her grandmother sent to school with her for lunch. Although she was embarrassed of the "poor" lunches she brought she remembered that she loved school and doesn't think she ever missed a day. She remembers some of her fondest memories of school as being in band, where she played the trumpet, even though she tells me with a gentle smile, "I can't say I was any good, but I loved it." My grandmother went to school from grade school through high school, which she graduated from in 1948. However, she recalls, "I never took many difficult classes—mostly home economics and typing classes. I never took chemistry or anything." Later she went to business college and went on to work at a bank for most of her career. "I was always encouraged to be independent, unlike a lot of Mexican girls I grew up with. The Mexican men wanted the women to stay home. They dressed up and went to the bars but the girls just stayed home. It was their way or no way."

At the age of five, Beatriz moved back in with her mother, Jenny, and her stepfather, Tom. Because Jenny was quiet and private, she remembers growing up hearing stories about Tom's life. "He had a hard life," she remembers, which makes her even more thankful for the comfortable and happy life he gave her. Although not her birth father, Tom raised and cared for her well. At 99 years old, he continues to play a large role in her life. She was raised as an only child, but two sons were adopted by her parents when she was married and living in Panama. Her youngest brother Ricky was born in 1952, a year after my father, her first child, was born. Ricky was adopted at birth and raised in the family from day one. Bernard, on the other hand, was adopted later, when Tom, who was working in Utah, discovered him in an abusive family and took him home to be raised as part of the family. Bernard was older than Ricky, and the two boys grew up very close. My grandma remembers Ricky being protective of Bernard even though he was the youngest. Because of the age difference and distance, my grandmother did not have much of a relationship with her brothers for many years until she settled back to Lompoc in 1966, where they were still living. However, Bernard, the family's wild child, died an early death in his 30s after serving in Vietnam spraying Agent Orange. He got sick and spent his last days, cared for by Ricky, in Alaska. Ricky has continued to live in the same area for his entire life and has grown into and maintained a very close relationship with his sister.

Growing up, my grandma said, "was happy times." Her stepfather Tom Mendoza was a well-off contractor who kept the family comfortable and who took extremely good care of his children. When speaking of her favorite memories from her youth, she speaks about when she was 13 and Tom started to teach her how to drive, but tires were rationed and the ones on the car were wearing down. She recalls one of their early lessons, when he told her to stop early in the driveway and when she did not stop fast enough and almost ran into the garage, he ended their driving lessons and let them continue with her Aunt Marta. These stories with her father are remembered with a smile and quiet laugh, the stories that form families.

"My mother was strict, but I don't remember ever being unhappy." My grandmother remembers the saddest time in her life as when her own grandmother passed away. After being raised by her grandmother in her young childhood, the two remained very close. During the war her mother rented every room possible to war brides. "All of the beds were full and I slept in the dining room on a day bed. But besides that, no one else ever lived with us. After I moved out of my grandma's, I only ever lived with my parents, and later with my own family."

Beatriz got married at the age of twenty, to Raul Villegas, a first-generation Mexican American. Raul joined the Army in 1948 and in December of 1950 Beatriz flew to the Panama Canal where he was stationed and they were married. "My mother, even though she encouraged me to be independent and do what I wanted, did not want me to get married. She was really unhappy about the marriage, but eventually she came to love him. But she was not happy." In 1951, in Panama, she had her first child, Michael; in 1957 her second, Celia, in Texas; in Germany in 1959 a third, Robert; and again in Texas in 1963, Marie, her fourth and last. "Being a wife and mother in that generation was what you did. I liked to cook and be home and I was fortunate to be home with the children. It was hard to go back to work." When her youngest daughter Marie was three, she returned to work, leaving childcare to the older children and other aunts and cousins who lived in the area. While she occasionally paid for childcare, but it was always family who did the looking after. "But that's what I was most proud of, being a mother."

In addition to the bank, my grandmother worked for a brief five-month period at a secondhand store for $1 an hour. The pay was good, she recalls, compared to the 50 cents an hour she was paid over the summers during WWII when she worked in the petunia fields of Lompoc. "We worked in one field and German prisoners of war from Camp Cooke (where Corporal Joe Dimaggio played baseball!) worked in ones right next to us, in the vegetable garden. On our lunch breaks we'd talk to them." But she always felt she was paid enough; the money went for school clothes. "Things didn't cost that much."

My family is built on strong women, so when I asked my nana which women in her life made the most influence on her in her life, I was anxious to hear the answer.

A long pause preceded the answer, "I would say my cousin Anna. I've always liked her attitude in life. I was raised with her until I was five. I remember her coming to me and asking me to be in her wedding. And even though my mother said no, it was a nice feeling and I went to her wedding anyway. She was always such as giving person. And her mother, my Aunt Magdalena, was the same way."

Growing up as a Mexican American, my grandmother lived within a subculture, although she asserts that "being from California you did not feel like you would if you were from some other places in the country. Like, in Texas, Mexicans were held to be inferior. You could look at them and know they did not feel the same way you did. It was like being Black in the south, being Mexican in Texas." Living in Texas for a time, she remembers seeing these reactions to people and the difference in subcultures but could never connect to it completely. Although she recalls seeing the effects of these cultural divides in Texas, she also remembered when her "stepdad went to Utah to work and saw 'No Mexicans Allowed Signs'; he was furious. But we never had to live with that."

And as a member of yet another subculture, she could, once again, see but not directly relate to the effects of this subculture. "Well you see a lot of changes in the way women have developed, they were not treated very well in the workplace. I do not know if I ever thought about it myself, but I think in the old days you accepted it." But my grandmother does not feel she fits those confines of women, especially Mexican women. She worked and went out, although she remembers other girls not being allowed to date at all. Although families were strongly patriarchal, with the men making their expectations clear, she was raised to make her own choices and do what she wanted.

"Out of everything, I just remember when I was younger at the grandmother's, all the girls, Marta, Susanna and Magdalena, they all lived in one house, and Juan, Guillermo, and Arturo they'd all go to Grandma's too and they all worked and gave their pay checks right to her. And she'd chaperone their dances because you had to have a chaperone. I loved to watch them get ready to go. They had these mascara brushes they had to rub over the mascara before they put it on. They were poor, but they loved getting ready for the dances. When I got older, I went with them. We would all sit in chairs around the room and the boys would come ask us to dance. I loved going to dances."

Living through Pearl Harbor, the Kennedy assassination, and September 11, my nana has seen America in perhaps its most memorable mourning periods. "I don't remember where I was when Pearl Harbor was bombed," she shared, "but I remember listening to Roosevelt on the radio, during his fireside speeches. We admired him. There were no televisions to hear any bad things, if there were bad things, so all we heard was good and we thought well of him." And, although she may not have remembered where she was when Pearl Harbor was bombed, she can recall with no doubt where she was when she found out that Kennedy was killed. "It was exactly one month after Marie was born, we were on base in Texas and I was taking her for her one-month checkup. Our next-door neighbor ran in and told us.

I called Tata [Raul] right away. He was working in Army Intelligence at the time and they were processing it right away." She recalls this day as more memorably devastating than Pearl Harbor. The nation mourned. And she remembers being in the kitchen on September 11, making breakfast and Raul in the bathroom shaving, with the radio on, and him running out to the kitchen saying, "Something has happened," and turning on the television. "And we kept it on all day. We watched the second tower fall. It was horrible." From child, to mother, to grandmother, she can measure years in national tragedies. But more so, she can measure her life in happy memories. She would not change much.

"If I could live my life over? I guess I most regret that I did not go to Germany[1] with Tata the last two years of his service. I am sorry now, and if I could do it over I would have gone. It was two long years without him. But we made it."

"These tortillas from La Vallerta are the best. They taste like the ones Anna used to make with butter." We merge from her history back into the present, pozole bubbling on the stove.

"I made some last weekend. They turned out pretty well for flour. Not as easy as corn, you really just need masa for corn tortillas, huh?" I reply, wondering if this woman who taught me how to make tortillas when I was much younger would be disappointed with the odd-shaped outcome of my cooking attempts.

"Yeah. You will have to give me your recipe, I do not have one."

"But you have never needed a recipe." I try to keep the confusion from my voice. But this is my nana, who taught me all the Mexican cooking I know.

"I used to make them every day, and we did not ever have a recipe. We just knew how much of everything to put in. But I tried that the other day, and just throwing things in does not work anymore, not when you're not making them every day."

I guess she would have been disappointed in the tortillas I turned out, because although they are not as I was taught to make them, those days and that recipe is gone now, forgotten, but the effort to keep our family traditions, that remains.

CREDIT

Fig. 3.2.1: Source: https://commons.wikimedia.org/wiki/File:U-118_Besatzung.jpg.

---

1   In his last two years of service, Raul Villegas was stationed in Korea. He had been stationed in Germany earlier in his Army career.

China (1931)

As told by the interviewer's grandmother.

FIGURE 3.3.1 Shanghai Burns after Japanese Attack, 1937

My grandmother was born on August 22, 1931. She was very lovely with a little flush in her face, so her mother liked her very much. Because she looked like her mother, all the neighbors said she would be a beautiful lady in the future. Although her father liked boys better, this was the first child, and she was good looking, so he was very happy. Her father asked a knowledgeable elder to name his daughter as Mingyun Li.

There was a family in the Zhao Jiabang village. The father, An Shi Li, worked as a manager in a hotel in Chenghuang Temple. He was talkative, knowledgeable, and hard-working. An Shi Li's family was very famous in the village. He had two wives and a two-year-old son. The second wife of An Shi Li had a good relationship with Mingyun's mother and came to their house often. The second wife liked this beautiful baby very much, so they made an arranged marriage to have Mingyun be their daughter-in-law, but their son, the future husband of Mingyun, died at the age of five. From then on An Shi Li treated Mingyun as their adopted daughter and Mingyun called them her godmother and godfather. Mingyun's godmother and godfather helped them a lot.

Mingyun Chin was born during the period of Anti-Japanese War between China and the Empire of Japan, also called the Chinese People's War of Resistance against Japan (1931). All her family suffered greatly during the war, and they made their first escape to the refugee camp when she was less than one year old.

On January 28, 1932, the first Shanghai incident[1] occurred. The Japanese army entered Shanghai at Baoshan Lion Forest. They attacked Wusong and Jiangwan. Songnan, the place where Mingyun lived, was one of the places where the Japanese attacked. At that time, the National Government of Nineteenth Route Army was resisting the attack. But the Chinese Army could not defend it anymore. Mingyun was scared by the sound of the guns. With the help of her godmother and godfather, Mingyun's family first escaped to the place near Hengbang Bridge and then they escaped to a refuge near the Dapu Bridge and the Tanjing Temple.[2] Mingyun had two uncles, but because they were ill, they could not escape. Three months after the war ended, the whole family moved back to their house again, but they could not find her uncles anymore. Some people said they died during the bombing by the Japanese army.

In 1935, the Chins had their second daughter, who they named Rueling Chin. Mingyun's father was very sad. He wished he could have a boy to help him and inherit his farm, because Mingyun's father earned a lot of money during those years and the Chins gained position in the village of Xu Bang. Mingyun's father could not stand it anymore. At that time, there was a Xu family who had a son two years old. Mingyun's father adopted the son and hoped they could rely on him later. Unfortunately, he passed away a few years later.

Three years later, the Chins had their third daughter named Jia Li Chin. At that time, people were all very busy. They needed to do farm work as well as sell the products. Because Mingyun was the eldest daughter in the family, she needed to help her parents. She needed to take care of her younger sisters and do housework. Although it was hard, Mingyun felt happy.

In 1937, when Mingyun was eight years old, the Lugou Bridge incident[3] broke out in Beijing. The Japanese made trouble in Shanghai as well. The atmosphere in Shanghai became more warlike. So, Mingyun's father asked her godfather to get a house near Tanjing Temple in the French Diplomatic Concession. All her family moved to this refuge except Mingyun's father, for he needed to do the farm work to support them. On August 13, 1937, the second Shanghai incident broke out. It was also called the Songhu War. Most of the people escaped to the concession for safety, including Mingyun's father. The Japanese army did not attack the concession in Shanghai, so refugees were safe. However, there were too many refugees, and life there was extremely hard. Because the Chins did all the preparatory work, they had fewer problems than the others. They lived in the refuge for two years.

---

1   In order to make the Nanjing government capitulate, the Japanese attacked
Shanghai constantly.

2   At that time it was the place belonging to the French Concession.

3   The Japanese army used the excuse of a missing solider to enter Wanping City to search, but
the Chinese refused. The war broke out on Lugou Bridge.

At that time, the sister of Mingyun's godfather, with her children and parents, lived in that refuge, too. Because they had a hard life, they were looking for some family who could adopt their children. Mingyun's father adopted a boy, Koshing Wu, who was three years older than Mingyun, and changed his name to Koshing Chin. From then on, the Chins had their son. Although Koshing was skinny and silent, Mingyun's father was happy because they had their son.

At the end of the war, people all moved back to their houses. Nine-year-old Mingyun followed her parents back to their house again. It could not be called a house anymore. All the walls were collapsed and all of the farm was destroyed. Having no time to cry, the Chins started to repair the house. Mingyun led her sisters and brother to pick grass in the farm.

There was a private school in the village. Mingyun wanted to go to the school with other kids, but her father did not agree because it cost a lot to go to school and there would be no one to take care of the younger kids. At that time, it was useless to go to school. The goal for all girls was to marry and have children.

At the end of the Songhu War, the Japanese built a military industrial base around Wusong, Jiangwan, and Daba Temple. There was a lot of military industry around Mingyun's house, too. At that time, the Japanese searched the village often. If they found people resting in the house and not working, the Japanese beat them. There were not enough young adults to work for them, so they ordered kids to work for them. Twelve-year-old Koshing worked in the gas plant, and nine-year-old Mingyun, together with Anchi Sheng and Lanfen Xu, worked in the Maqiao Warehouse, Sanheli Warehouse, Jiangwan Airport and the soy sauce factory for four years.

Mingyun went to the Sanheli Warehouse first. In the warehouse, there were a lot of quilts, clothing, and canned food. Two Japanese men were in charge of hundreds of Chinese workers. Every day Mingyun got one package of rice, and every half month she could have her salary. Every day the Japanese checked the Chinese workers' bags; they even searched their clothes. If they found people stealing things they beat them. One day, the Japanese ordered the workers together. They beat a young man in front of them and finally broke his leg. The reason was that the Japanese thought the man stole some canned food from the warehouse.

The Chins became rich. They had a 6 *mou* farm, brought 2 *mou* more, and raised a buffalo.[4] During May and June, the Chins lacked farm workers, and Mingyun began to help with the farm work. The children's work was to irrigate. Mingyun always led her sisters and brother to irrigate. There were a lot of leeches in the paddy field, which was flooded with water. The leeches stuck on the legs of animals and people, which scared Mingyun a lot. She checked her legs every few minutes and worked slowly, which made her mother angry. Her mother said, "Let them drink your blood, if they full they will leave." They always worked after the sun went down. It was scary at night, but with Koshing's help, Mingyun and her sisters felt safe.

When it was not the time for farm work, Mingyun's father always did some small business. They brought the rice, vegetables, and animals to the country to sell. With

---

4   A *mou* is about one-tenth of an acre.

the lack of transportation, people used their shoulders to tote goods. Koshing quit his job in the gas plant and helped his parents sell products, while Mingyun and her sisters did the cooking, washing, and sewing.

In 1945, the Chinese army defeated the Japanese army, so all Chinese could live their normal life. At that time, Koshing was 18, Mingyun was 15, and Rueling was 11, and all could help the family do the work. Jia Li was just eight years old, and Mingyun's parents found they needed people who could read and write at home, so they sent their third daughter to study. Three years later in 1948, the Communist Party of China won the civil war. They were against the upper class, so those who owned a lot of land sold their land for money. One day, Mingyun's father heard exciting news that the landowner Chongshi Zhou could not support his family so he sold his land for money. Mingyun's father used all his money to buy another two *mou* farm. All together, they had a twelve *mou* farm.

People began to envy the Chins. They said, "The Chins bought a lot of land. They were the rich. Why did they buy that much land? They just have an adopted son. All daughters need to marry." Hearing these things, Mingyun's parents got their idea. When she was 18 years old, there were a lot of families asking for her hand in marriage. There was a young man called Lingfu Yen who was smart and good at hunting. He always gave Mingyun some beautiful birds as a gift. However, Mingyun did not consider him a reliable person, and both of her parents did not like the man.

There was a relative of the Chins whose son graduated from the university and worked in the bank. He had a good income and was honest. His parents wanted Mingyun to be their daughter-in-law, so they invited Mingyun and her mother to watch a film and go for dinner. Mingyun wanted to marry that man but her parents did not want her to marry him. They wanted to have a son-in-law who could continue their family name so that they could have the Chins' grandchildren. So her parents let their adopted son marry Mingyun. They did not care whether they loved each other or not. Mingyun knew that Koshing was not the man she wanted to marry, but it was their parents' order, so they needed to obey. In the autumn of 1949, Mingyun married Koshing. All the people in the village came and congratulated them. After a few months of Mingyun's marriage, Shanghai was released by the Communist Party of China. At that time, some soldiers lived with Mingyun's family for almost half a year. They lived peacefully.

The Kuomintang (KMT), who fought against the Communist Party, left Shanghai in a hurry and threw their guns into the river and pretended to be the common people to escape. A few years later people could get these guns when they were fishing. Those who did not report guns were punished by the Communist Party of China. Many people were punished, and some lost their family. When they lost the war, they moved to the island off the shore of China named Formosa (now Taiwan).

In September of 1950, the first daughter, Yulan Chin, was born. Mingyun was happy and excited with her first child. After having their own child, Mingyun and her husband separated with their parents and lived their own lives. Although Koshing was not Mingyun's favorite, she decided to take care of their family and their child. Mingyun was just twenty years old at that time; she did all the things, including work in the farm, take care of child, and cook. She always said, "Men have their own things to do; housework is for women." Since Mingyun took care of the family, Koshing did not need to worry about any housework and did not know how to take care of the family. Nevertheless, Mingyun did not complain.

At that time, workers could earn more money than farmers, so Mingyun and Koshing decided not to be farmers; instead, she encouraged him to work in the first steel plant in Shanghai. Although there was a lot of competition, Koshing won the opportunity. While he worked in the factory, Mingyun helped her parents and sisters do the farm work. Every day she waited for Koshing to return home for dinner, and when Koshing gave her the first month's salary, she found herself the happiest woman in the world.

In 1954, Mingyun gave birth to a boy they named Lok Wei Chin. Because he was the only son in the family everyone liked him very much. In 1956, another daughter was born named Chu Bo. But she died when she was one year old. With the low level of medical care, the doctor misdiagnosed her and thought she only had a sore throat. Because Mingyun was busy doing the farm work, she asked her mother to take care of the baby. But she was still ill and Mingyun's mother was so tired that she fell into the septic tank and died a few days later. A month later her daughter Chu Bo died. Mingyun was so sad, but she did not give up because the family could not run without her.

In the autumn of 1958, another girl was born, Li Hua Chin. That year, throughout the country, people held the People's Commune Movement. They gathered all the tools and shovels to be the source of the steel, but the movement had little impact. As part of the "Great Leap Forward" the success of the movement was mandatory. The leader considered the reason for the movement's failure the work of the counter revolutionaries. A movement to find and kill hidden counter revolutionaries was organized. In the village, there was a man named Au Luo who was considered a spy for the Taiwan Kuomintang, and he was shot. Mingyun's father's godson, Xingen Xu, was also considered a counter revolutionary. A few months later, there was news that the government was investigating Koshing, because in 1955, a friend gave Koshing a gun and he kept it for about an hour and then reported it. Mingyun was shocked and wondered if Koshing would be shot, but because Koshing worked hard in the factory, he was not shot.

After 1960, the national famine came as agricultural food was shipped to the cities to support the Great Leap Forward. The government called people to return to farms. But no one wanted to quit the job in the factory; the leaders forced Koshing to go back to the farm or they would report him as a counter revolutionary. Unwillingly, Koshing returned home.

Because of the famine, Mingyun did not want any more children. "We can't have children anymore," she told Koshing. "I will go to the hospital to do the sterilization operation tomorrow." Koshing agreed. But six months later, Mingyun told Koshing the bad news that she was pregnant. At the Mid-Autumn Festival in 1962, another boy was born; they named him Qing Yuan. The boy was skinny because of the lack of nutrition. "We need to let the boy live!" With strong hope, Mingyun found everything for the boy to eat and Qing Yuan survived.

Three years later, the national famine was over. But in 1966, the Great Cultural Revolution began.[5] The revolution movement destroyed many families. If one person was regarded guilty, all their family was involved. Because of the gun problem, Koshing was regarded guilty. He could not leave the village, he had no holiday, and he had no right to speak freely. As the family members, they were looked down on. Some people suggested to Mingyun she should "divorce and find a better man to live with." But she said firmly, "No, I can't. The children cannot live without me. They need a complete family. For my children, I can bear this." After Koshing was considered guilty, they worked long hours but earned little. There were four children to feed; she did the jobs that no one else wanted to do.

One job she had was pushing the slops.[6] In order to gain more money, Mingyun did it twice a day. Pushing the slops to and from the destination took ten hours. In order to earn money, Mingyun did this job for ten years. In order to share responsibility, her daughter Yulan helped doing housework at 12 years of age, and helped her mother doing the slops push when she was 17. Lok Wei helped do this at 16, and at 18 he could do it by himself. Jianming helped his parents do farm work.

The last son in the family, Qing Yuan, was a clever boy. He was the only one who entered university. After his graduation, with the help of his teacher and himself, he found a good job and earned a lot of money. During this time, the Great Cultural Revolution ended.

At the end of the 1970s, the economy grew, so and Mingyun and Koshing decided to build a house. Because they did not have enough money, some people suggested, "Build a two-floor building first to solve the problem of marriage for the first two sons." Mingyun responded, "No, we can't do this. All the three sons should have one floor." In the autumn of 1980, the Chins finished the building. All Mingyun's sons had their own floor.

In 1986, the first and the second sons were married and Mingyun had her first two granddaughters. But in the spring of the second year, Jianming was hurt when he was working. Jianming's wife divorced him and left the family and her two-year-old daughter. Mingyun held her granddaughter, Juhua Chin, and said, "Don't cry. Mom is here. Mom is me." This was not a sentence for comfort; this was a sentence for promise. In the next twenty years, Mingyun took care of both Jianming and her granddaughter Juhua. In April of 2011, Juhua Luo married. She thanked Mingyun and said, "You are my grandmother, and, more, you are my mother!"

CREDIT

Fig. 3.3.1: Source: https://commons.wikimedia.org/wiki/File:Shanghai1937city_zhabei_fire.jpg.

---

5   The political movement led by Zedong Mao and other leaders.

6   It is a wooden cart full of over a thousand pounds of swill feeding. Swill is collected garbage, e.g. old food and vegetables, to feed hogs. You need to push it to another village far away from yours and feed the pigs.

Philippines (1936)

Written in third person by the boyfriend of the interviewee's granddaughter.

FIGURE 3.4.1   Painting of Sulu Home and Coconut Plantation, Philippines, 1913

Nose over toes. Nose over toes. The nurses burned this into her brain. She needed her nose over her toes to shift her weight and stand up from wherever she was sitting. It was part of her stroke recovery program, and she was not liking it. Even though only a week had gone by since a massive right brain blood clot, she was already 85 percent back to the way she was, but this was not good enough for her. Being dependent on her daughter and son-in-law was so frustrating for her. But, like she had for the entirety of her life, she believed the impossible could be possible.

All that she had to do was not let anyone get in her way. Even if it meant listening to the nurse say nose over toes one more time, she was going to get back to living her life by her own rules. Doreen was born on August 24, 1936, to an Anglo-American father and a Taosug mother in Jolo, the capital city of the primarily Islamic province of Sulu in the Philippines. This was also the birthplace of her mother. Doreen was one of multiple children as she has a total of nine siblings. Her father, Louis Johnson, was a man of action and was in the US military. This is why he found himself in the Philippines in the early 1930s. He was a medic to the US Cavalry fighting against the Moros in their early rebellion. It was during his time there that he met her mother, a native Taosug living in Jolo. One of six siblings, she fell in love with him and was prepared to add to the family. After the war ended and he had an honorary discharge from the military, he stayed in the Philippines to be with her. Together they began a family in Jolo, and he started a coconut plantation on their land.

Over the years many children were had, ten total, and they became quite prominent figures in the community. He was well known in the area and had become fairly wealthy, notably the only American in the community. He was quite tall, so he stood over most of the locals. They were a very close-knit family, and her father was in charge of the bunch. Soon, however, unforeseen circumstances were to test the strength of them all.

A war had once again begun in the region, but this time the impact would be far more troubling for Doreen and her family. It was the beginning of World War II. She was only five years old in 1941 when the Japanese invaded and occupied the region. Fearing the worst, her father decided the best thing he could do for his family was surrender himself to the Japanese, as he was an American, in hopes that they would be safe from the horrifying conditions that were now surrounding them. The village was at their mercy as well. Anyone who refused their leadership was killed on the spot. He was kept in the concentration camp for the four years following the Japanese occupation.

It was during this time that true strength and perseverance were shown in the face of adversity. While her father was interned, her eldest brother and mother stepped up to keep them alive and fed. They often did not have enough food to go around for the entire family, and sometimes some would not have had enough to eat but they were surviving. Survival was key; this was their only goal until the occupation was lifted and her father could return to them.

Terrifying images became embedded in her mind during these horrific years. She clearly recalls what a P-38 Lightening split body aircraft looks like, as one would make machine gun runs down the center of town, spraying bullets into the posts of market buildings. People would be screaming and running around in a panic with faces of sheer terror; some were shot in the middle of the street and left for dead. She witnessed all of this as a young girl, before the age of ten. After four long years of horror, which including the burning down of her family house and slaughter of her father's livestock, the Japanese left the region and the internees were released. Her father then rejoined them and they could once again be a nuclear family. However, it would not last. It was to once again to change as circumstances called for drastic measures.

In the years following World War II, Mr. Johnson found it even more necessary to take action to protect his family. It was in 1954 that at the age of 18, Doreen, along with the rest of her family, except her father, moved to America. The Korean War was going on and, fearing another world war was lurking in the shadows, he utilized his American citizenship to move his family into the country for safety. He decided to stay behind in Jolo to continue working and send money over to provide for them.

However, four years later tragedy struck the family. The princess of Jolo, as there was a rudimentary hierarchy in the region at the time, had been in need of funds several years prior and had come to Mr. Johnson, being the prominent figure that he was, to borrow some money. He knew that some type of collateral would be necessary in the case that she could not repay him directly. Her collateral was then the one thing she had to offer: land. But, when the loans came due, she was not too keen on giving up her land. On February 1, 1958, she ordered him to be brutally murdered so that she would not have to pay this debt and lose her land. He died from multiple gunshot wounds. This is by far her saddest memory and was a terrible tragedy to the family. They were now left in a land foreign to them with neither money nor a way to support themselves.

Something had be done then, so it was decided that all the women of the family were to go to work to support everyone while some of her brothers were drafted into the military. They had no formal education, so they found the only jobs they could at local packing and sewing sweat shops. They were able to put food on the table without a single handout, even though they often battled poverty. They did not believe in any help and did not use a single penny of welfare. They were very proud of that fact and kept their honor through it all. The workplace was not easy for her though; she faced many prejudices there. Even though she was half Caucasian, she was still discriminated against for her limited English and foreign appearance. After years of these prejudices and cultural isolation, she had had enough and decided to make a change once again.

It was in January of 1961 that she returned to Jolo. The discrimination she had faced in America was too difficult to bear, and she realized it could be solved by retiring back home. It was there in the Philippines soon after her return that she met her husband, Javier Pantao. They married in 1962, when she was 26. She had her first child, Celeste, in Manila, the capital of the Philippines, on October 3, 1964. Soon after, they returned to America, making Sarah a foreign-born American citizen.

Three years later, on September 3, 1967, her son, Paulo, was born in America. Despite already having two children and given the rarity in her culture, she soon wanted a divorce from her abusive husband. In 1984, this was finalized and she was able to move on with more strength and courage than ever before. She had stood up to her culture and chose to do what was best for not only her, but her children as well.

It was in these coming years that many of her proudest accomplishments occurred. Her son graduated from high school and her daughter graduated from nursing school and got her first job as a nurse at a children's hospital in Los Angeles. Being a single mother came with some hardships though. It is never easy to do the job of two people all on your own. Her children had to work as well as go to school to keep food on the table. She had to cash out her pension for a down payment on a car for Sarah's transportation to school and to finalize the divorce.

She also found herself getting a job as a keypunch operator for Los Angeles County. There she took property tax information and input it into computers, along with processing the data of vital records, such as birth, death, and marriage into the county systems. She did this job to provide for and take care of her family, because at the end of the day all we have is our family. She continued her work even after her first grandchild was born, taking care of her during the day for 16 months and working night shifts.

Family is there for you through thick and thin; they will always be there when you need them the most. Many hardships had been faced throughout her life, but none like what was to come. From Jolo to America and back again she had always had her strength and independence. This helped keep her survive everything she had encountered, be it good or bad, celebratory or horrific.

In 2009, she was struck with a pulmonary embolism or blood clot in her lung that led to many problems, such as chronic high blood pressure and diabetes. But, as throughout the rest of her life, she kept a strong will through this new adversity, bounced back remarkably, and remained independent. Unfortunately she was once again faced with another health issue. Just a week prior to this interview, she suffered from a major stroke that attacked the right side of her brain. Within this week, she made astonishing progress and was already back to 85 percent to how she was prior to the stroke, which from a medical viewpoint is quite an amazing feat. Her speedy recoveries further prove just how strong-willed she truly is and that when we set our minds to a goal, no matter what it may be, and if we try hard enough, nothing is impossible. That has all of her attention now, trying her best to get well. She believes, as many do, that she can recover from this with her strength, willpower, and faith.

If she had to life all over again, would she do anything differently? No. "Life is good. Why change it?" After all that is life, we try our best to achieve what seems like the impossible one day and make it the reality the next. Her father's murder gave her appreciation for family, and marrying Javier gave her Celeste and Paulo, and later their marriages lead to her four wonderful grandchildren. Her challenges built the life she loves to live today.

Nose over toes. Nose over toes. The saying said over and over again by her nurses has become imbedded in her brain. She will listen to what they say, but in her mind she is following her own road to recovery. She is not letting anyone or anything stand in her way. After all, she needs to be around to see her four grand-children get married and begin families of their own and to share those same values that have brought her to where she is now. She never underestimated herself, and when faced with impossible hardship, she took it head on and it took her amazing places that she could have never expected.

CREDIT

Fig. 3.4.1: Source: https://en.wikipedia.org/wiki/File:Sulu_house_%26_coconut_plantation. JPG.

Moscow (1937)

In the voice of the interviewee's grandmother.

FIGURE 3.5.1   Russians Refugees from USSR in Shanghai, 1930

Quite simply, I was born in Moscow, in what was at the time the United Soviet Socialist Republic, in the year 1937. Josef Stalin was in power at that time, and Russia was in turmoil, shifting its extreme revolutionary demands into the background in favor of numerous political alliances. A civil war broke out in Spain a year before I was born, and my country sent aid to the Spanish republicans. My father was sent there as a military specialist and ironically never survived the trip back to Moscow, for his train derailed at the Czechoslovakian border, and there were unfortunately no survivors in the crash.

My father's death was a tragedy for my mother, who had two other children besides me (I, by the way, was not born yet), one boy four years older than I and a girl a year and a half older than I. With advent of Adolf Hitler, Russians became anxious, as we watched him come more and more into power, and the successes of the German nation were quite disturbing. Despite efforts at diplomacy on Russia's side, the die was cast, and on June 22, 1941, Hitler attacked without warning.

I have vague recollections of being rushed off from train to train, through rainy weather and otherwise difficult conditions, with my older brother holding both me and my sister Arina by our little hands, doing his best, in turn, to keep up with our mother. I was four years old then, and World War II had just begun. The first five months of the war were devastating to the Russians and almost fatal to the Soviet Union. My mother was sent off with us and our grandparents to China, in order to escape the war. We were lucky, because we came from a fairly influential Russian family; our lives were spared and tentatively put out of danger. We were to live on the outskirts of Peking (now Beijing) for the next 11 years.

We lived in a closely quartered apartment, my grandmother from my mother's side, my mother, my two older siblings, and of course me. Oddly enough, even though we were located in a Russian settlement, there were only two other households with children, and they were all older than my sister and me; my brother was closer to their ages than we were. As a result, the bonds between the three of us grew stronger, and we were an inseparable trio: It was actually my brother who raised my sister and me, for my mother was too preoccupied with caring for her mother, who was sick all the time as a result of the humid climate and the difference in diet that our temporary move to China brought with it.

Our favorite pastimes in China, while we were there, included playing tag and hide-and-seek barefoot in the soft young bamboo fields, as well as going swimming in the river that was close to our place; my sister and I did everything our brother did, and pretty soon, as we caught up to him in age, we set him quite a few challenges, if not outdid him in a few things, like wading through rice paddies and the like.

By the time I was 13 years old, I had picked up some of the language of the Chinese, as well as some of their customs. Arina, my older sister was, by that time, 14 years old and my brother, with whom I was the closest and adored more than anyone on earth, was 17. In him a saw a mother, father, best friend, and teacher, not only a brother; he was responsible for our education as well as his own and disciplined himself and us to study and read the works of Cicero, Plutarch, and Ovid out of the great three tome volumes that my mother brought with her from Russia. Vladmir, my brother, was a highly intelligent, sensitive, and trustworthy young man, and his looks were unmatchable: an artistically defined aquiline nose; sharp, almond-shaped eyes that were of the deepest brown; fresh young lips that had determination written all over them, as well as kindness; and to top it all off, a head of thick, ebony black hair. It is not wonder that I wept for four months straight when he was taken off to the army on his 17th birthday. I was never to see him again. The happiest memories of my childhood revolved around my brother Vladmir and the things we did together; I still remember the way my heart warmed inside of me every time he would comfort my mother silently, as he sensed the deep pain she harbored in her soul at the death of her husband, our father, as well as at the news of her homeland faring badly with Hitler's aggressions. I'll never forget how my heartbroken mother would take comfort in my brother and hold all of us so close to her, and cheer up, as she saw our father in each of our eyes.

At this point, Mrs. Komolov left off speaking about her brother, and I opted not to pursue the subject any further, as it was an obviously painful one for her. As I gathered, however, from my family, it seems that Vladmir was shot by a firing squad in Kazakhstan, for apparently not obeying orders in shooting a Russian political dissident and his family, who fled to Kazakhstan; moreover, the family learned of the plot and subsequently escaped death by fleeing the USSR to France.

We moved back to Moscow when I was 15 years old. My mother's first impression of the city caused her to weep bitter tears, for as she told me later, nothing was the same, and Hitler had left an evil mark on the land, as well as scars on the people's minds. Every single one of my mother's friends had lost at least one son, husband, or brother in the war. My sister and I were both sent to the Academy of Sciences in Moscow, a preparatory school for the best scientific university in Russia, Moscow Technic Institute, after having received our preliminary educations at home. My sister and I were placed at the same grade level, so we had the advantage of taking classes together, and studying together as well. We were both taking biochemistry, and that field of study is highly demanding, so we had to devote practically every waking hour to study; the potential for having many friends was greatly decreased as a result of this. We basically kept to each other and went on to university together for the following five years.

Both my mother and grandmother were proud of the fact that my sister and I were studying so hard to become something. My grandmother often told me stories of how she regretted never having had the type of education that we were getting. My grandmother was raised to be married and to be a good wife and mother; she was taught to read and write in Russian, German, and French, like all ladies of quality were expected to do. She was well read in poetry and could play the clavichord, as well as do needlepoint and tapestries. She always wanted to be better, though, and felt inadequate in front of her husband intellectually. That is why when my mother was born, my grandmother managed to talk my grandfather into hiring an additional tutor for her to expand her education in include the study of Latin and history.

My mother married my father when she was almost 16 years old; he was 20 years old at the time. My mother was very lucky, because she was happy with her marriage to him and loved him more than the world, and as it happened, he returned her love. My mother got married too young, I think; I myself married at the age of 23, right when I came out of university. I met my husband there; his name was Grigory Komolov, and he was a year and a half older than I. He was a student of neuro physics and spoke five languages; we were a perfect match and married after six weeks of knowing each other (even though we went to the same university, we were caught up in our separate areas of study; we met accidentally outside of the university).

Grigory was Armenian, and my mother did not approve of our union at all, because she wanted me to marry a Russian and keep the tradition in our family. But I loved him, and he returned my feelings, and I think that the decision I made to marry him was the best one I made in my life. We were to spend the rest of our lives together and be blessed with five beautiful children, who in turn have provided us with 13 grandchildren between them. I am very proud of myself that I could stand up to almost everyone I knew and go through with what I knew would lead to my ultimate happiness. I am proud that I had enough strength in me to realize what was going on in my native country, the way in which the government would discourage people from being individuals and doing things that were morally acceptable to them. I won't go any further in saying how restrictive the Soviet regime was; however, it was the reason my husband and I packed out bags and left for America in search of a better and more fulfilling life. Armenia was no option for us either, because of similar circumstances, so I followed Grigory to the United States and was prepared to start a completely new life, language and all, at the age of 26.

My husband spoke English fluently, and with his educational background had no problem getting a job teaching physics at the University of New York, or NYU. I myself unfortunately did not take a job, for our first baby was born in America six months after we arrived, and I was taking care of things at home. The highly advanced education I received and worked so hard for was basically no use to me, other than in making my mind sharper and giving me something in common with my husband. Things were relatively easy for us here, and my only obstacle to overcome was learning the English language; this came quickly to me, however, because I had trained my brain in memorization of scientific formulas and so on, so it was not as difficult for me as it might have been for someone else.

With a happy marriage, and a wonderful family and friends, I believe that I was lucky, even though I had a hard life the first twenty or so years of my life. If I could live my life over again, I probably would not have changed anything, even though I sometimes wish that I had held off with having my own family for a while and had a chance to pursue my own career, something my mother wanted me to do. I raised my two girls that way: education and career at the foremost of their agenda, then friends and social life. Women's roles have changed greatly through the course of my lifetime: When my grandmother and my mother were growing up, the role of a female was to keep her husband contented and happy, as well as bring him many children. Today, women are in the workforce and are encouraged to pursue a great career, in addition to having a family. The change I see is that responsibility for the family is now more 50/50, and that is the way it should be, I believe. Also, a woman does not have as much pressure from family, at least here in America, to marry someone from her own culture or ethnic background. In the old days, in

Russia, the parents would have all the say, and if the daughter wanted to "go her own way" and make her own choice in marriage, the door would be closed on her forever, like it was for me.

> *Mrs. Komolov and her husband have been married almost fifty years and claim to be as much in love as they were when they met.*

CREDIT

Fig. 3.5.1: Source: https://commons.wikimedia.org/wiki/File:Girls_of_the_Shanghai_Ghetto. png.

Los Angeles, California (1938)

FIGURE 3.6.1 Japanese Child Waiting to go to Assembly Center , California, 1942

I was born in Glendale, California, in 1938. It is unusual for people in California to be natives. Most people in my generation from California were from somewhere else. They came from another state, they came from the Midwest, and they came from the East. I have lived in Southern California my entire life.

My earliest memories are of the war, World War II. My father was an air raid warden. During those years they had air raid drills, because of where we lived, in

Sun Valley, California, which is right next to Burbank, just where Lockheed aircraft was. That was where they made the P-38 planes for the war. My father worked at Lockheed aircraft. There would be periodic times when you would have to pull down all of your shades and turn off all the fires in your house or any gas flame, or anything that might show. Then they would have what they called an air raid drill. Everyone had to darken their house and you would have to stay that way for about thirty minutes and then these air raid wardens, they were volunteers from the community, would go around and make sure that everyone had pulled their shades down. Later there would be a big signal, kind of a whine sound that everyone could hear, to signal that it was all clear and you could put your lights on again. We were in the Pacific coast and Japan at that time had just bombed Pearl Harbor, and so we were getting into the war. It was a defense mechanism to protect us, particularly with an aircraft factory nearby; they felt that the Japanese might bomb it. That was a security thing. My father had a helmet with an insignia on it that showed that he was the air raid warden. He would go around and check, and after it was over, everyone would turn their lights on and go back to normal. I remember knowing this as a child.

I attended Roscoe Elementary because Sun Valley was named Roscoe (from 1896–1948). I went there until I was six, in the first grade. As you may know, during World War II, after the Japanese bombed Pearl Harbor, there was strong anti-Japanese sentiment. The president of the United States signed a decree that all persons of Japanese descent would be placed in internment camps all around the US. Many Japanese American families were taken away from their farms and homes and kept under guard in these camps until the end of the war. It was very unfair, since some were US citizens and many had their property confiscated in the process.

Just after the end of World War II (1945), I was in second grade, and there was still a lot of anti-Japanese sentiment due to the loss of so many American service-men at the hands of the Japanese. There had been people in our agricultural area of Japanese descent who had been placed in the detention facility at the Los Angeles County Fairgrounds in Pomona, California. When the families were released from the camps after the war, they had to start their lives again, including their children attending school. Our second-grade teacher said that we would receive a new boy in our class. His name was Bobby Dan, and he was Japanese. She said he was to be part of our class and that she expected we would treat him well and as one of our classmates. The reason she did this was because many of the children's parents still harbored anti-Japanese sentiments that they transferred to their children. She did not want to have those negative sentiments persist since the war was over. As it turned out, Bobby became a class favorite because he was very personable and all the children liked him; however, it could have gone another way if the teacher had not prepared the class beforehand.

This was at the end of the war because it was when we sold our house. I lived on a chicken ranch in Sun Valley. There were not a bunch of houses around; people had horses, and they had chickens, and they had land around. My father would always grow a vegetable garden. In the war everyone grew what they called victory gardens to help save food, and you grew your own food so you could put food to the war effort. Also, I remember going to the gas station with my father. To get gas he would have to give them these little coupons out of a book. It was a little book, and he would pull out a little stamp and could only have so much gas to get him back and forth to work.

You got these coupons that were the size of a dime. They were like cardboard and were red and blue. The red ones were worth something, and the blue ones were worth something, and then you could use these tokens. They also had books where you could only have so much sugar. When I went to the grocery story with my mother, she could only have so much meat or so much sugar. Different things were rationed. Ladies could not get nylon stockings at the time because they made parachutes out of nylon. There were many things that you could not get—like chewing gum. I forget why; I do not know what they did with the *chicle*, but it did something for the war effort. (It was part of each soldier's rations and so popular a synthetic replacement had to be found.) They wanted us to save tin foil. Gum used to have tin foil on it. You were supposed to save tin foil from something. There were a lot of things you did, and I was never really sure why.

Everyone was very conscious of the war. You did not know when it was going to end. How the war ended was of course with the atom bomb in Japan. That was something that changed the world because then there was the threat of someone else getting the bomb and using it on us or someone else. That began the next decade. You had the 1940s, say, which were influenced by World War II, but then you went into the 1950s and you had the nuclear cloud hanging on you, in terms of people's mind-sets. In the 1950s some people made bomb shelters for fear that there would be a nuclear attack. In school they would teach you to duck and cover under your desk in case there was a war attack. It was kind of in your mind that way.

My family happened to go to the movies every week since there was no TV; there was radio, but no TV. The movies had what they called movie tone news; they were news reels. You would go to the movies and see a cartoon, the movie tone news, and two features, not one, but two features in a movie for the same price. In the movie tone news they would show footage of the war. They would tell you what was happening and that was where you would be brought up to date on the war, plus through the radio. As a child, I went often to the movies, so I do remember seeing movies about the war and seeing some clips of the war scenes.

That was how they did it then, no TV, nothing showing it all the time. You got your information through radio or the newspaper. The president at that time, Franklin D. Roosevelt, would have what they called "fireside chats," and he would talk on the radio every week to the people. Most families sat around the radio and listened to him because they wanted to know what was happening. That was fairly common during that time. In the 50s we moved to a dairy farm in Chino. This was a totally different life. It was very rural, a lot of dairying out there, still is. It has changed, but back then it was very rural, but it was nice. I liked it a lot. It was a very nice community and we lived on the dairy for one year. I was very lonely there because there was no one to play with. We were out in the farm, in the country with nothing to do. My parents were working all the time, because it was hard work. In the 50s we moved to town. It was a small community, and it was really fun.

I have one sister who is six years older than I am. She was very active in high school and was the queen of the Future Farmers of America (FFA) dance. It was a rural community and that was one of the big clubs, the Future Farmers. They had clubs on campus that were called the Girls Athletic Association (GAA); I was in that, and I was on the student council, and all the different kinds of high school activities, I participated in them. In grade school, we roller skated down the block all the time. We wore shoe skates that were key skates. They were skates with a heel part with a strap, and you would put your shoe on this thing and tighten it with a key. We would skate up and down the front of the sidewalk of our house.

I had to fight my mother for my first pair of jeans. She never liked to wear pants. She thought little girls should wear dresses. She always wanted to me to wear dresses, but I did not like wearing dresses. When little girls started to wear jeans, at least to play in, I begged for my first pair. I was probably 8 or 10. I think I wore those jeans until they were so dirty they could stand up, because I did not want to take them off. I was so happy to have jeans.

We had balls and tricycles and bicycles. We played jacks in the spring with a small ball. You would bounce the ball and try to pick up the jacks. Jump rope had its own season when it came around. The boys had a game that involved milk bottle caps. The top of the glass milk bottle caps had a cardboard cap to keep the milk in. Once you pulled the cardboard cap out and the milk bottle was empty, the kids would save the caps and the boys would play a game with all of the bottle caps. They would throw them on the ground and try to put one on top of another and whoever won would get all the bottle caps.

That was also the day when the milkman brought you milk and put it by the front door. They would deliver milk in glass bottles. I was having milk delivered to me when my children were newborn; that would have been the early 1960s. It still exists today, but I think it just got expensive and supermarkets were more available, so some of that has changed.

In the early years my mom was home, but then later she worked. She worked all the time I was growing up. She was a secretary in the schools. I was very comfortable being in a school setting because that was familiar to me. I later worked in the schools, and here I am again.

In high school I was the Girls League president and was also into sports. We went to camp for the summer. Learning to drive was also a big thing. My dad taught me how to drive. I wanted to learn how to drive since my dad taught my sister. I used to go out and ride with them when he taught her. I was ten years old and she was sixteen and learned, and I could hardly wait until I could drive at sixteen. That was exciting. We only had one car, so I did not get to drive very much. My dad worked in another town, so on the weekend I sometimes got to drive.

During high school I had a little part-time job at a soda fountain in a pharmacy. I remember going to look for the job. I took the bus into town, and I went into the pharmacy and the owner told me to come back in a little while. I was concerned about not making my bus, so I went to catch the bus instead of going back to the pharmacy. I went back the next day and I explained about the bus and he was kind to give me the job. He understood I was 16 and did not know. It was a good experience. I learned how to make burgers and shakes. It was really fun. That was part of my senior year. People did that; my sister had done that, too. You would usually have a part-time job to be able to pay for clothes and have extra money. It was a good time. Once in a while I would go out with friends. Usually we would be going to an event. A friend of mine and I were in an organization called Job's Daughters, which is a fraternal organization that did charity work.[1] We would take the car and go to a meeting in another town. After the meeting we might go by the drive-in restaurant. They did not have roller skates at this one, but they did have car hops, people who would deliver your food on a tray to your car. There were boys at the restaurant. Believe it or not, I happened to meet my husband, Edward, after a Job's Daughters meeting. I was 16, still in high school, and he was 23. I had to ask my mother if I could go out with him when he asked me out. He was a friend of a boy I knew from school. They both worked for the telephone company. I started dating him. He dated me all through my junior and senior year of high school. We got married that summer. We have been married for fifty years. I was married in July 1956.

There was not an actual proposal; we just decided and started talking about the wedding. We wanted to do it at a certain time, and his parents were planning on going to England, because they were from Wales and they had not been back in thirty years. They had been planning to go in August ,and they asked us to move the wedding to July, and then we could live in their house and take care of it while they were gone. We ended up getting married in July because of that. It was a beautiful wedding, with the white dress and the church. We had my sister as the matron of honor, my best friend and my future sister-in-law as part of the wedding party, and my niece as the flower girl. It was small, but it was nice. After I was married we lived in Pomona, which is a few miles from Chino.

Television came in when I was in junior high school. There was no TV until then; that was a big deal. Until then people used to have pianos in their houses, and they would play piano and sing around it. All of a sudden TV came in and everyone sold their pianos and bought a TV. Then people did not get together like they used to. It changed the way people interacted. Television did not come out until 1949, and most people could not afford them. As they became more affordable, more people had them. We had one in 1950. Then it was only black and white. Color did not

---

1   A Masonic-affiliated organization for young women.

come until later. We did not have a TV at all when we first got married. I think our children had a color TV when they were about four years old.

Going back and looking at the different styles, I never wore poodle skirts, but I did have saddle shoes. Dancing was popular growing up; "Rock Around the Clock" was very popular. During the 60s they were not much different. I did not wear high school–type fashions; I wore business fashions like dresses. That was another thing in school when I was growing up—you never wore pants to school. I do not think they let you wear pants to school even through high school. That was in the 50s; you could wear dresses, but you could not wear pants to school. That would seem odd now, that they had dress codes.

The 60s were all the flower children, all the protest, and about that time they started protesting dress codes in schools. After that they started to let girls wear pants to school, like slacks or capris or whatever was the style. I do not know if jeans were allowed. I think they kind of evolved. In the 50s I wore pants for casual things but not for school. You had to wear a dress or a skirt, it was just expected. It was the same in the workplace: You wore dresses or skirts. That's how I dressed in the 60s. When I had the little kids I dressed in comfortable clothing and things that if the baby spit up on you it was not going to matter. I was really was not a fashion plate! We had three little kids and only one salary, so sometimes I sewed my own clothes. I got a little bit into the styles of the 70s because I was working, but I tended to be a little conservative so I did not have anything that was too way out.

Ed and I were married for five years before we had our first child. We adopted our first; it was a boy, Robert. When he was about nine months old, I got pregnant with our second child, Richard. The first was 18 months old when I had the second, and after 16 months I was pregnant again with Karen. Then we decided that was enough. Robert had cancer when he was a baby; we had gotten him at two and a half months, and he kept getting sick with different things. At five months he got very sick and the doctor found out he had a tumor in his chest. They sent him to the children's hospital in Los Angeles. They removed the tumor, but he had to have X-ray therapy that left him crippled for the rest of his life. He had a lot of surgeries and things like that, but he was a bright kid and did okay and went to regular school for the most part.

All I remember of the Vietnam War is news clips. I do not remember much because I was so tired all of the time. When Karen was born I had three children younger than four years old. Then Robert turned five just a couple of months after she was born. I was just busy with three little kids. Then one would want to eat, and then I did not have time to do anything. I just remember news clips. That is all I remember about those years.

We lived in a suburb of Pomona for 15 years. Then Ed got transferred with General Telephone and Electronic Corporation, which is now Verizon. We moved to Whittier. The kids finished growing up and went to high school there; that is home for them. That was a fun place. It was not real urban, not too country, but semi country and city. They had places to play, and they could go dig in the dirt and make forts and things like that. They had a good time doing that.

I worked for the first three years I was married and then I did not work after that until my daughter was in second grade. I worked in the schools, where I had the summers off and vacations that were the same as the kids'. I worked at a health office with the school nurses. I also got an Emergency Medical Technician (EMT) certificate, so that I could do that when the nurse was not there.

My friend and I did that. That's what got us to go back to school. That was in 1973, when I went back to work. In 1974, we went back to school. A coworker and I started back to school together, to the emergency medical technician training and got our certificates. We said that if we could do that, we could take another class. That meant nine years to get an AA, doing one class at a time. By then it was time to either quit my job or finish school and get a bachelor's degree. My job ended at that time; they cut it to half time and I didn't think I could do that.

I went full time and finished my bachelor's in 1985 at California State University Dominguez Hills. It was a really good program in the human services. I liked it a lot. It was a good school for me. It was a small state school and a really good program that connected with everyone. Taking the AA, I was sandwiching it in with all the family and obligations at work. I went full time to get my bachelor's; it was fun. I got it done in two years.

At that time Ed got transferred again; that was in 1985. I worked a little bit out here, and then I went back to school again at Cal State Northridge. I started back to school again in 1989. I worked part time for Chapman College; now it's Chapman University. I was an academic advisor there and ran a program for a taped series that led to an associate degree. It was for working adults, and I would go to different places where I would give them the tapes and the test and sign up new people. I had a small office where people came to learn about the program. I did that for about two years until they decided to close that center down and bring it closer to LA.

It was different living in a rural area and in a suburban area. I was really lonely living in the country as a child. I prefer to live where there is at least a small city. Even in Whittier we were away from a city. We made friends more through our church or through the kids and their activities. The families we met through those things were our friends. When we moved to Los Angeles we did not get involved in a church, and I was really lonely, initially. Then we finally did connect with a church and the community as well as with my work. I had gone back to school for the master's by 1989 and earned it in counseling. It is a little harder changing from when you have children to when you go without them. You usually meet friends through the children's activities and it's a little harder to make those connections unless you get involved in something.

Unfortunately, Robert died of cancer at 25. He had cancer when he was young, but he died of a different cancer. Richard married at age 25 and just celebrated twenty years of marriage, but they did not have children for a long time. Now they have an eight-year-old and a three-year-old. Karen did not marry until later. She married in 2000. That marriage did not last. She is now single but happy. She lives up north in the Bay area. I have two grandchildren, and they are probably the only two I am going to have. They waited twelve years for the first one and then five years later they had Jennifer. They are fun and help keep you young. You can play with them and you do not have all the responsibility. That part is fun.

My two best jobs my husband found for me in the newspaper. It's not where they say you should look for jobs anymore. One was my job with the school district before I knew I was ready to have a job—he said, "This looks like a job you could do." I looked at it and said, "Yeah, I think so." I went ahead and it was about time for me to go to work again. All the kids were in school. I think I was getting a little bored and money was starting to get a little tight. I worked for the public school district for ten years.

When it came time for a new job opportunity, he again found it in the paper. He said, "Here's a part-time job that looks pretty good. You know, it looks like something you could do." I looked at it and could not make up my mind, but I tried for it. The one I went for was in the education school, but that one was filled. The women in the office said there was one at the business school. My degrees are not in that, so I was not sure. I had worked in business before, so I applied for it and that's the one I got.

The year before I started back, before I finished my bachelor's, my husband and I took a trip to the United Kingdom. We met relatives of his we had never met, so that was really fun. It was a really good time to do it because now all of them are dead except the younger cousins, who would be my children's age. They are the only ones we know of who are alive. We are glad we did that. It was really interesting and wonderful seeing his family.

The other trip I got to take outside the US was in 1987, which was a tour. It was a recruitment tour for undergraduate and graduate students. (She took out a magazine to show me where she had gone for the recruitment tour.) Believe it or not in this little picture this lady is me; we were in Indonesia. It was a three-week tour to recruit students all over Southeast Asia. That was the first time I had been to Asia. I thought it was really interesting and had a good time. We worked very hard. Every other day we were in a new city doing educational exhibitions. We were talking to students and going to international high schools. They were really neat. It was a really eye-opening experience. That was quite unusual, I think, to go to so many places in one trip. I mean that was amazing. I think we went to more places than that; it seems like we did. We went to Malaysia, and Macau, at the bottom of China.

In 1996, I went to Hong Kong and in 1998 I went to Macau. Macau was interesting because it's all gambling. It was all casinos and now it is even more so. It is like going to Las Vegas. The time I was there they just had one big casino. We got to meet the educational agents who recruit students to us, so now when we receive emails from them we know who we are working with. That is very good.

I'm trying to think of other things. (She takes a moment to search her memory.) The passing of my parents: My dad died in 1990 and my mom in 1992. She died right at the time I was finishing my master's degree. That was hard because she died the week I was supposed to have my comprehensive exams. Because they had such a to-do after the verdict of the Rodney King trial everyone was under curfew. They had to change my comprehensive exam for the week later. That was just as well for me because we had to get my mother's funeral in some place. I did not think I was going to be able to take my exams. Fortunately that did work out.

I remember the night Bobby Kennedy got shot. I was watching TV, and I mean I was just stunned. For John F. Kennedy I was shopping in Sears for Christmas when the news came out. I always remember that; people always say they remember where they were, and I do. That was less shocking than Robert Kennedy being shot though, because I was watching the political things on TV. They were trying to herd Robert Kennedy out through the kitchen and the next thing you know he was shot dead on the floor. I was watching this on television, and it was just stunning. Like, here we go again a second time.

Another thing that was kind of upsetting was the earthquake in 1994. Our house took a good shaking. It did not have any damage to it, but I lost a lot of dishes, and there was a lot of interior damage. It was kind of unsettling. I had lived through many earthquakes, living in Southern California, but none like that. That was quite traumatic. Also 9/11, everyone has their own memories about that in 2001. It was such a shock because you never think something like that is going to happen on your own soil.

As far as in my life personally, I had several mentors. You know, we never do these things in a vacuum. We always have people along the way who help us. I had teachers at school who encouraged me all along. I had friends of my mother and ladies in my church who would encourage me to go on in school. I had teachers in high school who said even though I married young I would go on to school, and I never forgot it. I think that's why I went back later. I never forgot that they said that I would go back. I did go back, and I think that encouraged my daughter to go ahead and finish her schooling and get her degree. She saw how much it took me to get done, but my son did not finish his. He took a different route, but for her I think the role model of me as a woman, I think it caused her to go ahead and finish it. It gave her better jobs and better opportunities because she finished her degree. I think that was important.

I have been at this job for 17 years in basically the same position. It has changed a little because I changed from US students to international students. It is very convenient. It's only seven minutes from my house, so that's easy. It's a pleasant place to work. People ask me when I'm going to retire and I say "I don't know." They say you will know when it's time and it does not feel like it is time.

CREDIT

Fig. 3.6.1: Source: https://commons.wikimedia.org/wiki/File:A_young_evacuee_of_Japanese_ancestry_waits_with_the_family_baggage_before_leaving_by_bus_for_an_assembly_center..._-_NARA_-_539959.tif.

Pillau, East Prussia (1941)

In the voice of the interviewee's grandmother.

FIGURE 3.7.1   Evacuation of Pillau, East Prussia, January 1945

I was born in Pillau,[1] East Prussia on December 25, 1941, during World War II. I was born to Gustav and Auguste Joetzki. My father, Gustav Joetzki, was in his forties when I was born, and he worked as a brick mason before joining the German army. My mother, Auguste Joetzki, was 39-year-old when she had me, and she was a housewife. They were married to each other pretty early on. I have one sister who is 16 years older than me, and one brother, who is also older than me.

---

1   Known by this name prior to 1946. Known today as the Russian city, Baltiysk.

We did not stay in Pillau for very long. It was probably in winter 1944–45, during World War II, when German soldiers came to my parent's house and told my mother that the Russians were coming and to run for their lives.[2] At this time, my father was in a Norwegian prison camp in Norway, and my older sister, who was part of the German army, was caught and put into an American prison camp in Italy. When my mother was told to run, she grabbed a knapsack and put the bread that she had baked the night before in the pack. She took my brother and carried me—as the snow was too deep for me to walk—and hurried through the snow, not knowing where to flee. She ran into a husband and wife who dragged a sled with them, and they asked her where she was going. After informing them that she did not know where she was going, the man said that he and his wife were going to the train station and invited my mother to go too. They let my mother share the sled for us children and my mother gave them the bread that she had baked. At the train station, my mother was fortunate enough to get a seat in a closed car with seats, whereas others were put in the open freight cars. I remember my mother telling me that there were parents with children and babies who had to travel in the open freight cars and many of the children froze overnight. The soldiers had to throw those frozen babies out of the cars as the train continued on its way. We rode the train as far as it would take us, and it stopped at Konigsberg (now part of Kalingrad, Russia, then the Soviet Union).[3] At Konigsberg, we were laid up in the basement of a school with other refugees. We lived on hard candy and water, and we were told that we were going to get out of Germany and sent to Denmark, because they were taking in refugees. This effort by the German Navy was called "Operation Hannibal."

The day we were supposed to board the ship to Denmark, my mother could not find my brother who had run off with another boy to play. She told the captain that we were not going because she could not find him, and we were left behind. As it turned out, that ship that we had not boarded was bombed and there were no survivors. My mother, brother, and I went on a second ship, which took us to a refugee camp in Copenhagen, Denmark.[4] My earliest memory took place in the Denmark refugee camp. We were in the barracks with a lot of people where we were given partition bunk beds and a stand-in closet. We were fed mostly soup and given rationed bread. I remember one thing about a lunch we were given where there were worms swimming in the soup because the flour was old. Perhaps the flour in the soup was from dumplings, I cannot remember, but we still ate it because the worms were extra protein. One other memory I have was also in the refugee camp. I asked my mother for some of the rationed bread we were given per week, but she

---

2   Pillau was captured by the Soviets on April 25, 1945.

3   A port city part of Prussia until it was destroyed during World War II and overrun by Russia in 1946. Renamed Kaliningrad.

4   "Immigrant Museet: Indvandringens Kulturhistorie," *Furesø Museer* (accessed December 3, 2015), http://www.danishimmigrationmuseum.com/index.php?page=tyske-flygtninge.

said that we did not have any left. I stepped onto a stool from where I could see inside our cupboard where she kept the bread. "See?" I said, "You have bread, you just don't want to give it to me." My poor mother was so skinny and I was quite plump because she gave all of the food to me and my brother, but she had to tell me that there was no bread because she knew that she had to ration it.

My happiest memory was when my mother, brother, and I were reunited with my father and sister after the war ended. After the war, the Red Cross did everything they could to find lost family members.[5] They gave each of us a card that we filled out and could claim a missing person. My mother claimed on her card that she was looking for my sister, and my card claimed that I was looking for my father. After all, that was how families found each other after the war, through the Red Cross. Miraculously, my father and sister found each other first, in Bavaria,[6] and they thought that the rest of us were dead. But through the Red Cross, all five of us were reunited in Bavaria. My happiest memory was being reunited because that was also where I first met my father, for I did not remember him. I cannot recall any really sad memories; I was always a pretty happy kid and I had a good life. I really do not remember any sad memories.

After being reunited and officially released from the camps in Denmark, my father, mother, brother, and I moved to Hamburg.[7] My sister remained in Bavaria and got married. Hamburg was where we rebuilt our life. At first, when we returned to Germany, things were not good. We lived off food rations (roasted wheat was a substitute for coffee), we lived in a single room, and we were given sheets. But my father continued his brick masonry work in downtown Hamburg and rebuilt houses, so that was good. My brother picked up my father's trade a little later on. My mother did housework. This was the structure of my family during my life in Hamburg, and my father had the authority in the household, but that did not exclude my mother's influence or voice.

Growing up in Germany, my favorite holiday was Christmas, and it was also my birthday. At Christmas, my father would bring home a fir branch and my mother would go out to buy special candies. These candies were chocolate rings that we decorated the tree with,[8] but my brother and I had the most fun eating them. Most of the time they did not make it on the tree. In Germany, unlike America, we celebrated Christmas Day twice. Germany has, in a sense, two Christmas days. The

---

5   The Red Cross still works today, in 2015, to reconnect families separated by World War II and other wars. Found at American Red Cross. "Reconnecting Families: Finding Loved Ones After A Crisis" Find Family Internationally After Crisis," *American Red Cross* (accessed December 3, 2015), https://www.redcross.org/about-us/our-work/international-services/reconnecting-families.html#:~:text=The%20Red%20Cross%20helped%20reconnect,able%20to%20help%20you%20too.&text=Our%20Restoring%20Family%20Links%20services,your%20family%20and%20loved%20ones.

6   A free state located in southeast Germany.

7   A city of northern Germany close to Denmark.

8   Chocolate Christmas ornaments are a German holiday tradition.

25th of December was the regular Christmas celebration with immediate family. The 26th of December was the second day of Christmas for people to get together from out of town and celebrate. For example, the second day was when my sister would come down with her husband and her baby bringing gifts, and we all had a great dinner. Of course, this described Christmas when Germany was economically improving and the city was being built up again.

On a typical day when I was a child in Germany, I walked to school and back. I did homework and played with friends. Then I would eat dinner and do more homework. When my father returned from work at the end of the day, we would all sit around the table and talk. I do not know how my typical day experience was similar or dissimilar to the experiences of other children. I only knew about us, my family, because we always shared what happened in our day.

We lived in Hamburg until I was 12 years old, at which point my father had the crazy idea of moving to America. He got this idea because the Red Cross put my family in contact with my mother's sister who had already immigrated to America. My parents actually thought she was dead. You have to understand that in the chaos of World War II, everyone in a family thought that everyone else was dead; there was no real reason to believe or hope otherwise. My father, who had a very adventurous spirit, acknowledged that we had lost everything in the war (including our farm in East Prussia that we only had one more payment on before we had to leave), so he decided that we would go to the United States of America. Subsequently, my parents started the immigration process. It turned out that someone in the United States sponsored my family so we could come over. But with this immigration process, that meant that that family was also responsible for us for five years. Sponsored and ready for our new home, we sailed to the United States on the SS *Italia* on January 22, 1954.[9] We sailed right past the Statue of Liberty and it was amazing, just simply amazing. From there we took a train to Portland, Oregon, where my aunt lived. Eventually, my family was also able to sponsor my sister, who was still in Bavaria, to come to America too.

My family and I stayed in Portland for a couple of years. My father and brother both got jobs right away as landscapers, employed by a fellow German, oddly enough. We saved up enough money to then move to Sherwood, Oregon, when I was about 15 years old. There, we purchased a 5 acre farm. We had all sorts of animals on that farm, including the usual chicken and cows. We also had one dog and about fifteen cats.

While in America, the Red Cross, once again, put my family in contact with my grandmother and my aunts who were still in Germany. We went back to visit her in 1957 when I was about 16 years old. We met my grandmother, along with my aunts, and had another family reunion, except my grandfather who had died rather

---

9   "Records of the Immigration and Neutralization Service of 1891-1957, Record Group 85 New York, New York," *National Archives* (accessed December 3, 2015), http://www.archives.gov/research/microfilm/t715.pdf.

young of stomach cancer. At this family reunion, I remember my parents and the other adults talking about the war and how they were all in refugee camps from the same area of East Prussia, now Bremerhaven.[10] But I was more concerned about playing with my cousins. I wish I had spoken more to my grandmother about her stories and such, but I did not.

Both in Germany and America, my family was well off; I would say middle class for that time. Back in Germany my father had a pretty good job as a brick mason because all the houses were made of brick and his occupation was in high demand since everything was bombed out. In the United States, my family was still well off. My father was never out of work and we had a farm with chickens and cows. He worked as a landscaper, as I mentioned earlier. Later on, he and my brother even went into their own landscaping business. The major difference from Germany's middle class and America's was that, both during and after the war in Germany, I can remember that I never felt that I ever had enough to eat. We had food to eat, but never enough for seconds. I was never full. It really made me appreciate everything. Even to this day, I clean my plate of all food. I always eat everything. I never throw anything away. That situation just makes you incredibly thankful for what you have. In the United States, my family never lacked for food. We always had plenty to eat.

Other than going from a lack to an abundance of food, other things influenced and affected my family, mainly our church and our belief in God. God was the most important thing that led us through our lives in Germany. My family and I were part of the church body known as the New Apostolic Church, which actually originated in Germany in 1863. I was part of that church in Germany, and I am still a part of that church today in America. I believe that God influences us every day, if we let Him. My parents were the strongest influence in my life, especially with everything that we had to go through. God, our family, and friends are what our identity was rooted in and what gave us strength. God, family, and friends and the memories of them are what stay with you. I am so thankful that life has changed and that life is not like what it was in Germany anymore. I would say that my family was close-knit because of these things, but when I met my husband I experienced what a true close-knit family was. His family got together every Sunday for dinners and really cared about each other. My family was close, but not that close. When we got together, I said that I wanted our family to be like his, to really love and care about each other.

I always enjoyed school. I went to school in Germany for six years. I attended school in Trittau, a district in Hamburg. I did not attend kindergarten, there was no such thing, so I went to school from the age of six to twelve. In the United States, I went to school right away, since the second day we arrived in America, in fact. I attended a private Lutheran school in Portland, Oregon. I remember going to this school and not knowing any English. Every day at the beginning of the school day,

---

10   A seaport city in Germany, west of Hamburg.

the school had us read from the Bible out loud in class and all the kids would take turns. When it was my turn, my teacher knew that I did not know English yet so she would let me read young children's books like *Little Red Riding Hood* as practice in front of the entire class, which terrified me, but I did it. While learning English, the phrase I learned the best was "Please speak slowly and distinctly." I always said that. Whether the other kids made fun of me or not, I do not know, but I do know this: I always smiled.

Funny story and a little off topic, at this time, we stayed with my aunt and uncle (my mother's sister who found us through the Red Cross) who lived in a Black neighborhood. I was afraid of Black people; that is why my parents put me in a private, all-White person school. I was a kid, and I was just afraid, no other reason. I attended Lutheran school until the end of sixth grade, so for about a half a year. After that, I attended a regular grade school in Portland with all different ethnic groups. I was no longer afraid at that point. I had gotten over my fear because the Blacks in my aunt's neighborhood were friendly and very nice, so I became unafraid of them. I trusted them and that was the end of that. In seventh grade, I attended a public school in Portland. After my family and I moved to Sherwood where we bought the farm, I attended the eighth grade at Tualatin Grade School in Oregon. I even finished grade school and was voted "most outstanding student." Then I went to Sherwood Union High School for four years and graduated.

I enjoyed school, and my favorite subject was English. I was always good at it even though it was my second language. It just clicked and came easy to me, and I was very good at writing essays and stories. I also loved the subjects of shorthand,[11] homemaking, and art. Shorthand taught me to use symbols for words, which helped me immensely when I got a secretary job after high school in 1960. I worked at Sawyer's Incorporated[12] (they sold cameras and the view-master's trademark) and wrote letters on an electric typewriter, dictated to me by my boss. My boss told me to write something, and I wrote in shorthand. I also loved the homemaking class because I loved to cook and sew. That class was how I first learned how to sew. In school, I was not very good with math, however. I never had any problems with the other kids even though I was the weirdo, the German girl. I just smiled.

From my teen years, I remember that I always studied, I was a happy kid, I had friends, and I even had a job at a little restaurant that I worked at after school and on Saturdays. My brother would pick me up after every shift. I belonged to the youth group at my church with whom we traveled to the Seattle New Apostolic Church occasionally. That was where I met my husband in 1959.

I was engaged to my husband in September of 1960 and we were married in Portland, Oregon, on February 12, 1961. I was 19 years old. I then moved up to Seattle, Washington, with him and we had four children. Our first son was born on

---

11   System of rapid handwriting including the simplification of letters and using symbols to represent certain sounds, words, or phrases.

12   Original manufacturer of the view-master line of products.

January 21, 1962, our second son was born August 11, 1963, our first daughter was born on March 11, 1966, and our second daughter was born on February 9, 1970. My husband made pretty good money as he worked in management at a grocery store, so I did not have to work. I had chosen to be a mother as my career until our eldest son was 12. I really wanted to learn how to sew well, so I got a job in a sewing factory, at the encouragement of one of my closest friends. She insisted that I get a job at the factory because they were looking for people, and even though I did not know how to sew all that well, my friend insisted that they would teach me. Well, I was hired on the spot and became a sewer. I worked in that factory for a couple years until the manager opened her own factory, called Cascade Sportswear, and asked me to go with her. I worked there as a supervisor until 1984. After that, I got the best job ever: a job with Boeing.[13] You do not choose Boeing as a profession; you had to be lucky to get this kind of job. Thankfully, my eldest daughter (my third child) got an office job for Boeing right out of high school. She actually told her boss about me because I could sew and they needed people for the blanket shop (throw blankets with Boeing planes and such on them). This branch was soon outsourced to Mexico, and I was sent there to train the workers. When I got back to Washington, along with a few others who taught the workers with me, I was promoted. We blanket workers were sent all over the place after we trained workers in Mexico. I was sent to Auburn, Washington, just outside of Seattle. It was there that I learned how to become an aerospace mechanic. I built airplanes. I was there for 14 years then I retired.

Over my lifetime, the times that were most important to me was when I was in the refugee camp with my mother and brother, when I came to the United States, when I married my beloved husband, and when I had my children and watched them grow up. My whole life has been outstanding. These things taught me to love life and to treasure every moment. I am most proud of my marriage of 54 years, which takes true work. I am proud of all four of my children who are wonderful and successful, of my grandchildren who are wonderful, and even my two great-grand-children who are wonderful.

I believe that everything we go through shapes our lives and helps us become a stronger person. I have really had a happy life. Even today, though I struggle with and am challenged by my husband's health issues as he suffers from Parkinson's and other degenerative diseases, I would not change my life if I had the choice. And as for the future, if I have plans, that is fine, and if I do not, that is fine, too.

---

13   Still an American multinational corporation.

Port Orchard, Washington (1942)

As told to the interviewer's granddaughter.

FIGURE 3.8.1 Mount St. Helen's Volcanic Eruption, Washington, USA, May 1980

Margarita (Margie) Sartucci is my grandmother on my mother's side. She is currently 69 years old. She is living in Port Ludlow, Washington, and enjoying life after retirement. She is a wonderful person who loves to bestow her knowledge on any who will listen. This is the story of her life.

Margie was born on November 15, 1942, in Spokane, Washington, to Felipe and Benedetta Sartucci. Margie's parents were both born in the United States; however, Margie's grandparents were born in Italy and migrated to the United States. Margie's Italian heritage was evident throughout the early stages of her life. Margie was the second of two children; her sister Alisa, who was nicknamed "Oldest," was put in charge of Margie. This meant that Alisa decided what Margie could and could not do. This strained their relationship because Margie did not like that Alisa had so much control over her. Needless to say, Margie and Alisa did not have the best relationship growing up; however, it mended with time.

Felipe owned a small Italian grocery store and Benedetta helped him run it. Margie remembers her dad telling her that during the Great Depression "he made some kind of coin that he used for his grocery store to help people buy things." Regardless, Margie does not remember any time when her family was struggling with money. Margie and her family lived in Spokane for all of her schooling. They lived in a 1,200 square foot home with a basement, three bedrooms, two bathrooms, kitchen, and living room. Her family owned a swing set in the backyard, and this was Margie's favorite place to be when she was alone. She swears that she "could have been a gymnast." One of the more memorable memories Margie had while growing up was the Sunday drives. Felipe would just drive, with no destination and no time schedule. Margie remembered that these drives would sometimes last a very long time because they would get lost. Nonetheless, this was family bonding. Margie's family purchased their first television in 1954. It was a very heavy box with a 12-inch screen. Nancy regularly would watch the *Mickey Mouse Club*, but, at the time, enjoyed the radio more because it allowed her imagination to take over. Margie lived in a very Italian community; many of her friends shared the same heritage. Her parents had a group of Italian friends who did everything together; they called themselves the "Tanto Vino." Their name means exactly what it sounds like: They drank a lot of wine. Most of the couples in "Tanto Vino" had children, and these were the friends Margie had. They went to school and church together and hung out on the weekends. They played a large influence in Margie's life.

Margie attended an all-girls Catholic school until college. She was not particularly fond of school because she struggled with grades, whereas her sister achieved straight As. Margie did not feel extremely religious either, so most of the Catholic teachings were more laborious than enlightening. For example, once every week, she had to go to confession. Before confession, she would "see to it that [she] would hit [her] sister ... so [she] would have something to confess." The family moved to a new house in 1956. This new house was a "very nice brick home" on a hill that overlooked Spokane. She remembers going to a little pond, not more than two blocks from her new house, and just relaxing in the weeds or picking buttercups. This was her favorite place to be alone. She graduated from high school in 1960.

After high school, Margie attended Washington State University from 1960–1964. Contrary to high school, Nancy really enjoyed college. Tuition was only about $100 a quarter, so her parents were able to pay for all of her expenses. This was the first time that she felt as if she had complete freedom to do what she chose, rather than having to listen to her sister. Margie was very interested in interior design and was finally able to find her niche in school. She lived in Ferry Hall for her first two years and later moved to housing on the golf course. It was in her second year of college that she met her future husband, Bruce McInery. He lived in the fire station that Margie had to walk by every day in order to get breakfast, lunch, and dinner. She swears that the fire station guys made sure that they were outside when the Ferry Hall girls passed by. With the dorms segregated by sex, this was prime time to meet someone of the opposite sex. The girls also had more restrictions than the guys when it came to school rules. For example, the guys did not have any hours, but the girls had to be in their dorms by 10 p.m. or they would get locked out. Margie made sure that she was never late; however, her roommate had to climb through the window a couple times. Margie and Bruce began dating at the end of her sophomore year. They dated for one year and got married on May 11, 1963. Once married, Margie and Bruce moved into the married students' apartments on the golf course. Rent was $50 per month and Bruce made $100 per month. Margie never worked during college other than when she went home and worked in her dad's grocery store. She did work an internship with a furniture company between her junior and senior year, but it was for the experience rather than the pay. Despite going to college during the 1960s, Nancy never drank before she was 21 and never participated in smoking pot. She even attended an Elvis Presley concert, but despite all of the screaming girls around her, all she could think about Elvis was "he's a good singer." Margie never fell into the lifestyle that the 60s were commonly known for.

Throughout Margie's college experience, many political events and movements occurred that were momentous in US history. Most of these had very little effect on Margie's life. She never witnessed any boycotts or speeches for the civil rights movement and never even felt threatened by the Cuban Missile Crisis. The one event that did enter into the Washington State campus was President John Kennedy's assassination. Nancy was walking back to her dorm from class when people began yelling and screaming that the president had been assassinated. She immediately thought "Oh my goodness. How could something like that happen? I mean, this is a president that, I thought, was really good and most people liked, and here he was shot." Directly after the assassination, the Washington State campus had a somber atmosphere for about a month.

Margie became pregnant with her first son toward the end of her senior year of college. Being pregnant in college had its ups and downs though; for instance, on the day of her design class final, she had terrible morning sickness. She talked to the professor, and because she had an A in the class, she just skipped the final and finished the class with a B. After Margie graduated with a degree in home economics, she and Bruce moved to Spokane where he began his student teaching. Shortly after, Margie gave birth to Patrick on December 25, 1964. They lived in Spokane for just over a year as Bruce worked as a student teacher while finishing his last year of college. Once Bruce graduated, he enlisted into the Army and Nancy officially became a military wife with one child. This was at the beginning of the Vietnam War.

After enlisting, Bruce had to go to Fort Knox for his training. He was there for two months before being deployed to Germany. In those two months, Margie and her son, Pat, lived with her parents. Before Bruce left for Germany, he had heard about a program where his family could accompany him to Germany if they already had military housing in the US. Without actually living in a military house, Bruce had heard that if he were to just write down a random address on his papers, Margie and Pat would be allowed to accompany him to Germany. So that is what he did, and the family moved to Germany. Finding a house in Germany, however, was not very easy. Margie, Bruce, and Pat jumped from hotel to hotel for the first four months before finding a little apartment. Right after moving in, Bruce was sent to the East German border. Luckily for Margie, the German couple living in the apartment below, the Brakenhofers, helped Margie and took her in as part of the family. Frau Brakenhofer and Margie became very good buddies; they created their own language consisting of hand motions and short phrases. At this time, Margie and Bruce were very poor, so they did most of their shopping at the military base. Margie experienced a culture shock while driving to visit Bruce for Christmas at the military base, because she drove on the autobahn. She could not believe that there was no speed limit and cars just drove as fast as they wanted. Bruce, Margie, and Pat were only in Germany for about a year before being called back to Fort Lewis, early in 1966, so Bruce could help train the newly enlisted troops.

They lived on the base in Fort Lewis for the remaining two years of Bruce's service. During that time, Nancy became pregnant her second child. Laura "Laurie" McInery was born on October 11, 1966 and was Nancy's only daughter. With Bruce still in the Army, Margie did not have to pay anything for the delivery of Laurie. The only thing Margie had to pay for was her $5 meal. While Bruce was in the military, Nancy took on the role of housewife. She raised the kids and took care of the family. The Vietnam War was also becoming more controversial. Margie did not know very much about what was going on but having a husband in the military made her believe that US citizens should be supporting the men in the military regardless of what the government had them do. Needless to say, Nancy opposed the anti-war protests specifically because she thought they should support the troops.

After Bruce's three years in the military, he immediately received a job as a shop teacher at Port Orchard High School. This led to the family moving to a small, one-story house in Port Orchard, Washington. Margie's last child, Michael McInery, was born on June 28, 1968, just a couple months after moving to their new home. Mathew's birth was a lot more expensive than Laurie's. Bruce and Margie had no insurance, and his birth cost a couple thousand dollars because Bruce was no longer in the Army. With her three kids and Bruce working as a schoolteacher, Margie began babysitting some of the other neighborhood kids. This was a win-win situation because Margie was able to stay at home with her kids as well as make some extra, much needed, money. Margie babysat until all of her kids began going to school. At that point, she started teaching preschool in order to have the same work hours as her kids had school hours. She did this for three years before working full-time at the local grocery delicatessen in 1974.

Raising children was Margie's greatest accomplishment in her eyes. She remembered when Michael did not want to go to school because he could not let Mom be home by herself. When she started working full-time, Pat felt like it was wrong for her to have to work because he wanted her home when he got home. Margie described raising children as being able to get "one stage figured out, and then they go to another stage and you have to start all over again." She attempted multiple times to try to enforce a daily chores routine with her kids, but every method seemed to fail. She tried charts, allowances, and spreadsheets, but eventually fell back to simply telling her kids what they had to do and when. One particular chore that Margie was able to control very well was doing the dishes. She came up with the idea that the first kid to leave the dinner table had to do dishes. She remembered her kids sitting for hours at the table until someone, usually Pat or Michael, gave in and did the dishes. Overall, Margie's experience raising children was one that she cherished.

On May 18, 1980, Mt. St. Helens erupted. This is an event every Washingtonian remembers. Margie remembered it because everywhere she went there was a fine layer of ash covering everything. Television stations were telling people to wash their cars with water otherwise the ash would scratch the paint. When she called her parents about it, her parents, who still lived in Spokane, relayed that the entire sky became as dark as night from all of the ash. This happened within the time it took them to drive home from Sunday Mass. It was quite an event, and Nancy claimed she would never forget it.

When all of Margie's children went off to college, she went through some difficult times. She was depressed because her kids had become her life for the last twenty years. She was still able to get on with her daily life, as she was working full-time, but it took her a couple years before she was able to find herself, without kids. Things like making the right-sized portions for meals and coming home from work to only Bruce were difficult for her to deal with. Things became more difficult when Pat married. Margie and Bruce did not approve of the woman Pat was marrying and were, therefore, not invited to his wedding. This specifically hurt Margie because she felt very distant from her first child. When Laurie married Douglas Hale, Nancy was very proud as Bruce walked her down the aisle. Unfortunately, Pat was not invited to Susie's wedding. When Michael got married, Margie felt like her family was whole for the first time since Pat's marriage, because all of her kids attended. She was especially proud of Michael because he wore his Army uniform for the wedding. After Michael's wedding, Nancy was content with the way her family turned out, considering Pat and his wife divorced a few years after Michael's wedding and she now had grandchildren. Between her three kids, she would have eight grandkids. Margie was a proud grandmother, but even more proud to be a mother because her kids were able to start families on their own. The entire family came together for every Thanksgiving, Christmas, and most major holidays.

In 1998, Margie and Bruce, along with Margie's parents, moved to Puget Sound in Washington. They built their own house, and it took eight months to complete. It had a magnificent view over the Sound. Nancy enjoyed gardening and landscaping in her new house, particularly because she had more land to landscape. In 2001, Felipe Sartucci passed away at age 87. This was a particularly difficult time for Margie considering she had to watch her mother deal with the loss of her father. In 2003, Margie retired and became very involved in her community. She volunteered at the church most Sundays and enjoyed all the extra time. Unfortunately her retirement was interrupted by the death of her mother, Benedetta, in 2005. A beautiful funeral was held at Margie's home, in Benedetta's garden. The passing of her mom was comforted by the knowledge that her parents were together again.

Margie and Bruce have since hosted neighborhood events every other month, and Margie became a dedicated bridge player. They own a fishing boat that they take out nearly every week during crab season. For Christmas, Bruce and Margie usually plan a very fun activity or trip where they take their kids, and grandkids, for family bonding. In addition, Margie has been able to travel more than she ever has in her life. She and Bruce have road tripped to the East Coast and traveled to Italy. The rest of Margie McInerny's life has yet to be written.

CREDIT

Things to Think About

1. In what ways were the women in the oral histories impacted by the Great Depression? Did you notice that children in the 1930s and 40s expected to work either at home or for pay before they were in junior high school? Is this still common today? Why or why not?

2. The intriguing thing about oral histories is that they introduce the reader to individual experiences. In one case, the German "Operation Hannibal" was the largest amphibious rescue in history, although many never hear of it. Does this humanitarian effort by the "enemy" in World War II surprise you? How might you explain why this mission is rarely discussed?

3. Many of the oral histories discuss social inequities. Can you find specific examples that impacted three *different* groups?

4. Many people are familiar with the history of Argentina through the vehicle of the Broadway play *Evita*. What many people find less familiar is the crackdown of freedom in the 1970s and 1980s in Argentina, Chile, Bolivia, Brazil, Paraguay, and Uruguay from military *juntas* and other authoritarian governments. Women in many of these countries used nonviolent means to tell the stories of what was happening, including works of art, called *arpilleras*. Look up the "Mother of the Plaza de Mayo." Who are the "disappeared" they march to remember?

5. Three different oral histories touch on activities in communist countries during the Cold War. Moreover, two of the stories are from women who still live in those countries. Considering the Cold War defined much of the latter half of the twentieth century, how do these women describe their homelands? How might they have perceived the Cold War?

For Further Reading

Great Depression
The Forgotten Man: A New History of the Great Depression (2008) by Amity Shlaes

Holocaust
Night-Dawn-Day (1961) by Elie Wiesel

World War II
The Catcher Was a Spy: The Mysterious Life of Moe Berg (1995) by Nicholas Dawidoff

China
Wild Swans: Three Daughters of China (2003) by Jung Chang

Philippines
When the Elephants Dance: A Novel (2002) by Tess Uriza Holthe

Armenia
My Grandmother: An Armenian-Turkish Memoir (2012) by Fethiye Cetin

Eastern Europe
Between East and West: Across the Borderlands of Europe (2017) by Anne Applebaum

Argentina
The Little School: Tales of Disappearance and Survival (1998) by Alicia Partnoy and Julia Alvarez

TIMELINE

- **1950-1953**

  Korean War

- **1953**

  Dr. Jonas Salk announces polio vaccine

- **1954**

  Dien Bien Phu falls in Vietnam, US Supreme Court outlaws segregation

- **1955**

  Emmett Till murdered, Montgomery Bus boycott

- **1961**

  Berlin Wall built, pulled down in 1989.

- **1963**

  JFK Assassinated; Vice-President Lyndon B. Johnson (LBJ) is sworn in.

- **1965**

  LBJ lands ground troops in Vietnam

- **1969**

  Americans land on the moon

- **1972**

  Nixon visits China and the Soviet Union, Watergate

- **1973**

  US withdraws from Vietnam

- **1979**

  Iranian Revolution, US hostages

- **1980**

  Moral Majority; Ronald Reagan elected president

1945–1960

Introduction

The oral histories you will read in part IV represent women born in the first era of the baby boom. Some entered the workforce, while others did not. Some became activists and others watched. Many married, and still others became career women. Whichever path they chose, the women of the mid-twentieth century were modern women, influenced by the generation and events before them, but, overall, an outspoken and confident group of more educated, healthier, and more willing to

FIGURE 0.1   Grandma Moses Stamp, 1969

FIGURE 0.2   Peter Max Stamp, 1974

work outside the home females. A television ad of the period said that women "had come a long, baby," and they had.

So how does one visualize the views of this era? One way is to use art, as you did in part I. In 1938, an agent saw a painting of the American countryside in a drugstore window. He bought the painting, plus ten more, and sought out the artist. She turned out to be 78-year-old Anna Mary Moses, better known as Grandma Moses. She was born the year before the Civil War in 1860 and lived to be 101. By 1961 she was eulogized upon her death by President Kennedy. Her type of work was called "folk art" and she was given a stamp featuring her painting of the Fourth of July that hangs in the White House. Her work pays homage to the agrarian world of the nineteenth and early twentieth centuries and was wildly popular with the greatest generation.

Now take a look at the art of the 60s by Peter Max, a noted psychedelic poster artist. His view of the world was one that appeared on every book cover and Pee Chee folder for school children each September for over a decade. The work was colorful and was said to represent the colors of an LSD "trip." His postage stamp appeared five years after Grandma Moses's stamp. One can clearly see that these two types of very divergent art were favorites of two very different groups of people. One harked back to the world of the the past and one was said to recall the mind expansion of ingested drugs. Were the differences a matter of generation, of economics, or of something else? As you read the oral histories try to imagine which style of art would resonate with each speaker.

The baby boom began in 1945 when the soldiers and sailors returned from World War II. Their offspring would include the large number of children born between 1946 and 1964 in the United States and around the world as booms and "boomlets" occurred in many developed nations. The 1960s population boom in China was so large that by 1980 they passed the "one-child" rule, allowing couples to only bear one child, a rule that was not reversed until 2016. For the United States this meant expansion and consumerism ruled the day. Cities grew, suburbs marched across farmland, and new schools were built to accommodate the influx of children. Despite the worry of nuclear confrontation over the Berlin Wall or the Cuban Missile Crisis, each evening one could hear children's voices as games of kick the can and hide and seek echoed through the backyards of the new suburban, "picture window" homes. Little attention was paid to the bomb shelters tucked below the suburban driveways in some developments.

Children born in this period learned to read with Dick and Jane,[1] went to church every Sunday, and joined the Boy Scouts and Campfire girls. With no seatbelt laws yet passed eight kids could clamber into station wagons for outings to the seashore or a baseball game. Dads worked long hours, often until late into the evening in order to earn that raise to pay for all of the children's futures. Moms began to take part-time jobs to help pay for baseball cleats and ballet lessons, but they also had an ulterior motive. Prior to the war young married couples lived in cities, near friends and relatives, but after the GIs returned home the young families moved to the suburbs, often a significant drive from friends and family. Being home with six children each day could be tiring, so opportunities to interact with other adults were cherished. In 1963, a feminist writer, Betty Friedan, discussed this in the *Feminist Mystique.* She called it the "problem that has no name."

Along with the rising costs of child raising, some women wanted to limit the number of children they bore for health reasons. In 1963, the birth control pill became widely available and women could begin to think about having two children rather than six. By the 1960s many middle-class families believed in helping the planet by having smaller families. In addition to these changes, President John F. Kennedy's Commission on the Status of Women, led by Eleanor Roosevelt, began to advocate for equal pay for women and equal opportunities for jobs. These changes were embraced by the young people who grew up in the 50s and 60s. As the new demographic group of "teenagers" grew up, marketing aimed at this group encouraged buying all of the latest music and gadgets. For the most part, these young people

---

1   Books for teaching children to read created by Zerna Sharp and written by William S. Gray in 1930.

worked for spending money, learned to drive at 16, and planned to attend college in large numbers. Thanks to the postwar economic boom, families had the money to pay for their children to be educated since costs were relatively low. By 1964 the first wave set off to college, not to war as their parents had. Once ensconced in their dormitories, they often embraced a new brand of activism.

Initially, many were drawn to the civil rights movement that had been kicked off by the Double V campaign and reinforced by the *Brown vs. Board of Education, Topeka, Kansas* decision in 1954 that overturned the 1896 *Plessy vs. Ferguson* decision that had allowed that "separate was equal." In 1955 the murder of a 14-year-old African American male, Emmitt Till, for allegedly whistling at a White woman, coupled with Rosa Parks and the Montgomery bus boycott, committed college students and others to the cause of equal rights. Young people, from Michigan to Greensboro, Tennessee, held sit-ins at lunch counters, joined efforts to integrate interstate busing, and joined voter registration drives in the South. Two new laws, the Civil Rights Act (1964) and the Voting Rights Act (1965) changed the landscape and strove to improve the rights of African Americans.

From this movement grew awareness of poverty, pending environmental damage, and the knowledge that a war was brewing in Southeast Asia. This was a war begun after World War II by France and supported by US funding to retain France's colony of French Indochina. When the French lost to Ho Chi Minh's troops at Dien Bien Phu in 1954, the US faced a dilemma. Should Vietnam be unified under its communist leader, Ho Chi Minh, or should further steps be taken to prevent the fall of another communist "domino." The Eisenhower administration decided to hold the line against communism and continued the support of South Vietnam. The Kennedy administration initially continued this policy, but by 1963 Kennedy reversed the course and signed to begin the process of withdrawal in October 1963. Two weeks later he was dead from an assassin's bullet in Dallas, Texas, and his successor, Lyndon B. Johnson, committed himself to the war. While the president might have been committed, the new generation of students was not. They burned their draft cards, sought asylum in Canada, and took over the administrative offices of the colleges they attended with sit-ins. As the music of Bob Dylan and the Beatles portended, the "times they were a-changing."

Unlike their parents, raised on hardship and travail through the Depression and war years, these young people were more like their grandparents from the 1920s, rebellious, sexually charged, and experimental. The pill allowed the sexual revolution to happen, the drugs allowed the mind-bending trips that later led to serious flashbacks, and the "establishment," specifically anyone over thirty, was their nemesis. Encouraged by rock and roll, the British music invasion, and the driving beats of the Rolling Stones, young men grew their hair long and their beards longer, smoked weed, and "shacked up" with their significant others, who were mostly girls wearing mini-skirts and white go-go boots, surfer straight hair, white lipstick, and fake eyelashes—all of which generally outraged their World War II and Korean War veteran parents.

Nightly news began in the early 60s and covered sit-ins and walk-outs, as well as maintaining a body count of the dead in Vietnam. Not imbued with the anti-communism of their parents, these students declined to fight in the jungles of Vietnam. Many were drafted, some resisted, others marched, and, in 1970, war resistors were shot by National Guardsmen at Kent State. Unlike previous wars, young men who fought came home to abuse and were called "baby killers" by their peers rather than being named heroes. The country split into Hawks (pro-war) and Doves (anti-war.)

While the 50s had been generally perceived as calm and safe, the 60s became something else altogether. After the assassination of JFK, Malcolm X was assassinated in 1965, Martin Luther King, Jr. was assassinated in April 1968, and less than two months later, Bobby Kennedy, JFK's brother who was running for president, was assassinated in June. The hope infused into Americans by Kennedy when he said the country would put a man on the moon by the end of the decade was lost in scenes from Woodstock, riots at the Democratic Convention in 1968, and the election of Richard Nixon as president with the promise he would pull out of Vietnam, even as he expanded the war. And then came the Watergate scandal.

World War II veteran Richard Nixon became a red-baiter or anti-communist after World War II. As Eisenhower's vice president, he anticipated being elected president in 1960 until John F. Kennedy beat him at the polls. Undeterred, he ran again in 1968 and won. History would later record that he saw Vietnam as a footnote to history. He was more interested in securing oil in the Middle East to keep the US economy booming than fighting the Viet Cong. He therefore focused on the Arab-Israeli conflict, which had reached a new crisis when terrorists attacked and killed the Israeli wrestling team at the Munich Olympics in 1972. In order to end the Vietnam stalemate he determined to thaw US relations with its communist opponents, China and the Soviet Union. He visited both in 1972 as the world applauded, but he also arranged for electronic bugs to be placed in the Democratic National Headquarters, and his "plumbers" were caught red-handed that summer. The ensuing two-year investigation led to his resignation on August 9, 1974, and Gerald Ford became president.

By 1974 the country was restive, but the US withdrew from Vietnam in 1973, the sit-ins slowed when civil rights seemed within reach, and the students who entered college in 1964 married and went to work. The later baby boomers had watched the 60s as young children, and those students became yuppies, that is young, upwardly mobile people looking for material success and financial stability. This group would later include those born between 1964 and 1980, or Generation X. As young adults they saw the Berlin Wall come down in 1989 and the Soviet Union collapse two years later. What they could not have foreseen was that the idea of superpowers had restricted regional powers and their supporters who used terrorism to make their political agenda clear over the next three decades.

The last set of oral histories explores this period of transition in the mid to late twentieth century. In general, the outcry of the 60s raised awareness of inequities and abuse for segments of the population, including minorities, the disabled, and the impoverished. In addition, the issues of preserving the planet became important as small children learned to "reduce, reuse, and recycle." The legacy of the hippies included the ideas of healthier food, more limited pesticide use, and cleaner air. By 1980, these concerns were reflected around the globe as nations came together to discuss environmental issues.

The oral histories demonstrate just how much the lives of women had changed. Fewer children were born and 50 percent of marriages ended in divorce. By 1970 women had learned from the National Organization of Women (NOW) that women had brains and did not have to major in home economics. Women could be lawyers, doctors, and pilots, if they chose. They even had credit ratings by 1990 that did not depend on their husband's income. In many ways the women's movement grew out of the activism of the civil rights movement. This catalyst encouraged other movements, including the American Indian movement (AIM), the Brown Berets, and the gay pride movement after the Stonewall Riots in 1969. These fields became areas of study in colleges and universities.

Of course, this tide did not impact everyone equally. One of the results of World War II became a commitment to national self-determination by the United Nations. By 1960 this meant that many former colonies were now independent nations. However, some lacked a trained workforce and appropriate infrastructure. In addition, many felt that the lands afforded them did not represent that ones that culture and heritage said were theirs. This perception led to increased intertribal wars, like those in the Congo. In other places, access to ports became vital, as with Iraq, and still others could not readily shake the yoke of the Soviet Union. Ideas of latent imperialism lingered and often resulted in nationalizing the companies built by foreign investors. Often the conflicts were complicated by differences in religious values, the status of women, and ethnicity. These battles became much more prominent once the bipolar Cold War ended.

As many former colonies embraced beliefs predating their colonization, others disintegrated into tribal and ethnic conflict, like Rwanda. These more traditional beliefs often included strict religious observance, while the developed world moved toward a more secular structure. During the Cold War, the Soviet Union was staunchly atheist, or godless, in the terms of the day. By the 1920s they had allowed unlimited female abortion, so issues of female bodies became part of moral decision making. By 1980, the backlash to the

60s and the liberal court decisions, like the liberalization of abortion with the *Roe v. Wade* decision, became integral to the rise of the moral majority in the United States. This movement elected President Ronald Reagan and George H.W. Bush to three consecutive terms in the 1980s. By 2000 the clash regarding the future trajectory of the United States was becoming more and more divisive.

CREDITS

Holland (1945)

Written in third person by the interviewee's grandchild.

FIGURE 4.1.1   Hongerwinter, Dutch famine, 1944–45

She was born on September 3, 1945, in the small town of Nijverdal near the German border in war-torn Holland. She was the youngest of three children born into a family of two loving and caring parents. At the time of her birth her father, Wilhelm, was around the age of 36 and her mother, Annette, was around the age of 35. Her older brother, Ansel, was eight years older than she, and her older sister Kristin was four years older. From an early age she remembers her parents being very loving and nurturing toward her and her siblings and working hard to provide the best life they could for them. This was not an easy task in postwar Holland, so at the age of four her whole world was turned upside down when her parents made the decision to leave everything they had and moved the family to the United States. What a drastic event for a little girl! Everything she had come to understand was about to change. And so, in December of 1949, Great Aunt Lieke Hoerder van Buren began her new life in America.

Her mother, Annette, grew up in a tough setting but was determined for a better life. Annette's life began as a result of a pregnancy out of wedlock. Her mother passed away when she was five years old, and she never knew her father. She grew up thinking her grandmother was her mother and her mother was her sister. It was not until after her grandmother's death that she found out the truth. After the death of her grandmother she was left an orphan. Eventually she was shipped to some distant relatives in another part of Holland. These relatives were in the later years of their lives and did not really want her around, so she moved from house to house a lot. She started working at a very young age as a nanny and housekeeper for a family who owned a business; she continued working as a domestic servant for them until her early twenties when she met Wilhelm.

Lieke's father, Wilhelm, came from a very poor family of eight children. Of the eight children, one died of pneumonia at a young age. Wilhelm was only able to attend school until the sixth grade because all the children were needed to work and help the family gain some income. He worked as a bread delivery boy, in which he had a route and would go deliver bread to houses and businesses. He later became a baker and continued to pursue that profession for several years, all the way up until their first son, Ansel, was born. Once they started having children he began to work in a thread factory. Wilhelm and Annette met in their teens, as many teenagers from different churches in the area would all walk to youth group together. They could not afford to get married and so they remained together for eight years before being able to afford to get married. They did not live together during those eight years; rather, she lived with a family who took her in and allowed her to stay with them. After eventually getting married around the ages of 26 and 27, they had their first son a quick nine months later.

Lieke only knew her grandparents on her father's side of the family; she has vivid memories of her grandfather. Her grandfather lost his arm during World War I as a result of no doctors being available to take care of the blood poisoning that started as a sore on his little finger; by the time a doctor was found it was too advanced and his arm had to be amputated. Her grandfather could do almost anything with his one arm; this was especially shown in the fact that he was able to work in a factory after the amputation. She heard many stories growing up from her father giving credit to the many ways her grandfather supported their large family in aiding them through the Depression in Europe. Faced with low food sources and little money, her grandmother would make soup out of potato peelings and survived off of meat a farmer her grandfather worked for provided to them.

Lieke's childhood in Nijverdal, although she was very young, was filled with many small memories both good and bad. In Holland, she remembers living in a duplex that her family shared with her aunt and uncle who lived on the other side. Not remembering much detail to the context or other aspects of the story, she has a memory of a scary man who would walk past their house everyday singing when she was playing outside; she would get so frightened she ran inside. She remembers one Easter her whole family went to a hill and would roll eggs down the hill. She also has some distinct memories of the Christmas season, remembering Sinter Claus and his companion or servant Zwarte Piet. They would stand by the chimney and sing to Santa to bring them presents. Due to her young age while living in Holland, she does not remember many specific details, but rather little glimpses. She has heard many stories over the years from other family members, which she references for what life was like for her family during this time.

Her brother has shared some stories and memories over the years of what he remembers from the time they lived in Holland. One of these stories was their mother coming home on her bike covered in shrapnel and scratched up a little bit because she had been near a bombing site when a bomb went off. He remembers them cleaning her up and making sure she was okay. She explained that many of the boarding towns and railroads had many bombs that went off, and so in later years her family talked about how even in their own home they did not feel safe. Many times people dug trenches in their backyard that they would go and hide in if there was a declared bomb dropping. Her older siblings described the fear they often felt in their own homes and the lack of comfort they even felt hiding in the trenches.

Lieke and her family left the Netherlands in December of 1949, after two aunts came to visit from the United States and give them the idea to move. Ultimately it was her father who made the decision for them to move to the United States. He asked their relatives to sponsor them since you had to have someone sponsor you if something went wrong. They had to wait about a year until they could board the ship to the United States. They boarded a big ocean liner called *The New Amsterdam* in Rotterdam; and after a week's journey and one major storm, they ported in New York. In New York, they were given "stickers" to put on their shirts saying they were heading to Hollandale, Minnesota. They then got on a train and arrived in Hollandale, where Lieke's father had a job lined up as a carpenter. Her father made the decision to move for several reasons, all of which he believed would benefit the family and their well-being. He was working in a factory in Holland at the time and did not want to do that for the rest of his life, nor did he want to pass that profession down to his children. He also felt that religion had become too repressed in Holland during those years and decided to move to start a new and better life for his family.

After sometime in Hollandale, they moved to Pease, Minnesota, and then Everson, Washington. Her years in Minnesota as a child were filled with fun memories of playing in the snow. She remembers going ice skating fairly often. With older siblings to look up to, her family played games together and had a lot of fun even in the cold Minnesota winters. She does not recall her transition to the United

States being overly difficult in reference to learning a new language; as a four-year-old she was able to learn it rather quickly. Her mother, on the other hand, never fully learned English. Lieke was able to learn most of her English by playing with a neighbor girl, who also happened to be her third cousin. In Minnesota she went to a Hollandale parochial for three years. This school was so small it had the first through fourth grade in one room with one teacher and the rest of the grades in another classroom with another teacher. She then attended Pease Christian School for one year before moving to Washington and attending Lynden Christian through high school. As a young student in elementary school, one of her favorite things to do was ring the bell for recess. Unfortunately, she felt moving all the time was a detriment to her learning and put her behind in school.

Her family's move to Everson, Washington, was influenced by the fact that her father was presented with an opportunity to rent a farm his cousin had told him about. In 1954, Lieke and her family drove to Washington from Minnesota in the car her family owned. Her father became his own boss and advanced his career. In Everson, he worked as a farmer the rest of his life. Lieke has many fond memories of riding her bike, swimming, and playing with her animals on the farm. She also started working on the farm at a very young age; she helped with the animals and in the garden very often. She believes her life on the farm was very different than the life other children enjoyed, but was still good. She learned how to sew with her mother, as well as how to can. Gardening, sewing, and canning were all expected and done on a regular basis.

Growing up, her favorite time of the year was Christmas, as some of her fondest memories came from this time. Lieke still remembers the Dutch prayers and songs they said and sung. Her dad would make *oliebollen*, which she describes as a Dutch dessert sort of like a donut. She also loved eating spice cookies during Christmas. Her siblings and she would normally get some version of what they had asked for from Santa. This meant a lot because her father worked very hard to provide for his family and they greatly appreciated it. During the Christmas season, the whole family would all pile in their car and shop in the "big" city. Some sad memories were also associated with the life on the farm. Her worst memory as a child on the farm was the loss of her dog, Bailey. She cried for days after Bailey was run over by a car and died.

Her father, being of European descent, was the definite head of the household. He was very firm, loving, and strict; he worked very hard to provide the best for his family. He wanted his children to grow up with good morals and good futures. While her father went to work on the farm, her mother was a full-time homemaker who took an occasional cleaning job for other people to raise a few extra funds. They were not extremely well off, so the extra money came in handy. Their family went to church twice every Sunday, as faith was of major importance and value to them. She was raised under the Christian Reform Denomination, as Catholicism and Christian Reform were two of the only religions in Holland at the time. They brought their faith with them in the move; and it continued to play a major role in her life, as she became a young and independent woman. Her father led them in devotions at every meal and she said her prayers on her knees every night. Her parents were born into a socialist economy, but they wanted to immigrate in order to escape to a free country. Even though they immigrated and wanted some change in lifestyle, their European cultural influences still remained prominent. She described her family as being very outspoken, somewhat stubborn, and not afraid of hard work. Her family loved tradition and keeping with their Dutch roots. Her parents worked hard and were associated with the middle class; they were not rich but worked very hard to make a good living. She grew up in a very adventuresome family that loved to explore and was not afraid of the changes that came as a result of the moves.

After finishing high school, at the age of 18, she moved to California. Her life was filled with freedom, beaches, boys, and a young adults' church group. After growing up on the farm this time was an amazing experience and change, all presenting good, clean fun for her. Three short years later, she married Christopher Bakker at the age of 21. She and Chris first met when her family moved to Pease, Minnesota; she was only eight years old at the time and he was just one year older. They attended the same church as well as the same school, but her family left that summer for Washington. It was not until he was 16 and his family ended up moving to Everson, Washington, as well that they met again. They again ended up going to the same church and the same school. She was so excited to see him and his curly hair when his family moved. They attended youth group together and shortly started dating and eventually were married.

She went to secretarial school and worked for a bank for several years, as it was what made sense to her father, but her dream was to be a flight attendant. She still slightly wishes she had pursued her dreams to become a flight attendant but is very thankful for the life God blessed her with. She and her husband, Chris, are blessed with four wonderful children and now further grateful for their eleven grandchildren, ranging in ages from two to twenty-two. As she looks back on her life, she is proud and thankful for her marriage and children and the joy that comes in seeing her children happy and healthy.

Going back to Europe, especially Holland, has been her favorite vacation as she has strong ties there. She finds it amazing to go back and see where she came from. In Europe, she also loved being in Prague as it is surrounded with beauty and amazing architecture. She loves the vast history it offers, as she claims history is her passion. She has many places she wants to go in the coming years in order to check them off her bucket list. The top place she desires to visit is Israel, as well as go back to places like Prague and Africa. She feels blessed to have traveled and seen so much but still would love to go experience more parts of the world.

CREDIT

Fig. 4.1.1: Source: https://commons.wikimedia.org/wiki/File:BC856_HUI-2050.jpg.

Long Beach, California (1945)

In the voice of the interviewee's grandmother.

FIGURE 4.2.1   The Pike Amusement Park, Long Beach, California, 1960

Hello, I am Constance Isabel Linden. I was born on the beautiful sunny day of May 12, 1945. I was born at the General Hospital in San Francisco, California. As you can tell, I was brought into this world nearing the end of the Second World War. I was one of eight children in my family. In order from youngest to oldest, my siblings are as follows: Wayne, Yvette, Ruthie, Elaine, Pearl, myself, Cathy, and Dottie. We were all born within ten years of each other, so we remained a pretty close family, although I grew closest to Pearl and Yvette over the early years of my life. We moved around more often than I would have liked as a child, so as kids we used to stick together and play outside almost every day that we were not in school. Due to our family constantly relocating, I did not enjoy school very much because friends were difficult to make and would be lost when we moved next. This only emphasized the importance of the relationships I had with my siblings and parents since I would always have them to rely on.

We siblings would play games such as hide-and-seek, tic tac toe, hopscotch, and jump rope with each other along with our neighborhood friends. Due to the limited income my family had, one of my fondest memories as a child was receiving the gift of a store-bought doll. I had a couple of handmade dolls at this time, but to receive a gift such as this was a very exciting moment for me. I took very good care of this gift for many years. During these years, it was very common and expected for the older of the siblings to look after the rest of the siblings while away from the house. Our parents depended on the eldest of us kids to make sure we got back home after a long day at play. In my generation, it was common for aunts, uncles, and grandparents all to live in the same neighborhood or very nearby. My grandparents used to tell me stories of their experience during the Great Depression. The various tactics that they came up with to get money back then still leave me in awe. In a way, we were partially still feeling the impact of this time period in my early childhood. The importance of family was always a trademark of the Lindens. When I was a young girl, we lived near Napa, California, and would often take fishing trips as a family to a creek nearby. This was one of the few distinct memories among my family that I can recall having much enjoyment. Having quality time outside of the house such as this was very important to us kids to provide additional bonding time as a family.

At the age of 15, we were living in Long Beach, California as a family, and my father was working at the time. By this time, I had grown especially close to my sister Elaine, and since we were not allowed to go out alone, we used to enjoy going out on walks on the Pike Boardwalk in order to get away from reality for a while. It was on one of these walks with "Lizzy" that I first ran into my husband Dennis Lang. Near dusk, we were walking around the Long Beach Naval base when we heard a couple of young sailors hollering at us. They were stationed here on the U.S.S *Thetis* aircraft carrier. After meeting these young men, my sister Elaine became fond of the sailor interested in her. I, on the other hand, wanted nothing to do with Dennis (even though he made it very apparent he liked me). Not long after this first meeting with the boys did they begin to make it a habit of throwing rocks at our window to get us to come out and meet them in our front yard. Over time, I began to grow fond of Dennis due to his gentlemanly behavior. Our father did not like the idea of us dating men in the Navy, but eventually they were allowed inside our house to be introduced to my parents and family.

It did not take long for me to fall for Dennis and run off with him to tie the knot. I was only 15 and a half and was already a married woman. Though it was not uncommon to get married at a much younger age in this day and age, I was among some of the youngest of my siblings to make the commitment. In a private hospital in Long Beach, at the age of 16, I had my first child, Dennis Lang, Jr. A couple years later, Dennis and I moved to Oakland, where he was stationed and where I had my first daughter, Marlena, at Oakland Naval Hospital. From this moment on, Marlena was my little playmate. I dressed her in cute outfits, took her shopping, and did all sorts of other activities with her. Dennis Jr. was with us most of the time as well but was much more interested in the activities of a boy at a young age. It was during this time in Oakland that I experienced one of the most memorable historical moments I can remember. I watched in horror as John F. Kennedy was shot in Dallas. I remember the shock that I felt and the feeling of vulnerability by the sight of his death. This was a terrible day for our country. Soon after this historical event, we moved into Washington State to Whidby Island where Dennis was stationed in the Navy. While living there I had my second son, Vance Lang, and only settled in for nine months before we moved back down to San Mateo, California for the last time. Over these next seven years, Dennis left the service and began working as an engineer. Meanwhile, I opened a daycare to look after my own children as well as many others. Throughout these years, I had several miscarriages that brought down our spirits, but only momentarily. To our surprise, I soon became pregnant yet again and gave birth to our final child, Jennifer Lang, in the hospital near the city of San Mateo. Jennie was our little surprise and, like youngest siblings, seemed to get spoiled much more than the others. I absolutely loved being a mother, involving myself in all of the children's school events, sports, and committees that were available, even the Boy Scouts. I made sure to include my children in many family activities so that they would also experience the importance of a close family as I had at a young age. We would often go to the San Francisco 49ers games as well as several Giants games. Camping was another frequent family event we had every year at the Russian River in Santa Rosa or at the beach at Coyote Point.

Since most of Dennis's family resided in Washington, we made our move up north once again. His parents and other family members were beginning to age, and he wished to be around them during their final years. Our final move up to Washington landed us in the city of Tacoma where I live today. Our first years up here I began to do some work on my own as a night janitor for churches and cleaning up construction from houses after they were finished. I also worked as the phone operator for Dennis's business, B & D Industrial, for some years after, making about $100 a week.

Some of my best accomplishments occurred in the 80s after living in Washington for several years. In July of 1986, Dennis was working when he took a spill down the cement stairs of the building. He suffered an enclosed head injury and terrible amnesia, losing memory of all his children except Dennis Jr. It took years to fully recover his memory from the accident. Although this was a horrific event for our family, it provided me with many new experiences of my own. When this happened, I was now responsible for the decisions of the family and Dennis's work. Still trying to work on my own, I was now also the caregiver for Dennis as well as taking over the responsibility of paying bills and driving Dennis around since he

Oregon (1945)

Written in third person by the interviewee's family friend.

FIGURE 4.3.1 Entrance to Disneyland, Anaheim, California, 1957

Cynthia Hanks, Cindy to her friends and family, was born on April 29, 1945, in Redding, California. She was the first child born to her parents Sam and Janet, their first girl. Sam's mother died when he was a child and, as a result, he spent most of his time caring for his siblings. Cindy remembers her father to be the most engaged parent out of the two. Her mom, Janet, grew up in Horse Creek,

California, but moved to Redding on her own when she was 14 to pursue a high school education. After Cindy was born the family moved to Oregon where they lived for about three years until they eventually moved back because Sam got a job with the railroad Freight Line; he was the youngest manager the company ever had. After working there for a couple years he left and started his own business in Redding renting logging trucks; Cindy's mother worked as a waitress.

Cindy's family eventually grew to six with the addition of her younger brother and sister. Her aunt and uncle, along with their two sons, lived in the same house with them, making their household busy with 11 people. Cindy loved having a lot of kids in the house; she thought it was really fun to always have other kids to play with. One activity that the kids would do was collect empty Coke bottles for which, in return, they would get five cents, which they would use to go to the movies. She did say that it was not always easy living with her cousins, though. Cindy did not think that her aunt liked her very much. She was the hired help and her aunt never appreciated all of the work she did for her family. Cindy's two cousins were older than she and were always trying to trick her into doing things that she knew would get her into trouble. She remembered one time when her cousins told her they would give her five dollars if she would dive to the bottom to see how deep a swimming hole was. After being in the water her dress was wet and she had to wait until her dress dried before she could go home and would not get in trouble with her mother. To make matters worse, she never got the five dollars. Looking back on this Cindy realized that the boys would not have even had five dollars to give her, but they always used that bribe to make her do things.

Because Cindy was the oldest girl and both her mom and aunt worked, she had the responsibility of the majority of the household chores. This was something she really did not like. Her parents were not home much, and Cindy always felt like she was in charge of all the younger kids; she would cook and clean up after them. At a young age it was instilled in her that the boys had more important things to do like basketball, Little League, and Boy Scouts. Her least favorite chore was washing the dishes for the 11 people in her house. One night she was particularly upset that she had to stay home to do the dishes and her brothers got to go to Boy Scouts, so she put all the dishes back wet to show her family how upset she was. This did not turn out well for her though; her aunt made her rewash all the dishes and dry them before putting them away, and she had to go to bed very late that night. Being in charge did come with at least one perk, though. Cindy's favorite holiday growing up was Easter because she always got to hide the Easter eggs from all of the younger kids and she really liked seeing how excited they were during the Easter egg hunt. Another fond memory she has from Easter is having her dad read them Easter books that she thought had very pretty illustrations.

Cindy lived in a low-income area; however, she considered her family to be lower middle class. They always had food to eat and owned their own home. Her family also went on vacation every year. Some places they went were Seaside, Oregon, the World's Fair in Seattle, Disneyland, and family camping trips. When asked about the World's Fair she said that she was young at the time but remembers being amazed by a large cylinder with one million $1 bills. At Disneyland she remembers going on "Peter Pan's Flight" with her two brothers. They hopped off the ride and ran around inside the ride and jumped back on just before the ride ended. She was convinced that they would get caught, but they were able to get away with this mischievous act. Cindy really liked going on camping trips with her family where she would fish and explore the campsite.

As a child Cindy loved playing outside. Her family lived on a large property where she could explore. When she was ten she got a pet donkey, Sadie, that she took on many adventures looking at mine shafts and cabins. Cindy said that these mine shafts and cabins were left over from the gold rush time period but that there were still spring beds and stoves in some of them. Also, her younger brother would help them pan for gold. Cindy said that her brother would pan for gold in their creek and then mix some dirt in it so his siblings could pan for gold easier. One time Cindy was so upset when she had come home from Girl Scouts because they would not let her fold the flag that she decided she would run away. She packed up her bags, took her donkey, and headed for the mineshafts. She was not gone for long, though, because as soon as it started to get dark and animals started making noises, she got scared and went home. When she was about ten she and her friends found "pirate food" that was marked with a skull and cross bones. While Cindy just sniffed it, her friend ate it, found out that it was actually rat poison, and had to get his stomach pumped.

Cindy also loved fishing in the dredger pond for perch; they built a raft so they could ride down the creek. Building these rafts was one of her favorite things to do because it made it easy for them to travel down the creek. Her favorite raft was about 8 to 10 feet long, 10 inches wide, and 10 inches thick. It was more like a plank, but it could fit three or four of the kids on it and take them down the creek easily. The raft had a hole in it for a rope and they left it tied up to their house. Cindy remembered the sad day when the creek flooded and her raft floated away. The next time she saw it the plank was lying in the middle of town. When she was young, she did not realize that her life was different than her other friends because she lived on a big lot and her friends lived in town. It was at her school reunion that she realized her friends had fond memories about the adventures they went on at her house.

Cindy always liked doing well in school; she was one of the top in her class up until sixth grade when school became more about socializing for her. Although she went to college and got her degree when she was older, she wishes that she were encouraged to go to college right out of high school. Cindy's dad told her that she was pretty enough to just get married, and her counselor told her that she would be a good waitress because she was friendly. She spent most of high school working, socializing, or partying. She made a lot of money waitressing and usually had more money than her friends. After high school she ended up moving to Sacramento, California, to go to court reporting school. This was around the time of the assassination of John F. Kennedy. The news of the assassination shocked

Cindy; she had actually had a picture taken with the former president just months before at the dedication of the Whiskeytown Reservoir in French Gulch, California. When Cindy heard the news that Kennedy had been shot she was in class at her court reporting school. Her class was dismissed early, and she went home to the boarding house she lived in at the time. She watched the news unfold on the television with the friends she lived in the house with. Cindy described the time as very sad because Kennedy was such a young president who was so well liked and the country was full of hope.

It was in Sacramento where she met her husband, Mark, who was in the Air Force. Cindy and Mark were married at 19 and moved to Germany shortly after they got married. At twenty years old she had her first child, her daughter Selena, and then at twenty-three she had her son Victor. Cindy remembered her time in Germany being tough as the locals always thought Cindy and her husband were wealthy Americans. She said that they always had to be careful and make sure that they were not over-charged for anything. She recalled one month when their electricity bill was outrageously expensive and realized that it was because the local people in their building were hooked up to her family's electricity. The bill ended up being much more than her family's income, and when she went to fight it, the tenants denied it. Once Mark was out of the Air Force, their first stop was Sacramento, but after Mark got a job in Oregon their family relocated to Lake Oswego. While this was a slight relief for Cindy, she did not enjoy living in Oregon either; she said it was always cloudy, rainy, and depressing. She also said that Oregon's cost of living was more than California.

After twenty years of marriage Cindy and Mark got divorced and Cindy moved back to Sacramento to pursue a degree in business communication at California State University, Sacramento. At the time she still had two children to support. Her daughter was involved in soccer when they got to Sacramento, and this led to Cindy start the first women's soccer team in Sacramento. It started because her daughter's team wanted to play the moms, but Cindy could not get enough participation from the moms on the team, so she had to ask other women in the community. Once the team was formed Cindy's team started playing men's teams. The next year another women's team formed and a year after that there were enough teams to start a league. She started working for the Pacific Gas and Electric Company (PG&E) because they paid for her tuition. Although she does not have any regrets from the life she has lived, this experience made Cindy realize the different kind of life that she could have had if she had gone to university right after high school. She wishes that it was made more of an option for her because she thinks that it would have helped her realize her potential. Cindy did not plan to stay at PG&E for long, but she said she got stuck there. Regardless, she ended up liking working there and stayed until her retirement. Cindy was on the Pacific Service Employees Association where she would organize events like talent shows, picnics, and casino nights. She loved working for the company and still keeps in touch with coworkers.

Currently, Cindy resides in northern California with her beloved dog, Tolly, and cat, Mischief. For the past couple of years her greatest challenge has been taking care of her 91-year-old mother who has Alzheimer's. Cindy really hopes that they find a cure for this disease as she has had a very hard time caring for her mother. She hopes that others will not have to worry about this disease in the future because of its emotional toll and expense. Overall, Cindy is proud of how she has managed her money and how frequently she travels. When she retired she had accumulated five rental properties that provide a good return that helps her travel. Some of her favorite places she has been include Finland, Guatemala, and Peru. Right now Cindy spends her time golfing, playing on a volleyball team, investing in the stock market, traveling, and spending time with her grandchildren. Cindy would like to continue traveling and going on more adventures; her bucket list includes going to places such as Thailand, Turkey, Cuba, and China, as well as going on a sailboat and snowmobiling.

CREDIT

Fig. 4.3.1: Source: https://commons.wikimedia.org/wiki/File:Entrance_to_Disneyland,_Aneka_Amerika_102_(1957),_p31.jpg.

Wisconsin (1945)

In the voice of the interviewee's grandmother.

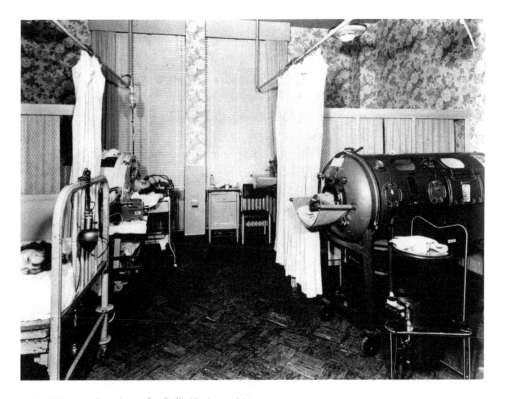

FIGURE 4.4.1   Iron Lung for Polio Victims, 1952

I, Deborah "Debbie" Jane Davidson, was born on July 8, 1945, at St. Joseph's Hospital in Marshfield, Wisconsin. It was one year and two days after D-Day, so World War II was just over. My status as the baby of the family lasted about ten minutes, and then my twin sister Donna Jo was born. We were the only children in our family of eight daughters to be born in a hospital, and my mom was under-whelmed by the hospital experience. A first-time mother got the delivery room before my mother, so Mom delivered us on a cot. Trust me when I say that this would not count as an optimal birthing environment.

I had seven sisters, and I loved them all pretty indiscriminately. Adeline, the eldest, was 16 years older than I, and left home when I was two years old. Beverly, the next, married right after World War II ended, so I cannot remember a lot about either one of them in the early years of my life. Cathy, Iris, and Easter were huge influences in Donna Jo's and my early life—especially Cathy, who gave awesome backrubs and was always the first line of defense against thunderstorms (which are common in Wisconsin). Genevieve, who was four years older than Donna Jo and I, was not enchanted with losing her status as the baby of the family and could be a bit of a challenge. Nonetheless, she turned out to be a great ally as we all grew up. I always felt loved by my siblings, and I loved them very much in return.

According to my mom, Donna Jo and I had our own universe—we slept in the same crib, frequently sucked each other's thumbs, and for a while as toddlers had our own language. With a few exceptions (Mom, Cathy, and Iris), most relatives and friends called both of us "Twin." This was not the best route to establishing an identity of my own. Our parents even dressed us alike until I rebelled in high school. I loved it when we attended high school, because teachers and our fellow students finally called us by our real first names.

When talking about what I enjoyed doing when I was younger, I use "us" instead of "me" because Donna Jo and I went nowhere without each other. Exploring the countryside was high on our list of fun things to do. We made forts in the woods, picked wildflowers, followed the creek that ran through our little village, and hung out with two cousins who lived nearby. As much as I loved the outdoors, once I learned to read, that was absolutely all I wanted to do for the rest of my life (until I discovered boys, of course, but I still read voraciously after that!). To this day, I still have at least four books going at any given time—and absolutely cannot fall asleep unless I can decompress for an hour or so with my daily devotional and a good book. I eventually settled on one "boy," which freed me up to read even more.

As a little girl, some of my happiest memories are of my mom lying down on her bed with my sisters and me and reading us books. I loved holidays, when all "the girls" would come home. I also loved to hide in a closet with a good book and a flashlight when Mom wanted me to work in the garden. Donna Jo and I would take turns helping while the other disappeared with a novel. I really enjoyed attending church with my family, especially during Lent. When we got sleepy, Daddy would put us on his lap and I'd fall asleep surrounded by peace and love. Since my dad died when I was still a teenager, he will always be "Daddy" to me, although I notice that my older sisters still call him Daddy, too. Shades of Southern womanhood in the Midwest!

Not all of my childhood memories are positive, though. The saddest memories of childhood for me were when, for several summers, we were not taken anywhere near crowds because of polio. These times made for quite an insular existence. Two of my sisters contracted mild cases of polio, and my parents were terrified of the disease because so many children died. The disease did not affect specific segments of the population; rather, even doctors "didn't know how to stop its spread, for it overran every boundary [they] tried to draw." I was very sad when my first cousin died of polio shortly after giving birth to her third child. It still makes me sad thinking of it. I was also frightened of war as a child because of the horror stories I heard about Korea from the older kids at school. That, and my interest in history, turned me into a passionate, lifelong pacifist.

I was told various stories about the lives of my mother and grandmothers. Mom's father was disabled in an industrial accident when she was very young. After the injury, he lived with the Salvation Army in Milwaukee and only occasionally visited his wife and six daughters in Central Wisconsin. My Grandma Delacroix supported her family by living and working in a central office in Arpin, Wisconsin, as a telephone operator. She came from Russia, but she was German. My mother's father, on the other hand, came from French Canada. My dad's parents came from Germany, and both sets of my grandparents settled in Central Wisconsin. When Mom was eight, she was sent to live with her maternal grandmother. At 15, she dropped out of school and was literally farmed out to a farmer and his family. She rarely spoke of that time in her life, and I got the feeling it was a hard childhood for her.

With the exception of my maternal grandfather, who was raised Roman Catholic, all of my grandparents were Lutheran. There are traditions and recipes from each family that I still maintain, but the strongest pull to me is the French connection. I love most things French and love the joy of living that is so much a part of France. My guess is that a lot of the intelligence in my family is thanks to the Germans, though—I raised two engineers!

Ours was a traditional family, but since my dad worked such long hours, Mom usually ruled the roost, albeit in a genteel way. Our family lived in Sherry, Wisconsin, during my early life, and once my folks built a house there in 1947 they were planted. The location was optimal for my dad's businesses, since it was equidistance to Marshfield, Wisconsin Rapids, and Stevens Point. My dad worked his way up, despite his eighth-grade education. He was entrepreneurial, owned his own cheese factory, logged his own lands, built an earthmoving construction company, and was president of an area bank. By the time of my earliest memories, the family was financially comfortable.

My sisters and I all attended Pershing Grade School, a three-room schoolhouse in Sherry, Wisconsin. It was heated by a pot-bellied stove (with a metal apron around it) in each room and had two outhouses and a well pump out in the yard. It did, fortunately, have electric lights. And books! The students were mostly from area farms, and by the time Donna Jo and I graduated from eighth grade, there were only eight children enrolled. We each taught one of the lower grades to help out the lone teacher, which was fine, because we had long since exhausted our little school library. A new consolidated school had been built, so Pershing was closed that spring. I hated, hated, hated going outside to the bathroom and would hold my bladder as long as possible to avoid it.

On a typical day when I was approximately ten years old, Donna Jo and I focused on avoiding polio. I do not know how the city kids fared, but we were limited to each other and our two cousins. My oldest sister, Adeline, took Donna Jo and me to Chicago for a week every summer, which we adored. She and her family lived a very upscale life in the penthouse of an apartment building my brother-in-law owned on Chicago's lakefront. Heaven!

When I was 19 years old, I married Sven Davidson. I had dropped out of a private women's college in Milwaukee, Wisconsin, during the second semester of my sophomore year to move home and help Mother take care of my dad, who had terminal cancer. Donna Jo had married the year before, so I was the only one left of the sisters who was able to do this. After his death, I transferred to University of Wisconsin-Stevens Point for the fall semester and met Sven there. I missed Donna Jo, I missed Milwaukee, I missed Daddy, and I was devastated by my mother's grief. Outside of that, I was pretty well adjusted!

Sven and I dated for only three months before we got married—and they said it wouldn't last. We'll celebrate our 47th wedding anniversary this February. I still laugh about the book I took along on our honeymoon: *The Feminine Mystique* by Betty Friedan. Poor, traditional Sven—he never knew what hit him! We had two sons, who have turned out wonderfully well. I always said I knew God had a sense of humor, giving someone who had never been around boys two little boys to raise. He made amends by giving me two granddaughters.

All the women in my family had careers outside the home, except for Mom. Adeline poured her heart into volunteer work after her marriage, but she was a pediatric nurse before she married. Although I was the first to earn a college degree, all of us had further training for our occupations and made our own career choices. Sven and I both had college degrees, so even though our early years of marriage were a struggle, we have always lived comfortably. My dad was adamant that his daughters should be educated beyond high school. He frequently told us that we could be anything we wanted to be—we would just have to work harder for it than men did. What a legacy!

Mom, with her insecure childhood, just wanted all her daughters to marry and be secure, but there was never, ever any hint of bias from either of my parents. The Bible was their basis and Jesus was their role model. They did not preach, they did not proselytize; they just lived their faith. What a remarkable lesson for all of us! My mom's mother was the only grandparent I had, and her life was so hard, she just wanted everyone to be happy. (My favorite quote of hers was, "Don't talk to me about the good old days—there was nothing good about them.") Grandma's greatest blessing was that all her children survived, referring to the high rate of infant mortality at that time and the terrible flu epidemic of 1918, when her daughters were youngsters. She also enjoyed television and her indoor toilet. Amazing, when you think that she crossed the Russian steppes in a covered wagon to immigrate to America and lived long enough to see a man on the moon!

Being a wife and mother was what I chose to be. It bore little resemblance to the lives of wives and mothers I had observed as I grew up. I was *finally* able to create an identity for myself, so I figured it better be something I could respect and, eventually, love. Once I figured out that little boys were more like puppies (probably black labs) than little girls, I started relaxing and enjoyed the experience. And my sons.

I personally worked as a humor columnist for the local newspaper for eight years and it was the culmination of my dreams. A dream job. A financial nightmare. Male columnists were hired and got benefits. I was paid as a freelancer, even though I was writing five columns a week, and the per-column rate was laughable. I had promised to get a "real job" when the kids were ready for college, so I packed up and joined the corporate public relations world when that time came. A nightmare job. (My first day, my manager took me on a coffee break, sat me at a table with six other men, and proceeded to tell the filthiest joke I had ever heard.) A dream financially. Eventually, I pulled myself together, made my job into something challenging and fulfilling, and got enough promotions to consider it a successful endeavor. The company sent me back to school for an MBA degree. This job helped get my kids through college and helped me amass a comfortable retirement nest egg.

Seventeen years later, the company was absorbed by a merger and my entire department was "outsourced." I could not stand the thought of another corporation, so I followed my passion and went to work for a jewelry store that had integrity, creative genius, and enough sparkly objects to keep me enchanted. After eight years, I just could not handle another Christmas season of working around the clock and being too exhausted to enjoy my family. I thought I would retire. Now, I work a couple days a week fitting dancers with their footwear. I always was intrigued by ballet and wanted to learn more. I'm getting the itch to write again, so this winter I'd like to try my hand at blogging. (Oh, yes, and I'm helping out a bit back at the jewelry store for the Christmas season.)

There are a few experiences and accomplishments in my life that I am most proud of. First, through my column, I was a voice for women's rights, peace, acceptance of alternative lifestyles, and tolerance of other cultures—and I did it through humor. Also, I am proud that I raised my sons into two fine young men who have given me great joy. Third, I developed a partnership with my husband and fell in love again (he traveled a lot during his career, so things were not always nirvana when the kids were growing up). Finally, I am proud that I can be a strong, loving influence on my granddaughters—what a joy!

Some women in particular have had a great influence on my life. My twin is one of these women because, through her, I learned to live closely with a person whose personality was very different from my own (great training for marriage!). My mother, as well, influenced me through her depth of faith and integrity, as did Hanna Allison, my high school English teacher, for her intelligence and belief in my writing talent. I greatly admire Eleanor Roosevelt for her resilience and empathy.

My other sisters, as well, influenced me with personality traits that I admired and continue to cultivate.

Historically, the polio vaccine influenced my life by lifting a huge pall that hung over our nation. Those poor parents! I cannot imagine the terror of watching that scourge on the heels of the Great Depression and World War II. I was also affected by the equal rights sit-ins and marches of the 1960s, which were scary but too important to sit out. I learned that it's okay to be scared if you believe in something strongly enough. As a woman, I empathized with minorities, so I probably was demonstrating as much for myself as I was for them. I loved all the computer breakthroughs (it was a drag to have to make three carbon copies in the newsroom when I first worked there). Long live Microsoft Word, the writer's salvation! In addition, if I was a pacifist before Vietnam, that "police action" really galvanized me.

In my life, one of the major psychological barriers I had to overcome was finding an identity that I could call "me" after almost 18 years of playing the role of clone. Socially, I had to overcome the difficulty of fighting sexual and racial discrimination in a "socially acceptable" manner in the 1970s, 1980s, and even 1990s. Also, I felt responsible for creating opportunities for young women who worked for me. I developed the first job-share arrangement, a practice often described as an employment solution for women and "a compromise between full-time housework and full-time employment," in a corporation of seventy thousand employees.

Since I was a child, ideas about women and women's roles have changed drastically. It's a different world, a different universe—thank God! Every time I hear a young woman say, "Oh, I'm not one of those strident women's libbers," I want to shake her until her teeth rattle and ask her how she thinks she was able to make it to the executive suite.

If I had to live my life over, I would not do *anything* differently. Every mistake I made (and there were many), every misstep I took (plenty of those, too), every wrong turn was a lesson learned. And along the way, I had epiphanies, met people whose lives have enriched mine, experienced things I swore I'd never have the courage to do but that have expanded my emotional frontiers and have, for good or bad, made me who I am today: Debbie.

CREDIT

Greeley, Colorado (1946)

Written in third person by the interviewee's grandson.

FIGURE 4.5.1   John F. Kennedy Presidential Campaign, Florida, 1960

When Elvira Schmidt was born in the Weld County General Hospital in Greeley, Colorado, on October 8, 1946, to many it probably looked like just another baby coming into this world, but they were wrong. This one was special for many reasons. For starters, Elvira was the last of four children to be born from German immigrants, all of whom were much older than she. As a matter of fact, they were 19, 18, and 14 years older to be precise. What is even more impressive about it is the fact that she was the first child to be born in a hospital; the rest were born "on the farm," so to say. But that is only one facet of the life and times of Elvira Schmidt. She is, and always has been, a working, independent woman, even in times when it was not socially acceptable to be one. She has traveled and lived in places many women from rural Colorado have not even seen or dreamed of before. She has lived through wars, rebellion, and riots, and she has some things to say about them.

When Anna Schmidt was brought into this world, little did her parents know that 19 years and two more children later, they would have her last child, Elvira. In between those two were Olga and Albert, respectively. Elvira was close to them all, but since the age difference was so great, her siblings were more like mother and father figures than sisters and brothers. Her sisters, Anna and Olga, were both married when Elvira was very young, and Olga lived near Elvira for as long as she could remember. Olga's husband, Dirk Huber, farmed with Elvira and Olga's father, so they were always nearby. By the time Elvira was two, she was already an aunt, but this did not really mean much to her until later in life. It is hard to imagine being an aunt and wanting to play with your nieces and nephews because they are as old as you are, have the same interests as you, and look on you as a friend as opposed to an adult. As a matter of fact, when Anna came home and brought her children along, it was almost like they were all trying to gain the attention of the older family members. Her brother Albert graduated college and became a premier pilot in the Air Force. All this occurred before Elvira was ten years old. It was almost like she was an only child, but that did not stop her from having an entertaining childhood.

As a young girl living on the farm, Elvira found many ways to entertain herself. She was not within walking distance of any of her schoolmates, and she was about 2 miles away from her school. "Sometimes I was with my mom, but I was never into cooking, or cleaning, or ironing. I was outside most of the time. I was either by myself or helping my dad. But I never remember being bored." With living on the farm came the usual menagerie of pets. They had a horse, a cow that Elvira never learned how to milk, and chickens that she did not care for too much. The most important of all the pets, though, was her parakeet, Pepper. Sometimes during the day, her mother would open the bottom of the birdcage and let the bird rest its feet on the warm cement. When one of the hired hands' children decided to lift the cage up so the bird could fly away, Pepper went missing. Elvira then spent the next three days running around with a cowbell looking for her bird calling out, "Pepper! Pepper!" She was too young to understand that Pepper would not be coming back, but her father knew the little bird could not survive for long on its own out in the wilderness of Colorado.

When Elvira talks about her grandparents, there is one thing that sticks out in her mind: the fact that her grandmother almost never spoke English. They lived in a mostly German community called Windsor. With her grandma being an immigrant, she had no use for speaking in anything except her native tongue. Even after her grandparents had been living in America for over fifty years, she did not hear her grandmother speak English. There was one exception she could think of, the time when her grandmother was talking to her granddaughter-in-law, Rosa, but it was only for a few sentences. Elvira's parents spoke in German as well, when they did not want her to understand what they were saying. Elvira was amazed to be born in the United States, saying, "It is amazing that we are first-generation born, and we are so 'Americanized.' It is hard to believe."

As Elvira became old enough to attend school, the school system had a country school up to the seventh grade. A country school is a public school that is located in the country. Being in the country, the school did not have an indoor bathroom until Elvira was in the fourth grade. It was very cold in the winter in Colorado, so walking outside the warm classroom to use the restroom in the middle of winter was not too pleasant. However, when the school finally did build indoor facilities, there was only one bathroom. Elvira remembers, "Girls had to understand that this was the only time that they got to go into the boy's room. I remember that the faculty was always real worried about that. It was funny stuff."

As Elvira was growing up, she learned about living in an environment that was not always forgiving, and when her father died of cancer when she was 14 years old, not only did her mother move them to the city, but they also began to drift apart. She states,

> After dad died, I was not the best kid, and my mother was not the best mother. It was interesting. I guess we were both dealing with our loss. She was in her fifties by then, and all of my friend's mothers were much younger than her. We did not communicate very well for years.

This was a very difficult time for her. All of her siblings were older than her and living elsewhere. They had lived on the farm her entire life, and now they had no one to tend to it. In 1961, they packed up the farm and headed to Greeley, Colorado.

As it turned out, the new house that Elvira would call home was only about a block away from the Greeley High School football field. As Elvira went through high school, there were just some subjects that she did not find interesting, such as science. She disliked it strongly, and math was not that much fun either, but it was at least tolerable. The one subject she did like was social studies, and she liked Mr. Klein, her teacher:

> He was gruff but interesting. I remember in November of 1963 when Kennedy was shot, they had just announced over the intercom that Kennedy was dead; we had already known that he had been shot, but the announcement came that he was dead. Mr. Klein just laid his head down on the desk and started crying. I had never seen a man cry before. Those were really hard times. Then that Sunday, I was waiting for my girlfriend to come pick me up to go to church, and I was watching the television and I saw Jack Ruby murder Lee Harvey Oswald live. I was one of millions of people to actually see someone murdered in live time. It made me sick to my stomach.

As a young woman in her teens, Elvira Schmidt had already seen her father die of cancer, made a big move to a place where she was the newcomer, and had been a witness to one of the most tragic happenings in the history of the United States.

In 1964, Elvira became extremely interested in politics. It was the election of 1960 that opened her eyes to the world of politics when John F. Kennedy was elected as president. Elvira says jokingly, "I had an aunt that just did not know what to do because she just could not accept that fact that a Catholic was going to be our next president." It was the 1964 election between Lyndon B. Johnson and Barry Goldwater and the Vietnam War that actually kept her up with everything that was going on in the society around her.

> In Greeley, everyone had the opinion that we should go in and bomb the Vietnamese, and that was what Goldwater was saying. Of course that is what Johnson did anyway, and I hated it. I was lucky enough to only lose two close friends in the war, but I had three really close friends who came back from the war and were never the same again. That hurt me. That is when I started to notice that drugs were becoming a big thing for veterans. It was about the time I was twenty or twenty-one.

By this time, Elvira had made up her mind that she did not want to live in the small, Midwestern environment any longer. She decided to pick up and move to California. Her family was unsure of her decision. At her age, all three of her older siblings were married and had children, but that was something that Elvira did not see in her future, and with that she moved to Los Angeles.

When Elvira reached California, it did not take her long to fit in, and she got a job working as a receptionist for a mortgage company. She made $320 a month. It was a substantial amount of money for her at the time, and she remembers always having enough spending money to make her happy. She lived in California for about two years and ended up moving back to Colorado for three years and getting married. She was married for four years, but soon realized that it was not something she wanted.

> I think it has been about twenty years since we split up, but I am not sorry that I did it. It was a good experience. It was not always pleasant, but it was a good experience. I am not very good marrying material. He just was not that I wanted, when I wanted it.

With that all behind her, Elvira had finally decided to make her last move and ended up back in Los Angeles and in a place that she feels was made for her.

Since 1987, Elvira has lived her life the way she has always wanted to, in a place that she feels is home. She has witnessed the great earthquake of 1991 and the Los Angeles race riots of 1993, but most importantly she has found a lifestyle that she likes and feels comfortable with. For many years, she had been working for different mortgage companies, and she felt that it was time to make a change.

I had been in mortgage all my life, and I was getting tired of management and being responsible for everyone else. Now I work for a software company and am the assistant to the president and vice presidents. I just do my job and do it as well as I can. One of my friends said that I had copped out, and maybe I have, but whatever job makes me happy, I will do it. I would rather be doing something that I want to do and something that is making me happy than anything that makes me unhappy. Of course I should not say that because if I did not have to work, then I probably would not. It's all about being happy.

For Elvira Schmidt's whole life, she has been an independent woman and thinker and doer, even in times when it was not politically correct to be so. But she does not mind it. She has lived her life the way that she has wanted to live it, and now she can sit back and look at the world and know that she had made something for herself without the help of anyone except herself. That is a good feeling to have, and one that she would not trade for the world.

CREDIT

Fig. 4.5.1: Source: https://commons.wikimedia.org/wiki/File:John_F._Kennedy_campaigning_in_Florida_1960.jpg.

Tennessee (1946)

Written in third person by the interviewee's granddaughter.

FIGURE 4.6.1 Sit-In at Lunch Counter in Nashville, Tennessee, 1960

William Fletcher said, "We live in a hectic, rapidly changing, highly mobile world, where family have become physically and emotionally disconnected … millions of people yearn to reconnect in some way with the continuity of their family's experience." Personally, this is a true statement, which is why interviewing my grandmother about her life experiences was so important. History books can only reveal so much about what it was like to live during a certain time. My 69-year-old grandmother could fill in the blanks and offer a unique perspective on the life in the 40s up to today. Tamara Peterson is not a famous figure, yet her story is an important source of family history, and her experience does offer a glimpse of the Black experience during her lifetime.

Tamara Gray Peterson remembers a good childhood experience. She was born on September 4, 1946, in Nashville, Tennessee. Connor, her brother, was the oldest and Lauren, her sister, was the youngest. For fun, Tamara and her siblings would tell scary stories to one another, and Lauren would always get scared. Sometimes they would camp out, but Tamara said she did not really like doing that sort of thing. They would also ride bikes, make mud pies outside, or even catch frogs at night. During the 1940s and 50s the manufacturing of paper dolls was very popular. As a young girl, Tamara especially liked to play with such dolls. She had movie star paper dolls, and she and her friends would dress them up like they were going to the hotel. She learned about staying in a hotel from seeing them on television. She recounts how her siblings had a sense of humor too. They once told their father that the local bus had broken down and that a plane came by and picked them up and dropped them off at home. Their father believed that story.

Tamara recalls that her everyday life growing up included school, church, and entertainment. She remembers going to school and doing homework. During this time, American education was segregated, especially in the South. Segregation made it harder for Blacks to be educated and keep a job, but her father did make more money than some of the educated teachers. Still living in the South, as a Black person, was difficult because there was a lot of racism. She used to walk clear across town to attend junior high, passing White schools that she was not allowed to attend. Her school was about 10 miles from her home. Traveling to school, she never could understand why she could not go to those other schools. They were after all, much closer to her home. Her mother would buy bus tokens once a month, but since there were three children, they could only take one bus ride per day. Tamara was tired after school, so she chose to use her token to take the public bus home. At this time there were no school buses. In the summer Tamara and her sibling sometimes chose to walk home, except it was very hot. She sometimes still dreams about taking a short cut.

Aside from walking a great distance to school, Tamara also did not like getting spankings at school. Back in this time teachers were allowed to hit their students, but Tamara's mother told her not to let the teachers spank her. Tamara's mother refused to let the teachers hit her because she did not think it was right. When Tamara told her teacher what her mother had said, she was sent to the office and given her walking papers. This is similar to being suspended from school. Her mother had to come back with Tamara and talk to the principal. By the time they came back there was a new principal named Master Dr. Powell. Her mother explained to the principal that Tamara "had a chip on her shoulder." Tamara turned and looked at her shoulder because she didn't know what her mother meant. Dr. Powell told her, "No one's ever going to hit you again." That was a defining moment for her and after she graduated from college she went back and looked him up and told him how he inspired her.

Another thing Tamara recalls about school is the clothes they wore. When she was in school they wore elastic halter tops, straight skirts, which are called pencil skirts today, Bermuda shorts made out of plaid, Orlon soft sweaters, and felt skirts with poodle dolls on them. She owned buckskin shoes, saddle oxford shoes, and also a pair of turquoise suede loafers. Ponytails were popular, but they did not have straighteners. She did not press her hair but instead washed it and pulled her curly hair into a bushy ponytail. Tamara also says that the cheerleaders wore their skirts below the thigh, not just below the butt like cheerleaders today.

Sara, Heather, and Nancy were her friends from the cheerleading team. Nancy was a true friend and the rest of the girls were, for the most part, how teen girls can be. Nancy meant a lot to her because usually one does not have a lot of true friends. Socially Tamara was very good. She performed in a lot of shows such as playing the role Little Red Riding Hood and Carmen, as well as singing and dancing in shows like Jambalaya.

She felt her experience was similar to other kids she knew because she had a mother and father and had a good home. Her family lived in a church-going neighborhood, and they always ate at the table because food was a big thing. Cooking was part of their culture; they ate soul food or Black cooking. She was proud of her heritage; however, she did not let the culture tell her how to live. She marched to the beat of her own drum. As middle-class Black people, her family did not feel like they could just get up and move away. There was always cautioned because neighbors or people could be racist.

Her church was also part of her culture; it was how she socialized. Every Sunday Tamara attended church service. The older people sang in the choir, but not the younger people. The pastor preached and yet she never understood what he was talking about. The pastor's wife would come to church late. She dressed up real nice as the other women did. The younger people were given a card with a picture and a Bible verse. Her mother would give her a nickel, and she thought it was to pay for the card. In reality, the nickel was for the church offering. In church the kids had to be on their best behavior because parents did give spankings at church. On Easter, the church hosted events for the kids. The old deacon would hide eggs in the schoolyard and give out paper bags filled with candy canes, apples, nuts, oranges, and other goodies. When she would play "Church" she told herself she was not going to wear a big frumpy hat or shout out in church like the parishioners commonly did.

Her parents brought her up in the church, which was good. They provided her a good life. She felt she had toys and clothes, a house, cars, and good food. Tamara never knew what it was like to go hungry. She thought that they were well off. Even during the hard times her mother fed the family grits, but she liked eating grits. Tamara had even more things she wanted from working part-time as a house cleaner, making just fifty cents an hour. That was good money. She lived in a decent home, but it was always cold because there was no ventilation. They had an oil stove and would heat brick and wrap it in newspaper. This was not safe since houses were always catching on fire. Her grandmother also made them quilts to help keep them warm. The temperature was the only thing that seemed a little wrong with her home. Her parents made a house of love. She would often stay up late with her family and watch movies. Dorothy Dandridge was one of her favorite actresses. Her family also liked to listen to the music of artists like Edda James and the Supremes. Sara didn't have a father.

When she compares herself to other families like Sara's, who had only one parent and was living in a shotgun house, she feels she was blessed to have her home and parents. She especially admires her mother, who was an amazing person. Tamara remembers her mother's cooking and spending time with her parents. She liked when her mother made hot chocolate after she came home from school. Her mother used to tell them stories and put them in good clothes. She says her mother wore real pretty clothes. A special memory is one day when it snowed and her mother stayed home from work. Tamara spent the whole day with her. Her mother was very educated because she went to a private school. She was later trained as a nurse, but at the time that was "dirty work," so she took a job with the Red Cross. Tamara's mother liked to cater parties, and she was a good cook. For example, on Christmas she whipped up Smithfield ham, biscuits, eggs, fried potatoes, and fried apples. She used to celebrate birthdays, but not every year. They were not as big of a deal. In fact, she does not remember attending many birthday parties. Tamara's mother also talked about politics and loved President Roosevelt and cried when he died. Her mother was very influenced by Eleanor Roosevelt, saying she was the kind of woman who could relate to anyone. Tamara never remembers her exercising. She was busy with other activities though. She used to write plays and perform in them, play the piano, and she could sing, too. She would help the neighbors as well as the poor. She was like a mother hen, meaning she was very protective but did not sound a trumpet about it.

Her mother sometimes used to argue with her father. This did not make her feel sad because she knew they loved each other. A sad day for her parents was when her father lost his job as a janitor at the Tennessee Valley Authority. He could hardly read but always found work. He was by no means a professional but worked odd jobs, like a chef cook. He was able to buy a home, and they had everything a family could ever want. Tamara's family had the latest commodities. He got them a television, which was nice to have. It was a black-and-white television, and they used to put a plastic cover on it to get color, but it did not work right. She had a transistor radio (plays it with batteries) and a track player, which was a big deal back then. He worked a lot and was tired, so he drank when he came home. He would drink from real glass jars. Her father was not a mean drunk; he was actually really funny. Whenever he drank he would start acting crazy. At five foot one, people used to call him a "Geechy." This refers to having a dialect that is a mixture of English and African languages. They were from the John's Island part of South Carolina, full of hard-working Black people. His ancestors were from Guiana. A doctor later affirmed them to Tamara, by analyzing her blood cells. Her mother adored her father, but there was not family support of the union. Tamara's maternal grandmother did not want them to marry because her father was not educated.

Her maternal grandmother and family were educated folks. She was very educated and sophisticated; some called her a snob. As a seamstress, people would bring her pictures and her grandmother would make them. They were descendants of a Cherokee Indian and African American slaves. Even though her great grandparents were slaves, they were able to acquire land and eventually were well off. Her grandparents had houses where they smoked meat and were likewise very prosperous. Her grandmother's hair was so long she could sit on it. People used to comment on her hair because it was so long; she would not cut it but instead burn the ends off. Sadly, her grandmother died of cancer when Tamara was just six weeks old.

Sixteen years later, Tamara was a young woman with a new life ahead of her. Her music teacher had helped put together music groups. Tamara sang with one of the groups. Her boyfriend, Franklin Miller Peterson, sang with another group called June as they traveled promoting their music. The manager of the groups was an ex-convict who was sleeping with the music teacher. The groups broke up. By this point, they were so disappointed and tired of school. Franklin decided to join the Navy and asked Tamara to marry him. She was not sure so she told him to go to boot camp and that she would think about it. She married Franklin in their last year of high school. She was okay being married because that was the thing to do. Her mom and dad were married and so were his parents, so marriage was not unusual. Going to school was not a big deal at this time. The television encouraged and socialized women to get married. After getting married, they moved to California, and Tamara attended high school. She was big and pregnant but had to go there, because they did not offer adult education. She was 17 when she graduated. It was very important to her mother that Tamara finished school, and Franklin promised he would see to it that she finished. He kept his promise. Tamara moved back to Nashville to go to nursing school when her husband went on leave.

During this time, she and her husband matured. Tamara was now a mother and had really grown up. She had a good marriage, with her kids and school keeping her balanced. She liked learning things, so school was good for her. When she became a nurse she worked in homes and felt she was paid fairly well and made a decent living. She later graduated from nursing school with a bachelor's degree and had one of the highest scores on the state board. Eventually she received her master's in counseling. If she could go back in time she would have gone to a university as a traditional student. There was a lot of immaturity as a teen, like how she tried to get pregnant. She says maybe she should not have had kids so soon. Still, she is thankful for the path God put her on. Like leaving home and growing up, getting out of the South was important for her life.

Although Tamara would have done things differently, she was proud of the role she played as wife and mother. Those women's liberation movements were not appealing to her. With working, she always felt there were differences between men and women. As a married woman she thought women were supposed to be submissive. It was not until after her husband died and she went into counseling did she understand women, like herself, could take leadership positions. This helped her to define who she was. In relationship to the feminist movements she says Black women were different. They never had a problem with the male/female discrepancy. Being a Black female, she never had a problem working. She was always free to work and never felt competition with men. Actually, she was fine staying at home with her and Franklin's five children. She never believed she needed to be liberated. White women were more likely not to have to work whereas Black women needed to work. She says as a Black woman she would have loved to stay at home.

Tamara acknowledges that the way women aspire for careers is different than when she grew up. This is because of the changing economic system. When she grew up only one parent needed to work, but today both man and wife have to work. This has created a lot more opportunities for women. The success of women represents the political and social changes that happened in her time.

Tamara has witnessed so many of these changes, starting with the civil rights movement. She felt defiant and chose not to protest because she was too angry from living in the racist South. For example, she refused to participate in a sit-in because she could not submit to that abusive situation. One time, when she needed to take her son to the bathroom she was told by the store owner that she would have to use a separate bathroom in the basement. She replied, "Not today." They did not have to use the basement bathroom. Working at a nursing home, she was the only one qualified to manage. The manager told her he did not want a Black woman working at the front desk. Another day she recounts was President Kennedy's death. That was the saddest day of her life. Everyone was dragging around that day. The war in Vietnam changed her life. There was so much despair in the world. They were making Woodstock, which is like a rowdy concert. Kids got naked and had orgies, lots of people were smoking dope, and the flower children were protesting. Tamara was afraid to raise her children in an immoral world. This is when she became a Christian. Most recently in her life was the inauguration of the first Black president, Barak Obama. All of her life she lived and never dreamed that would happen. It was phenomenal to see history in that way.

She has come a long way from childhood in Tennessee. Today she is remarried to Dale Underwood and is currently working on her PhD in adult education. She has five children and thirteen grandchildren, and if anyone of us ever tried to pull one over on my grandmother she would say, "Oh give me a break; I wasn't born yesterday."

CREDIT

Poland (1947)

Written in third person by the interviewee's grandson.

FIGURE 4.7.1   The *Palmach*, Immigration to Israel, 1947

Ruth Zaleski was born on February 9, 1947, in Walbrzych, Poland. Her young life was struck with tragedy early on when her father was murdered. He had gone into the city to search for family members after the end of World War II but never came back. Word reached Ruth and her mother that he was killed because he was Jewish. Despite the fact that in Poland women had many choices, were given many freedoms, and were allowed to work, life was still hard for a single mother and her young daughter. Ruth's mother thus taught her daughter to be strong.

That strength could be seen in Ruth's mother, even when she was a little girl. Her mother was a young ten-year-old girl when the Second World War began. She would see the people being taken away in the trains to the camps but had no idea where they were going or what was going to happen to them. Ruth's mother and sister were standing by one of the trains when a trusted relative saw them and called out to them. The relative told the girls to run away and never look back or return. The girls did what they were told and never saw the relative again. The girls ran into a forest so they would not be found and lived there for almost six years. They suffered living in such hard conditions, and Ruth's aunt even lost her toes to frostbite. Both girls had blonde hair, could speak Yiddish (which was very similar to German), and did not look "Jewish" and were thus saved from being caught by the soldiers.

In Poland during this time, it was common for multiple families to live together. Ruth's family lived with her aunts, uncles, and cousins. Ruth's mother was a central figure in the household because she worked so many hours and her husband was no longer there. Her uncle also had some influence, although not as much as Ruth's mother. Since her father died early on in her life, Ruth did not have any siblings, although she did have the two cousins who lived with her. They played together, especially in the snow. Ruth really enjoyed the snow. It was so white and the air was very crisp. She would slide up and down all over the tiny hills with the family sled. She had to share it with her cousins, but they still managed to have fun. They also had snowball fights.

When she was still young, her uncle sent her a doll from America. Everyone in town wanted the doll because it was from America. No one else had it. Everyone thought it was very special because it was American.

Ruth was very sad to leave Poland and all of her friends when she and her mother moved to America in 1956. It was common in Poland that when word went around that a family was leaving for the states, non-Jewish people robbed the family. Ruth was very scared that they would steal her from her mother. No such occurrence happened though, and they left Poland by train to Italy. From Italy, they took a ship to Israel. The voyage took two weeks. Those two weeks were enjoyable for her, since she felt safe on the boat even though she did get a bit seasick. In Israel, they then got on another boat and sailed to America. It was a beautiful ride, and Ruth remembers fondly seeing the Statue of Liberty for the first time. Once they arrived in New York, the family traveled by train frequently, looking for a job for her mother. They lived with Ruth's uncle for a while, and whenever he moved, Ruth and her mother moved with him.

So many moves looking for work and following an uncle made it hard for Ruth to make friends. As soon she made a friend it was time to move again. Ruth did manage to make a close friend who she said supported her no matter what, and who she still is in contact with today. She also had some friends from different backgrounds, which made it easier to understand each other's lifestyles. Ruth did go to school, attending all of the grades, and went to both Los Angeles High School and Fairfax High School. The children were cruel to her because it was difficult to learn English and she did not always speak correctly. She tried very hard to not let the teasing bother her and to try to better learn the language. She eventually became a citizen, something she is very proud of.

Ruth's family always strongly encouraged her to get married and have children. Even though her mother went against that familial expectation by working, it was understood to be a necessity for survival since Ruth's mother was the sole provider. Ruth did work for a while in a downtown Los Angeles clothing and shoe store before getting married when she was 21 years old. Her husband came from an Orthodox Jewish background and was a pharmacist. She had four children. Even though being a wife was a lot of work, she enjoyed it. From her mother, she learned how to raise her own children. Ruth credits her greatly, saying that she would not have been able to raise her four children without her mother's guidance. Ruth has other woman she greatly admires, in addition to her mother. Golda Meier, the Israeli prime minister, is very important to Ruth because she had many hopes and ideas for Israel. She was so involved in her country, especially as an educational speaker.

CREDIT

Fig. 4.7.1: Source: https://commons.wikimedia.org/wiki/File:PikiWiki_Israel_20841_The_Palmach.jpg.

Louisiana, US (1952)

As told by the interviewer's family friend.

FIGURE 4.8.1   Orphans in Kigali, Rwanda, 2000

I am a southern girl named Sherilynn Balsley, but everyone calls me Sherri. I was born in Shreveport, Louisiana, on October 4, 1952. My parents already had one child, my brother Alan, who was two years older that I was. We had a sweet relationship. We depended on each other since we really only had each other. My early life was constant change. One day we were at one school only to be moved the next day. We pretty much lived like street kids most of the time. When I was nine, a Christian juvenile judge placed us both in the home. Our relatives could not take care of us.

We interviewed for the Louisiana Baptist Children's Home at ages 9 and 11, but my brother did not want to go. Later a new superintendent came and we were admitted at ages 10 and 12 in 1962. They did not take children older than 12. My first impression was that there were many children to play with, tall swings, good roads to ride a bike, plenty of food to eat, and a bed of my own.

We moved to the home together. I brought my bike with me. I had to share it with forty other girls, so I did not get to ride it often. My most difficult time was my first day at the home. A little girl named Joan told me she hated me and that she wanted me to go back where I came from. She was a little bully, and I was the new girl. I was getting the attention that day. I cried that night and asked God why I was there. Years later He showed me the answer when God called me and my husband to serve with an international ministry for vulnerable children and adults.

After we moved to the home I was able to have a limited relationship with my parents. They were divorced, so I wrote them letters and could see them for holidays if my grandmother or aunt requested us being with them for holiday. My parents did not have legal custody of my brother or me.

At the home the boys lived on one side of the campus and the girls on the other. There were five boys' cottages and four girls' cottages. There were nine cottages on the campus. I lived in two of the cottages during my nine years at the home. My first one was designated for girls 6 to 10, with 21 girls in the cottage. The second one had older girls, and we had between 12 and 14 girls. We had a large dorm room with a partition down the middle with half the girls on each side. Later they divided it into four rooms to make it even more private. I had a wonderful housemother. She always had time for me, and I loved her like she was my mother. The home required her to take time off, and they would send in substitute house parents for the relief weekend or vacation.

My average day was getting up at 5:30, dressing in play clothes, doing chores, and eating breakfast in the central dining hall at 6:45. After breakfast we went back to the cottage to dress for school. As a high school student I had to help prepare breakfast, so the day started earlier. The girls had to clean the tables, wash and dry dishes, and set the tables for the next meal. Besides the dining room duties I mentioned earlier, I was assigned to clean the den of the housemother. I can run an industrial buffer with the best of them on hardwood floors.

Church was a big part of my life. We went to church on Sunday but had Wednesday night services on the campus. I was active in the youth group, youth choir, and mission activities of the church. There was also Christian training and the joy of attending church on the weekends. We were allowed to participate in children and youth activities at the local churches we attended. The children attended five different churches in Monroe, Louisiana.

Some women from the local churches would come for birthday celebrations each month. I always wanted my own cake but obviously the cake was for everyone having a birthday that month. I planned even as a child to have a cake for myself when I was grown and made sure my children always had their very own birthday cake. Christmas was a fun time. We would write letters to our sponsors and ask for three things. The sponsor was usually a church. They would send money to pay for clothes, allowances, plus give gifts at Christmas. Many people also brought gifts to the home. My first Christmas at the home as a ten-year-old is a favorite memory. I could not believe someone would give me all those gifts and not even know me.

I attended the public schools of Ouachita Parish in Monroe, fourth through twelfth grade, where my teachers treated me well. One high school teacher offered me her old clothes. They were a bit old for me, but she meant well. The home even provided scholarships for the children to attend college. I attended college after I left the home. I thought about nursing, but more than anything I wanted a family and to be a good mom. Ultimately, I studied home economics.

I met my husband, Eugene, when I was a junior in high school. We met at the church we were attending. He had known my brother in the sixth grade and always wondered what happened to him. He did not know my brother had a little sister. We had attended the same church in Shreveport before we moved away to live at the home. On our first date the car Eugene had borrowed broke down. His parents were visiting him at college that weekend and had to come get us. That was well before cell phones. Eugene had to meet with staff before they would let us date because he was a college guy. If we went out on Friday nights I had to be in by 11:00. On Saturday nights curfew was 10:00 because we had to get up early for church on Sunday, so we usually went out on Fridays. Phone calls were only for ten minutes. With at least six teenage girls the phone was rationed pretty carefully.

I wanted to marry a man who would love me and allow me to love him, and Eugene was that man. We married at the children's home. The home paid for the wedding, but I had worked and saved my money to buy my own wedding dress. We were very young, but we really loved each other. Eugene was taking a job in Texas and attending graduate school to be a minister. He did not want to leave me in Louisiana. We married young, but it has been a happy marriage for 44 years. We have two grown children and four beautiful grandchildren. Living at the home had huge impact on our home life. Little things like making your bed, keeping clothes picked up, and respecting other people's property were always things I emphasized. Saying "yessir" and "no ma'am" is important to me. We had many people who toured our cottage and we had to keep it clean at all times. My cottage was always the cleanest.

After Eugene completed his studies we served several churches throughout the South. I loved being a preacher's wife. A wise lady once told me to "just love the people" and I did. Our dearest and closest friends are those we served in our churches. We were part of their lives and they were part of ours as well. We tried to raise our kids to be "normal." We wanted them to experience life the way all children should. Eugene and I pushed back when people wanted our children to act like the "preacher's kids."

After that, Eugene served his ministry for nearly twenty years, with one of the foremost Christian service ministries in the United States serving children, families and senior adults. It truly is a ministry to the widows and orphans. That calling has allowed us to visit all over the US, Russia, Latvia, Kenya, Peru, China, Central America, Western Europe, and Ethiopia. I left my heart in Africa.

I am always amazed that a young girl could take the experience of a broken home and see God use people to bless her life and then be a blessing to thousands of others. I knew even as a child that living at the children's home was the best thing for my life. I was safe. I was loved and treated well. I got quality health care. I had never seen a dentist before I went to the home. Eugene and I believe in supporting the ministries to vulnerable children. Our philanthropy is certainly aimed in that direction. To this day I have maintained friendships with the children and staff from the home. I had a blast at the home. Many of my friends at school would say they wished they lived there. I think they thought it was a slumber party every night. I return for our homecoming events.

CREDIT

Things to Think About

1. Two of the stories emphasize the threat of polio to young people. Polio is passed though fecal matter, so children were not allowed to go swimming for fear of contracting it. Thanks to Dr. Salk and Dr. Sabin polio has not been a threat to children for several decades. How would your life be different if such a vaccine did not exist?

2. In many of the oral histories the women discuss one or two events that they remember more than others. For several, it is the assassination of President John F. Kennedy. If you were asked the same question in forty years, what do you think you might say?

3. One thing all these women have in common is that computers and the internet were inventions of their adulthood. Take a minute to think of the tools you used this morning to get breakfast and then look up when they were invented. Which ones were invented after 1980?

4. Which historical event that the oral histories discuss are you most familiar with? Why? Which events in your lifetime will be deemed historically significant?

5. Throughout the twentieth century there are certain common themes, and many are evident in the oral histories. Which twentieth-century trends have impacted the early part of the twenty-first century the most?

For Further Reading

Korean War

The General versus the President: MacArthur and Truman at the Brink of Nuclear War (2016) by H. W. Brands

Civil Rights

Warriors Don't Cry: A Searing Memoir of the Battle to Integrate Little Rock's Central High (1995) by Melba Pattillo Beals

Nuclear Power in America

A Girl's Guide to Missiles: Growing Up in America's Secret Desert (2018) by Karen Lynnea Piper

Cold War

Crossing the River: A Memoir of the American Left, the Cold War, and Life in East Germany (2003) by Victor Grossman

Vietnam

The Sorrow of War: A Novel of North Vietnam (1994) by Bao Ninh

Iranian Revolution

The Complete Persepolis (2007) by Marjane Satrapi

Migrant Workers in the United States

Under the Feet of Jesus (1996, novel) by Helena Maria Viramontes

9/11

Extremely Loud and Incredibly Close (2006) by Jonathan Safran Foer

INDEX